MW01625294

Confusion in the West

In their trenchant panoramic overview – ranging from antiquity to the present day – John and Anna Rist write with authority and ennui about nothing less than the loss of the foundational culture of the West. The authors characterise this culture as the 'original tradition', viewing its erosion as one which has led to anxiety about the entire value of Western thought. The causes of the disintegration are discussed with an intensity rare in academe. Critics of modernity ordinarily concentrate on the Enlightenment, and the book certainly offers deep analysis of Enlightenment thought. But it goes further. Thus, the cruelty of modern totalitarianism is now depicted as in the spirit of the French Revolution and its implacable hostility to a vanished primordial heritage, while scientism, bureaucracy and consumerism appear as the only rivals to a threatening nihilism. The book argues that Western thought has created a set of conflicting moral and spiritual customs: to the detriment of coherence, in individual minds as in society and culture.

ANNA RIST is a writer, and former lecturer in Classics at St Michael's College, Toronto. She has published two books of English verse translations of the ancient Greek poets Theocritus (1978) and Herodas (2015), an account of life in rural Tuscany (*We Etruscans*, 2006), a novel (*The Chain*, 2017) and a book of poems (*Festival and Ferial*, 2014). She is working on a second novel, a second book of poems and a five-act play on Catholic Shakespeare.

JOHN RIST is Fellow of the Royal Society of Canada and an Aquinas Medallist of the American Catholic Philosophical Association. The author of 18 books and of more than 100 articles, he has taught at the universities of Toronto and Aberdeen, the Catholic University of America, the Hebrew University of Jerusalem and the Istituto Patristico Augustinianum in Rome. His most recent book is *What Is a Person?* (Cambridge University Press, 2021).

Confusion in the West

Retrieving Tradition in the Modern and Post-Modern World

ANNA AND JOHN RIST

CAMBRIDGE
UNIVERSITY PRESS

Shaftesbury Road, Cambridge CB2 8EA, United Kingdom

One Liberty Plaza, 20th Floor, New York, NY 10006, USA

477 Williamstown Road, Port Melbourne, VIC 3207, Australia

314–321, 3rd Floor, Plot 3, Splendor Forum, Jasola District Centre, New Delhi – 110025, India

103 Penang Road, #05–06/07, Visioncrest Commercial, Singapore 238467

Cambridge University Press is part of Cambridge University Press & Assessment, a department of the University of Cambridge.

We share the University's mission to contribute to society through the pursuit of education, learning and research at the highest international levels of excellence.

www.cambridge.org
Information on this title: www.cambridge.org/9781009218375

DOI: 10.1017/9781009218429

First published 2023

Printed in the United Kingdom by TJ Books Limited, Padstow Cornwall

A catalogue record for this publication is available from the British Library.

Library of Congress Cataloging-in-Publication Data
Names: Rist, Anna, 1936– author. | Rist, John M., author.
Title: Confusion in the west : retrieving tradition in the modern and post-modern world / Anna Rist, John Rist, University of Toronto.
Description: Cambridge, United Kingdom ; New York, NY, USA : Cambridge University Press, 2023. | Includes bibliographical references and index.
Identifiers: LCCN 2022016950 (print) | LCCN 2022016951 (ebook) | ISBN 9781009218375 (hardback) | ISBN 9781009218412 (paperback) | ISBN 9781009218429 (epub)
Subjects: LCSH: Philosophy, Modern. | Postmodernism. | Civilization, Western. | BISAC: POLITICAL SCIENCE / History & Theory
Classification: LCC B791 .R57 2023 (print) | LCC B791 (ebook) | DDC 190–dc23/eng/20220608
LC record available at https://lccn.loc.gov/2022016950
LC ebook record available at https://lccn.loc.gov/2022016951

ISBN 978-1-009-21837-5 Hardback

To the rising generation, especially

Olivier (Frère Vincent-Thomas, O.P.), Vanessa, Ruth, Sarah, Zachary, Rachel and Joseph, who has no need to trudge upon this path

Contents

Preamble

Over the last few years, Cambridge University Press has published a further four of John Rist's books, namely *What Is Truth?*, *Real Ethics*, *Augustine Deformed* and *What Is a Person?* All four, in approaching their philosophical subject matter from different angles, are concerned to explain how, in the 'West', 'intellectuals', as less sophisticated folk, have lost a sense of cultural identity that – despite local and national peculiarities – we once took for granted, even when critical of specific features and evolutions.

These four books were written primarily for the said 'intellectuals' and for academic readers; hence these were fitted out with footnotes and bibliographies sufficient to give some idea of the monstrous quantity of studies available for 'further reading'. They are connected by an overarching theme in that they illustrate how Western culture and philosophy has driven itself into an intellectual space filled with a churning moral and spiritual confusion. Hence a number of persons, lacking specialist knowledge to enter into the books' academic material in depth, have asked if the ideas and conclusions might be presented to a wider readership in a less encumbered version.

This Anna has proposed be carried out before either of us should be any older, and for the purpose I have again enlisted (though in a more material way than hitherto) her co-operation as critic and as stylist in the joint engendering of the present work. The result should be viewed less as an academic monograph than as an 'essay' striving after the mode of the great essayists of the past: Milton in the *Areopagitica* or perhaps Edmund Burke in his *Reflections on the Revolution in France*.

By way of introduction we, being British, invite the reader to look at the British scene at the end of World War II when we were children – with consideration of the wider European backdrop – and compare it with what we find around us in 2022.

1 Confusion Introduced

> I am completely normal. Even while I was carrying out the task of extermination, I led a normal family life.
>
> Rudolf Höss, Commandant of Auschwitz

In 1945 Continental Europe was in ruins, Britannia on her knees. Political power had shifted to America and – in more raw and dreaded form – to Stalin's Soviet Union. Nevertheless, there was a certain confidence that, with the benefit of an American protective shield – a necessity often treated by Britons with an envious or mocking contempt sometimes expressed pithily of GIs as 'over-fed, over-sexed, over 'ere!' – things would return to an improved version of a cultural and intellectual 'Western' normality assumed to have remained more or less in place. Now that we were rid of Hitler and Mussolini, followed by Japan's Tojo and fellow militarists, we could set about establishing a fairer social order: better health, education, housing, better working conditions – something of the Utilitarian's vision of an ideal society.

Though we envisaged that society largely in material terms, some hoped that, especially with better and wider-spread education, there might be some sort of 'spiritual' – though not necessarily religious – revival. European art and culture would recover after the lengthy and literally devastating hiatus, with larger numbers equipped to share in it; thus, and with the despised Americans paying for our defence, we could go for a New Order – however bankrupt the 'we', not only fiscally but intellectually, morally, spiritually... Among us were still those who hankered for Revolution: Communist, even Stalinist. As did some in France, Germany, Italy, Greece. As did even a few in what to them was 'God's Own Country', our linguistic cousins in the United States.

The changes envisaged requiring clearance as the first stage, with the question of what we should improve arose the less openly discussed question of what we should eliminate. In Britain the problem seemed especially urgent with respect to education: this it was proposed to deal with by 'comprehensivisation' – raising the question of what to do with the existing 'public' and 'grammar' schools, the latter already offering bright children a superior educational experience attainable via examination: 'the Eleven-plus' (from the age at which it was sat by all primary school pupils) or just 'the Scholarship'. Those benefitting from the so-called public schools were of more mixed abilities, being limited – apart from some few on scholarships – by parental ability to pay. For these, 'Close down every fuckin' one', was the solution offered by Labour's Anthony Crosland, playing the working-class lad. Others thought that too extreme, even too Marxist, and that temporising was required.

Thus arose the fateful question much discussed when we were students at Cambridge in the 1950s: whether to raise the new 'comprehensives' – inevitably large and complex like their American originals – to the standard of the better 'public', 'private' and 'grammar' schools, by providing them with more teachers of more subjects in smaller classes, with 'streaming' in at least 'core' subjects; or alternatively to lower the standards set by the academically superior schools, therefore reducing elitism by a venture in social engineering.

It was probably inevitable that the latter option, involving spending a lot less money, would be accepted by default rather than decided upon. The British example would soon find analogues elsewhere in Europe, and in that outcome we can recognise factors contributing to the present cultural confusion which is our subject matter. The incoming changes in schooling would encourage a sometimes deliberately engineered ignorance and misunderstanding of our past, even where there was the wish to retain something of its outlook and virtues. Some of the cultural effects can be recognised in the general decline of knowledge of British and European literature and history as older works and older ages were adjudged either too demanding or 'irrelevant', so began to disappear from syllabuses in favour of less ambitious, more contemporary options. The decline in standards is well illustrated in the case of English literature. In 1945 Chaucer was a compulsory study at both Ordinary and Advanced Levels. By 2022 many University students of English have not read anything by 'the Father of English Literature'; some would seem to have barely heard of him. As for history, by now few in our schools acquire any coherent knowledge of the world before the nineteenth century – at best, for too often the cut-off comes in the twentieth.

Such educational 'reforms' are more widely informative, their implication and their effect being to hold that the world has changed and we must change with it; hence, in the rush to produce a social 'equality' too often viewed as homogenisation, an ulterior aim has been to eliminate the past from our common awareness. With this unthinking social progressivism has competed a wishful thinking about politics and history. In the United Kingdom (as in France over Algeria and 'Indo-China'), many assumed that the British Empire could carry on as before the War, with its ideals, real or projected. In 1956 the Suez crisis would put an end to that, with America waving the big stick to compel our withdrawal. Thereafter the United Kingdom would indulge a cut-and-run policy of abandoning her colonies, with 'imperialism' now adjudged a Bad Thing and the British Empire, with its drain on national income – and despite its by-and-large equitable system of government and provision for education and social relief – to be viewed as on a par with Mussolini's land-grabs – perhaps even Hitler's.

As students, many of us naively liked to assume that with black rule in Africa there would ensue a corruption-free Garden of Eden, 'original sin' (as the Christians remaining among us might have put it) being non-applicable to the untainted non-Europeans. In fact the largely European-educated – usually English- or French-speaking – native rulers who took over the Black Continent too often proved not merely more incompetent than their predecessors, but some decidedly rapacious and corrupt. That could be explained away as a secondary effect of imperialism – for another feature of our times has been European willingness to deny obvious and global facts. The ensuing and encroaching blending of reality and unreality would make for further conceptual confusion.

Traditional Europe had been, even with its quarrels, wars and oppressions, a Christian entity in which the clergy were generally respected if not obeyed – and after World War II the mainline churches prepared to continue as before. But not only were their congregations soon to diminish (after, in some cases, a wartime 'bubble') but their Christianity was already dissolving. For not only was contempt for a past deemed irrelevant eroding serious interest in Greek and Roman antiquity, but 'scientific' study was attacking that other root of an older Europe, the Christian church based in Judaism, its Bible and traditions. By a large constituency of European adults, most 'Bible stories' are by now unknown and many have barely heard of Moses, some even of Jesus. Attitudes to the post-war formation of the State of Israel as a haven for Jews and more generally to – and by – those Jews would contribute to this.

For while few earlier Christian believers had taken metaphysical accounts of the Trinity too seriously in what had become largely a national or tribal religion, theological ignorance did not keep bums off pews. By 1945, however, 'advanced' Protestants had more or less given up their belief in an historical Jesus with much resemblance to the icon previously worshipped or even to His New Testament portrait. In addition, they were finessing their traditional moral beliefs, particularly about sex and marriage. That hybrid conglomerate, the Church of England, had backed divorce and contraception since 1930 (though officially only in 2002 approving remarriage in the lifetime of a spouse). With morality uncertain and the Bible widely viewed as legendary (including by not a few clergy), the eventual disappearance of congregations, after a certain post-War burgeoning, could have been predicted. At the time of writing, the institutional Protestant churches still muddle along – with ever more 'chiefs' and fewer 'Indians' – exhibiting their confused and confusing combination of traditional religion and contemporary scepticism: to be joined latterly by the paradigm Western 'Roman Catholic' Church with a hierarchy long resistant to the *Zeitgeist* and members widely accepting a mental compartmentalism as the price of continuance in the faith. We shall inevitably be revisiting this, the Great Church under whose auspices the structures of what we call European civilisation had been developed out of Graeco-Roman and Jewish roots.

Meanwhile in Germany, fountainhead of Protestant theology, Christian behaviour – especially but not only as presented by the transmutation of much Lutheranism into 'German Christianity' under the Nazis – left many to conclude that Churches should, with the Nazis, pass into history (while still being allowed to collect tax revenues for social services such as marrying and burying). On the wider scene it could be recognised as something of the catastrophe of European Christianity predicted by many, most notably by both Nietzsche and Dostoyevsky. Too often it would seem as if all 'Christians' had to offer came down to outdated moralising coupled with a vague 'spirituality'.

Plus, it all happened so quickly: the remaining Church scaffolding torn away, leaving some clinging on (it might be to their benefices), others just confused.

This change in the 'West' from 1945 on – with the ensuing intellectual chaos – cannot be explained entirely in terms of world-events and the rise and fall of Empires; such may go hand in hand with literary and philosophical novelty. Neither Marx nor Nietzsche was an emperor or a general, and nor were those older gurus – Rousseau, Hume, Kant – whose works have been influential far beyond the ivory towers where they were conceived. In times of cultural reassessment, social and political changes – which may in part result from economic fluctuation – and the thoughts of philosophers (often inaccurately transmitted by journalists and publicists) will play into each other. Thinkers may offer ideas that a public has long, even secretly, been waiting to hear, while the public, exerting social and political pressure, encourages intellectual adventurism and careerism.

Never was such interaction so liable to produce cultural ferment as in this recent age, with its growing contempt for a past viewed not merely as irrelevant but as surely more wicked than our noble selves. And with communications made all but instantaneous: whereas decrees of earlier potentates, civil or ecclesiastical, might take weeks or months to reach the bounds of their authority, acceptance or rejection of orders and ideas can now occur within seconds; moreover, when imbibing the thoughts or feelings of varieties of 'celebs' on 'social media', the imbibers have little means of checking their truth, nor the instigators much suasion to be truthful. As we know – or can know – much 'fake news' is passed around anonymously.

So what – old or new – have Western philosophers, pundits and public intellectuals been passing around in the past half-century? That in part is what the following chapters set out to recount. First we should ask what happens more generally in those palmy university days when, as students, we are apt to take upon ourselves to settle the 'big' questions. At the outset our student – he or latterly more probably she – has (perhaps more than with any other 'humanities' subject) only a vague idea what 'Philosophy' is, or might or ought to be, and is inclined to think of those who teach it as 'doing' philosophy: thus philosophy must be what they do – and not only in general terms, but usually (though a few rebels – more commonly male – may dissent) in the specific questions and possible answers with which the student concerns him or herself.

But what if our teachers are asking the wrong questions? What if they are accepting (or rejecting) only the questions proposed by their own teachers, who have been doing likewise – and so on back into time. And what if those questions were originally confusingly posed? The new student of philosophy may believe that he or she is learning to be wise while actually confronting questions which have evolved to be ever and exponentially more malformed: in which case, one can expect the current philosophical scene to look trivial, absurd or even pointless. Already in the fifties of the last century some smarter undergraduates in our own *Alma Mater* were deciding that, with the philosophy on offer looking trivial, they would do well to study something else. And if our academic philosophy looks trivial, we should expect an inability to engage in ethical thinking and prioritising to permeate everyday life, accompanied by a growing irresponsibility – or perhaps a 'virtual' responsibility. Since World War II, and increasingly, that has been the case.

It might seem, indeed, that in addressing such questions that are 'on the (academic) table' or 'in the (broadcast) air', we have lost a sense of what philosophy is, or should be, *about*. Though admittedly that has been one of the perennial questions treated by philosophers, this will not be the forum in which to elaborate an answer to it. Instead we shall rely on the approach pioneered by Plato, who thought that philosophy could be recognised by comparison with sophistry, its shadow self. The sophist, says Plato, is like a bad carver, hacking up the meat into ill-assorted bits and so making rhetorical capital out of the ensuing confusion 'on the table'; the philosopher is he – the English pronoun he/him/his is throughout this work to be taken as gender-inclusive; likewise our use of the English word 'man' shall assume the reader not to be of that over-literalist breed of gender-warriors who insist on regarding it, erroneously, as denoting exclusively the male of our species – who is capable of looking at the world and at himself and 'cutting it up' – which is what the Greek-derived 'analysing' means – in terms of its natural and intelligible divisions: that is, he will *distinguish* (Latin *'Distinguo'*, as the medieval scholastic was taught to reiterate) between such pairs as: being-and-non-being, being-and-becoming, same-and-other, like-and-unlike, even-and-odd, right-and-left – even male-and-female.

It will be a major thesis of the present book that most Western heads are filled to bursting with a collection of incompatible ideas, even while their owners may believe they think coherently. As our analysis of these heads and their content aims to show, they will be at best intellectually compartmentalised, banalities jostling with important principles to produce a general philosophical confusion to serve as a guide for life. That this is often the case can be tested by a thought-experiment.

Pick three or four important moral themes on which you would take your stand: for example, to do with social justice, racism, capital punishment, population control – you name it! Then ask yourself on what principle you feel so strongly about each of them. If you go back far enough in your self-analysis you are liable to find that the essential first principle for one or more of your beliefs contradicts the first principle for one or more others: put in logical terms, that you believe 'p and not-p' (p being a proposition) at the same time. A good example is provided by the woman who urges that capital punishment be banned, even for serial murderers and torturers, because human life is somehow 'sacred', while simultaneously insisting on her 'right' to kill her innocent pre-born child a day or so before she would 'expect' to be born. (Of course, in attempting this test you will have to answer your own questions honestly; giving yourself the benefit of the doubt will weaken your chance of uncovering any possible truth.)

If the analysis we are about to undertake, of the history of Western thought from Socrates to Heidegger, Parfit and Rawls, is essentially correct, and if it shows the plethora of data to which we are now exposed to be an incoherent mass, then what is to be done? For a start, universities would have to be persuaded to rethink a narrow obsession – and not only in philosophy – with the contemporary, let alone with the merely economically advantageous. Philosophy departments in particular would have to give far more time to how our contemporary and supposedly 'relevant' questions became so contemporary and (supposedly) relevant. Thus the history of philosophy would have to be taken much more seriously, with older problems again admitted to 'the table' – not 'rephrased' as though they were our identical own: all this to clear the ground for a better understanding of what has proven compatible philosophically and culturally with what. Only then may we proceed to more contemporary observations.

But why, you may wonder, start with the Greeks? Since the first men, civilisations have come and gone, some few highly organised and literate: why not start in Babylon or ancient Egypt or China? Or with 'mitochondrial' Eve? The answer to that will depend on our keeping the actualities in mind. Yes, there were civilisations before Greece and Rome, though with limited intellectual influence on these which (along with Ancient Israel) provide our significant cultural inheritance. If others besides these three roots are to be called on to help us now, we need to discover whether they – or others yet more remote – have in fact produced anything philosophical or more generally cultural to help relieve our latter-day discontents; which is not a call for more cultural archaeology, however interesting such a study might in itself be.

If the answer to our question whether a specific pre-Greek culture has intellectual (as distinct from, let us say, architectural or artistic) interest is 'Yes', then let us indeed learn from that culture – even as thinkers in the Middle Ages and Renaissance were able to enrich their philosophical patrimony (consisting as it did of a limited number of the writings of Plato, Aristotle, the ancient Stoics, Sceptics and Epicureans) as further texts were recovered and those already known shown to allow of an improved understanding. Nothing need be ruled out *a priori*, but compatibility and coherence must be kept ever in mind – as it too often has not been in the recent European past.

But what if the answer to our question about the cultural and intellectual relevance to us of pre-Greek societies is 'No'? Then we need to face that reality without sentimentality, affected anti-Eurocentrism or other contemporary shibboleth.

2 Athens, Rome, Jerusalem

Plato is Moses speaking Attic Greek.

Numenius of Apamea (Second century AD)

Homer was not an Athenian, but by tradition a blind and wandering bard of the isle of Chios, off the Ionian coast. However, the first 'edition' of the Homeric poems was produced in sixth century BC Athens and marks the beginning of an intellectual and artistic achievement which laid the groundwork for the 'Western' culture we and the world have inherited and which we shall henceforth refer to as the Original Tradition.

Not that earlier Greece had contributed nothing to the enlightenment to come: apart from Homer, the variegated poetical output of such as Hesiod, Sappho, Alcaeus and Pindar and the intellectual originality of many of the Ionian Greeks – to include not least Heraclitus, Parmenides and the 'atomist' Democritus – lay behind the Athenian miracle.

Nor was that miracle to fade away, but to be handed on as Greek culture spread over the near East and beyond with the conquests of Alexander the Great and consequent 'Hellenization' of much of the known world. With the collapse of that 'Hellenistic' world and its subordination to Rome, the Romans too, with their practical appreciation of the powers of language, recognised their opportunity to pass on what the Greeks had given them while enriching their own civilisation. They thus formed a secondary source from which Europe and its worldwide offshoots were to be watered.

As for Athens, just as we have few original works (even counting copies) of her most famous ancient sculptors, Pheidias and Praxiteles, so the great majority of her literary output did not survive and played little more than a 'local' role in the development of Western civilisation. Of the hundreds of tragedies and comedies performed in fifth-century Athens, we have some forty masterpieces; they include Aeschylus' the *Oresteia*, Sophocles' *Oedipus the King* and *Antigone* (the former judged by Aristotle as the greatest of the tragedies), the *Hippolytus* and *Bacchae* of Euripides, and the *Clouds*, *Frogs* and *Lysistrata* of Aristophanes, to name some of the best known. Alongside these comes Thucydides' massive *History of the Peloponnesian War*: not the first *History* written in Greek, for Herodotus and others had preceded Thucydides, but foundational for historical methodology and political science.

Athens had thus become, in world intellectual history, a – indeed *the* – intellectual foundry from which were soon to emerge the basic structures of our Western *philosophical* tradition. Historically this tradition grew out of challenges to prevailing social mores crystallised by a cosmopolitan group of thinkers, the 'Sophists': not before Plato a pejorative term, but rather indicating professionally wise men lured to Athens, a cultural centre and home to rich patrons.

'Sophistic' reappraisals of Greek culture and society were preceded and accompanied by more widespread intellectual curiosity and moral puzzlings. Herodotus had suggested that the Olympian gods were invented by Homer and Hesiod 'some four hundred years before my time'. The heroine of Sophocles' tragedy *Antigone* challenges King Creon to explain why the laws of the state should override the laws of the gods. 'My tongue has sworn, my heart remains unsworn', claims a character of Euripides – while another asks, 'What is base unless the spectators think it so?' Meanwhile Thucydides exposes the thuggery of politicians who distort moral language, telling their hearers that moderation is lack of virility, justice the last resort of the weak.

Yet it was the 'Sophists' who provoked the replies of Socrates, that self-styled 'gadfly' who punctured, by holding up to scrutiny, the intellectual pretensions of the new teachers, as well as his fellow Athenians' unexamined acceptance of the conventions these disputed. That challenge, fatal to Socrates himself, would prompt the composition by his pupil Plato, then by Plato's pupil Aristotle, of those works of genius which even now can be seen to provide the rational foundation of our Western philosophical edifice.

The achievements of Plato and Aristotle – though by now long superseded in the areas of natural and biological science – rest primarily on foundational tenets in logic, mathematics, political theory, ethics, aesthetics and metaphysics (to include theology). Many of these advances would be scrutinised and supplemented in the various 'schools' of the Hellenistic and Roman worlds which, formal or informal, developed in the wake of Plato's 'Academy': a proliferating output of 'philosophical' (the Greek-derived word denotes 'love of wisdom') activity which would continue for centuries, and indeed never entirely die out.

Socrates, so far as we know, wrote nothing. His abiding significance was secured by Plato making him the central figure in the majority of his philosophical dialogues. Prior to that, we know that he had obtained instant acclaim – also notoriety – among his contemporaries, and after his hemlock-execution by admirers down the centuries. Though Socrates himself claimed to know nothing, the oracle of Apollo at Delphi – source of the philosophically seminal maxim 'Know Thyself' – had hailed him as the wisest of the Greeks.

Largely abandoning his intellectual predecessors' attempts to understand the physical universe in material, or rather in vitalist terms – a task which for some involved a 'cleaning up' of traditional religion and mythology – Socrates had set out to discover what the Oracle could have meant. His attention was on what he perceived to be intellectual confusion among his compatriots about those virtues, such as justice and 'holiness' or reverence, they thought they held dear, and on the clearing away of such confusion as a necessary first step to the acquisition of moral and political integrity. Beyond this preliminary demolition work, his aim was to ward off the threat of social and political chaos by 'fixing' moral language in such a way that his fellow Athenians – challenged to give up their 'unexamined' views and lifestyles and freed from the moral anarchy he (and others) saw inhering in the glib talk of well-paid sophists and demagogues – might render their society less unthinkingly conventional, less naive, less given over to material acquisition in both public and private spheres, and hence more worthily human.

Plato, a well-connected aristocrat and disciple of Socrates, became devoted, following his Master's execution, to continuing his attempts to correct the growing moral, social and intellectual chaos. He came to the conclusion that if, in the words of the Oracle, we are to 'know ourselves', only transcendent metaphysical realities independent of human greed, power-seeking and lust can provide the necessary standards for our individual and communal lives; we must recognise, that is, the immaterial and unchanging first principles of the universe in which we find ourselves. That project would eventually induce him to return to the physical world with its underlying mathematical structure; more immediately he argued that no well-regulated city state could be formed or develop unless moral ideas about human activity were seen as grounded in an objective Goodness.

Plato was the first thinker to argue – most cogently in the opening book of the *Republic* – that if we dare to be honest we are faced with the choice whether to live moral and spiritual lives – that 'examined' life which Socrates had urged on his hearers – recognising a providentially organised universe founded on unchanging *immaterial* realities that Plato called 'forms' or (from the Greek *idea*) 'ideas'. The alternative is a brutal warfare in which the rational option – as his anti-Socrates, Thrasymachus, explains – is to look out for oneself by force or by fraud perpetrated on those dim-wits who suppose they ought to live 'morally', and who indeed are to be encouraged in their soft-headed ignorance; that way they can be exploited for the purposes of 'the wise'. As we shall see, Thrasymachus' strategy of insolence and bamboozling has recurrently seemed to be worldly 'wisdom' and been adopted and adapted to handle historic problems and discontents.

Looking back after more than 2,000 years of philosophical thinking, it is easy to overlook the groundbreaking importance of Plato's positing of 'immateriality'. It is not just a matter of whether his account of the immaterial, and of what kind of immaterial items may exist, is factually correct; rather it is that before this breakthrough – and despite the contributions of some of his predecessors, especially Parmenides – thinkers scarcely could distinguish such apparently different propositions as 'I am fat' and 'I am unjust', except by reference to the four physical elements, or to those predecessors of 'sub-atomic' particles, the 'uncuttable' (so-called) atoms.

On Plato's basic 'metaphysical' propositions depend all subsequent non-materialist accounts of the universe – as also of the human person. That is not to make an obviously absurd claim that without some version of Plato's metaphysics religion is impossible, moral theories cannot be proposed or works of art produced. Rather it is that if we want to *explain* – rather than assert or enforce – religious, moral or aesthetic values, we cannot afford to neglect Plato's basic challenge. Thus to our earlier observation that Plato, following in the footsteps of Socrates, finds self-awareness ('knowing oneself') fundamental to philosophical progress, we add that self-awareness will immediately raise the necessity of non-material realities which might be mathematical, logical, moral or aesthetic – or a combination of these.

To these two Platonic axioms we can add a third: that when we think about ourselves, we can recognise that we are thinking of what we want or desire. All such desires will point to some basic underlying love: in Greek *eros*; hence Plato calls them 'erotic'. Some of our 'loves' are for basic needs, others for less necessary or unnecessary 'possessions', but underlying them all is a love of something we perceive as good, as *being* goodness or as 'Goodness itself'. This Goodness is no abstraction or projection; there really are goods, and so – Plato concludes – there must be a 'Goodness itself' which is immaterial and exists independently of our loving and 'intentional' minds. We are creatures of thought, of imagination (which may be deceptive) and of a gamut of desires which at their strongest are 'loves'. In sum, we are living beings capable of recognising material and immaterial objects and are driven ultimately by love of an objective goodness which, as the 'greatest object of thought', has, Plato held, to be the subject-matter of disciplined enquiry.

Such enquiry cannot, however, be carried out alone; like all his fellow Greeks, Plato recognises that for human development, individuals must be members of a community. Such a community – ideally for him the city state, the Greek *polis* – is essential in that it enables each of us to recognise ourselves as profiting from co-operating with others to achieve those 'common goods' beyond the reach of isolated and competing individuals. This leaves us with the question as to what kind of *polis* will best serve our needs. Plato's view (which would have been shared by most of his compatriots) was that it must be large enough to defend itself but not so large as to leave the citizen feeling lost in the crowd. Proceeding from that, Plato divided political constitutions into two groups. The first group (whether monarchy, aristocracy or 'moderate' democracy) is distinguished by having rulers who rule not for their own advantage but for that of their subjects. In the second, those in power are chiefly concerned with their own perceived advantage, whether they be 'tyrants', oligarchs or exponents of a 'majoritarian' democracy: that is where all citizens are theoretically reduced to a lowest common denominator, hence made pliant and rootless enough to be 'guided' by a 'Leader of the People'. (Such are known to our own times.)

The character of Plato's best city can only be determined by appeal to nature – to that of the universe itself and to human nature – and its 'causes'. To these he offers two approaches. The first, which we would call religious – and we have alluded to the work of his predecessors in this area – is to clean up traditional beliefs: to reject the myths of Homer, 'Bible of the Greeks', and the poets, and to insist that the gods are neither amoral, immoral nor deceitful; they are intelligent beings with some sort of providential care for the universe they formed and the human beings within it.

We note here that Greeks from Homer on will call 'god' or 'divine' whatever is the most important and powerful living force we can recognise. For Plato, that force is the immortal and self-moving Mind; thus 'god' – or 'the divine' – is to be identified as Constructive Mind. Both human minds and the divine mind are 'erotic' (we have already seen the sense in which the Greeks understood this word): hence they long to make things better and more 'beautiful'. As Plato, in his *Timaeus*, puts it in answer to the question of why the Maker ordered the cosmos: he did so because he is good and he wanted to. (We note that on this view God did not create the universe from nothing; Greek philosophers all accepted the axiom formulated by Parmenides: that 'nothing comes from nothing'.)

Plato's second approach to the best life is, as we have already seen, metaphysical: there exist immaterial 'Forms' corresponding to whatever meets various criteria, the first of which he seems to have identified as being in possession of a common name. As he proceeds, however, he whittles down the candidates for 'Forms' while continuing to hold that there are Forms of the different Virtues, and 'beyond' them a Form of Goodness itself. He apparently tried – but may not have succeeded – to determine the necessary relationship between the Divine Mind and the Good: between Mind and the Forms; between (philosophically reformed) religion and metaphysics. Later Platonists would come to identify God with the Good and assume – with some likelihood – that Plato must have done the same.

In his last, unfinished and rambling work, the *Laws*, Plato summed up many of the cultural features of his life's work under three heads: that God, not man, is the measure of all things; that even though the soul is immortal and the cause of all ordered movement in the cosmos, some souls become capable of evil; that well-formed political theories depend on recognising that good societies, like good individuals, are fashioned by observing and building on what we are by our nature: thus are not accidental, arbitrary or artificial constructs.

*

Aristotle, son of the court physician to King Philip II of Macedon, came to Athens, as did many others, because Plato's Academy was where the intellectual action was to be found. Though formed within the Athenian philosophical culture, he by temperament was quite different from the teacher in whose company he remained for twenty years until Plato's death in 347 BC. Plato was a metaphysical and political visionary whose bold claims were both inspiring and also obvious targets for correction. Plato had more or less invented metaphysics and, with his arguments for an immaterial world and an immortal soul, offered an account of human life which challenged his audience to face the consequences if moral norms could not be upheld as some sort of existents. From there he went on to urge a revolutionary politics he hoped would transcend the endless civil strife between 'democrats' and 'oligarchs' which had left the Greek cities a prey to one another and to larger predators such as the Persians.

Aristotle's philosophical approach was more careful, more systematic and in ethics more conventional, seeming more like a sophisticated version of a plentiful measure of common sense. He showed more respect than Plato for the views of the ordinary citizen and those of his philosophical predecessors, whose work he viewed as steps toward the project he would do much to complete.

Aristotle's range of intellectual activity, unparalleled in his time, arguably could never be repeated as the stock of knowledge increased. Within his purview came: serious criticism of Plato's Theory of Forms; the first attempt to construct a formal logic backed by what we would call the philosophy of logic; unprecedented investigation of species of animal life he could find around the Mediterranean and beyond; two lengthy treatises on ethics which laid the foundations for what is now referred to as virtue ethics and, starting with criticism of Plato and other theorists, a detailed examination of the form of 'natural' political life which would enable citizen virtue to flourish. Several books of what we would now regard as political science, in which he examined how regimes of any stripe could be effectively maintained, were to be backed by a multi-author series of discussions of the constitutional arrangements of dozens of city states in the Greek world and beyond; of these only the first, written by Aristotle himself on Athens, has survived. This is only a partial list of Aristotle's writings. Much of his early work – said to have been of far greater literary merit than what has come down to us mainly as expanded 'lecture-notes' – has perished or survives only in quotations.

In *Categories* and *Metaphysics* Aristotle replied to Plato's claims about an ultimate 'reality' by arguing that the basic items of our universe are individual singulars: that is, they are 'this' and 'that', and we can understand these singulars philosophically by trying (as Plato had tried) to sort them into distinct classes, distinguishing between different thought-objects as subjects and predicates. Thus water (subject) is qualified as wet (predicate); thus human beings are socio-political animals with varying mental and affective characteristics. Aristotle also held that we cannot talk philosophically about the individual: dictum that led to a neglect of anything other than *quantitative* individual differences within groups; this Aristotle's Stoic and Neoplatonist successors would find troubling. Since, in Aristotle's opinion, there is no *definition* of individuals, we recognise them not 'philosophically' – that is, schematically – but by perception or mental grasp within identified classes.

From the point of view of the history of Western culture, a number of proposals in Aristotle's biological writings and in his *Politics* would prove socially embarrassing. Thus, arguing that without slaves civilization is impossible, he held that there are 'natural slaves' (albeit his account of these would be widely misunderstood). Again, arguing against Plato that bodily difference is evidence of psychological difference, he concluded that males and females must differ psychologically – fatefully accompanying this conclusion by a sophisticated version of the popular view (presumably dependent on the fact that men are in general stronger than women) that females are 'defective males'. This assumption was supported by the conclusion – a rarely avoided type of mistake in his time – that the form of the newly conceived child was supplied entirely by the father, the mother being simply its nurse before as after birth.

Far more promising was Aristotle's account of the relationship between soul and body; while for Plato we are basically souls which, during earthly life, use their bodies as – often morally dangerous – instruments, Aristotle came to argue that this is a seriously inadequate account of human beings: that we are a combination of soul and body. While the soul being the 'form' of a living body possessed of organs. Thus (at least in life as empirically observed) souls cannot exist without bodies; only God (Aristotle's 'Prime Mover' of the universe, who remains himself unmoved, unlike Plato's God who is self-moving) comes near to the Platonic concept of the bodiless existence of mental agents (such as some souls after death).

There was a dispute in the Academy as to whether in *Timaeus* Plato indicates that the world is eternal or rather that it was constructed, together with time, from some (formless) 'matter' – as Aristotle seems to have taken Plato to mean, while Xenocrates denied it. Was Plato not asked? Perhaps he was, and gave some such reply as, 'I had been wondering about that': characteristically leaving the questioners to work out the answer. Be that as it may, Aristotle, though apparently rejecting Plato's belief in a divine Providence, held that the universe, while dependent for its motion on God, is in its raw materiality eternal.

If we are to sum up the joint impact of Plato and Aristotle on subsequent Western culture, we conclude that Plato teaches us to pursue a passionate desire for truth, beauty and goodness into an immaterial 'beyond' world, while his account of our composite nature needs the correction that Aristotle brought to it with his theory that we are active agents whose souls act as the 'form' of our bodies. Aristotle further offers a careful analysis of our powers and their limitations, of our virtues and vices, our capabilities (or potentialities) and our 'actualised' capacities. We shall flourish, Aristotle claims, by acknowledging both our likeness and our unlikeness to the divine;

also, as emphasised by Plato, that lacking such likeness – established as it is by unchanging moral truths – our common life must collapse into social anarchy: into the 'Hobbesian' war of all against all that resolves itself into the strong prevailing against the weak.

Throughout all this we need to hold in view that in antiquity moral obligation is to be translated not into respect for claimed 'rights', but into our duties to ourselves and the society in which we live: that is, into virtues. Though ancient society had – and this in view of its needs and lacks – little notion of 'systemic injustices' such as we now recognise in slavery or the oppression of women, its philosophers – in the footsteps of Socrates, Plato and Aristotle – placed enormous emphasis on a native inclination to cultivate honesty about ourselves, our society and the cosmos, and – where not corrupted by a society's 'sophists' – on our vocation to virtues even 'heroic' (such as those exemplified by Socrates) and a determined civic responsibility.

*

Thus were the major foundations of the non-Judaeo-Christian aspects of our subsequent Western culture built by Plato and Aristotle. However, their work was far from abandoned in the 'Hellenistic' age which followed this Athenian 'miracle'. With the spread of Greek culture among non-Greeks, many philosophers of subsequent centuries, both Hellenistic and Roman, arose from among non-Greek populations in centres far from Greece itself. Especially in Alexandria during the third-century BC – so contemporary with Menander's 'New Comedy' in Athens – we find a new flourishing of learned literature represented in the poetry of Theocritus, Callimachus and Herodas, as well as mathematical and scientific activity centred on the 'Museum' founded by Egypt's King Ptolemy II (and celebrated by those poets).

But while the schools of the Hellenistic period were often 'staffed' by Hellenised Orientals rather than by Greeks, Athens remained the philosophical centre until it was sacked by the Roman commander Sulla in the last century of the pre-Christian era. In those intervening centuries, philosophical work tended to become more systematised, while formal school structures which could, as with the Epicureans, require profession of a 'creed' of membership – created a more restricted intellectual milieu. By contrast, Plato's Academy had been filled with intellectually curious people – and notably female as well as male – even if often in significant philosophical disagreement with the Founder himself.

Of these many schools that flourished after Aristotle's death, three were of greatest significance: those of the Stoics, the Epicureans and the Sceptics – none of which would have arisen without the work of Plato and Aristotle and many of whose members looked back to Socrates as the source of philosophical inspiration. The Aristotelian School – called the Lyceum, from the portico where it was held – was only established after the Master's death by his pupil Theophrastus.

Platonic transcendentalism continued to be taught in the Academy after Plato's death until, in the middle of the third century, under Arcesilaus and claiming to go back to a more 'Socratic' style, it took up with a form of scepticism that questioned the possibility of obtaining certainty. This problem, coming to dominate the post-Aristotelian schools, renders the Hellenistic age something of an 'early modern', epistemological period in ancient thought. Among its basic questions were: How do we know that anything can be known for certain? What might be the possible objects of such certain knowledge?

The traditional scholarly account of Hellenistic philosophy is that it turned man back onto 'the care of the self', therefore, losing sight of wider political and social concerns and concentrating on ethical problems. Thus just as the Hellenistic poets we have mentioned abandoned the grand designs of the Athenian tragedians and national poets like Pindar or Simonides – agreeing thus with Plato that the 'big questions' should be left not to the poets but to philosophers – private rather than political virtue takes centre stage in philosophy itself. This view has been over easily dismissed, albeit we must recognise that logic and metaphysics – now tied into epistological debates about certainty – continued vigorously. Indeed, the Stoics developed, in contrast to the Aristotelian 'syllogistic' logic of terms, a form of propositional logic which has only come into its full flowering in quite recent times with the work of Frege and others.

Sceptical arguments were especially significant where the apparent impossibility of knowledge might seem to imply the dissolution of the person into a series of successive selves. This theme too would only come to loom large some twenty centuries later, in the destructive aspects of post-Reformation thought of the seventeenth century. In the Greece of our period, it was too easily dismissed rather than defeated. Metaphysics and the study of nature both seemed primarily directed to understanding, better than had Plato and Aristotle, how we can achieve the elusive *eudaimonia*: a word often mistranslated as happiness but indicating rather a conscious flourishing, or at least an understanding of what is possible within each man's capacities: what is 'up to us', what mere fantasising or delusion.

Such debates – in a period when Sceptics thought to guide their lives on the principle of 'doing as the Romans do' – were in Athens carried on primarily between the Epicureans of the 'Garden' and the Stoics, whose school, developed by the Hellenised Phoenician Zeno and his successors, met in the Painted Portico. These preached a providentialism, in some ways like Plato's (only devoid of the transcendental metaphysics judged by him to be essential) and a severe moralism in which virtue is the only good and vice the only 'real' evil, non-moral 'evils' being 'indifferent'. The followers of Epicurus (by this time the rare Athenian among school leaders) took a quite different tack, reviving the 'atomism' of the pre-Socratic thinkers Leucippus and Democritus, and denying final causes in nature.

For the Epicureans, the world (or better, worlds) results from chance collisions of atoms. (The chance is explained by Epicurus in a manner different from that of his atomist predecessors, as resulting from a 'swerve'.) Our habitat thus being a random construction; the task of the wise man is to seek protection against the storm: to experience as little pain, hence as much (calm) pleasure as possible: to achieve, that is, an untroubled contentment, free of the delusions of political power-seeking or moral obsessiveness. 'I spit on "virtue"', says Epicurus, 'unless it gives me pleasure'. And he found that in many ways it did; hence some have thought of him less as a hedonist than as a pragmatist, even as a utilitarian. He certainly resisted more obvious forms of hedonism, as immixing too much pain with the always calm pleasure sought.

There are clear resemblances between the self-protective views of Stoics and Epicureans. Stoics surrounded themselves with a hard shell, from under which the worst is to be expected and borne heroically: as a later member of the school, Epictetus, put it, 'Every time you kiss your child good-night, remember that he may die tomorrow'. Epicurus finds Stoic attitudes bizarre: there is no providential God, whether immanent and material (the Stoic view) or transcendent and bodiless (the Platonist); we must look after ourselves: not, however, in power-hungry mode, for that leaves us exposed to the mishaps and disasters which overtake public figures; even death may be the result of losing political battles. And why pursue Stoic virtue in a non-providentially-governed universe? Why, with the Stoics, even commit suicide if your lauded virtue will be unavoidably compromised? You will soon die anyway, and all pain is short-lived.

In the argument between Stoics and Epicureans we see another version of the battle between Socrates and Thrasymachus as depicted by Plato in the first book of the *Republic*. For while Epicurus has no time for Thrasymachean power-seeking, he agrees with Thrasymachus that we live in a non-moral universe in which we must survive as best we can. The Stoics, on the other hand – always provided they can defeat Sceptical arguments against the possibility of knowledge – look up to the moral hero as the providentially led guide to the 'best' life. Neither Stoics nor Epicureans accept Platonic 'salvation' through immaterialism. For the Stoics, while they agree with Plato as to providence, our best hope lies in a pantheist universe: foreshadowing much later developments in Hobbes and Spinoza.

In all this we need to bear in mind that in antiquity there is no materialism in the modern sense: that when the Stoics talk of the equivalence of God and matter and Epicurus proclaims that atoms and empty space are all there is, they are implying no absolute disjunction between living and inert matter; rather, matter for them is in some way the source of life. In the seventeenth century Locke will toy with the same idea.

While it might be supposed from the above that the Stoics could contribute little to a synthesis of Plato and Aristotle, such as would eventually be achieved in late antiquity and further developed in the Middle Ages, this is far from the case – as we can recognise if we compare Aristotle's account of the 'categories of being' with their Stoic equivalents. Aristotle envisages his categories ('substance', 'quality', 'quantity', etc.) as explanatory of physical objects, both living and non-living. They assume the existence of the universe as we know it: that it has always been, and will remain basically the same into the future.

But our conceptual world is not only composed of thoughts of what actually exists. Especially in literature and the arts, we fashion imaginary scenarios to inform, inspire, mislead, even terrorise readers and viewers. Constructs of the human mind are a part of the contents of the universe, therefore also demanding philosophical explanation: hence the first question of some Stoics is not 'What is this?' but 'Does this exist?' – thus opening up to philosophical reflection on 'possible universes'. Neither Plato (in *Timaeus*) nor Aristotle entirely neglected such questions, although both assume that it is good for things to exist. Yet to distinguish between what exists and what does not – and we should note that there is no word for 'existence' in Classical Greek – as the first step in metaphysical exploration, still leaves room for future speculation. Central to later thought would be a question the Stoics had failed to ask, namely: *Why is there something rather than nothing?*

*

Stoicism, Epicureanism and to a lesser degree Scepticism, dominated the philosophical scene from roughly the death of Alexander the Great in 323 BC to the establishment of the Roman Empire under Augustus at what we regard as the turn of eras. By then the Roman elite was culturally Hellenised, with a fair number being bilingual in Greek and Latin: thus able to read philosophy in the language of its original exposition. Significant among them, the Roman orator and statesman Cicero would transmit Greek philosophy, especially that of the Hellenistic Age, to his Latin speaking contemporaries and their descendants, while the long didactic poem *On the Nature of Things* by Lucretius, Cicero's contemporary, became a reliable source for our understanding of Epicureanism from its rediscovery in the Renaissance down to our own time, when further fragments of Epicurus himself have been dug from the Egyptian sands. To our understanding of Stoicism have further contributed the works of Roman Stoics: of Nero's minister and victim Seneca, of Epictetus, a manumitted slave lecturing Epicurus in Greek and of the bilingual Emperor Marcus Aurelius. Since some ninety-five per cent of Hellenistic prose writing has been lost, we readily grasp the importance of such a legacy, however imperfect, in perpetuating important intimations of a fading Greek deposit. When the time came for the recovery of larger quantities of original Greek philosophical material, texts newly brought to Western attention could, from the twelfth century on, be instructively inserted into this matrix.

By the time of Augustus and the Christian era – and despite Seneca and others still to come – the stars of Stoicism and Epicureanism had begun to pale. Scepticism too, after a brief zenith in early Imperial times, disappeared for many centuries almost without trace. Marcus Aurelius would write his Stoic meditations – apparently as an aid to 'care of the self' – and endow Chairs of Platonism, Aristotelianism, Stoicism and Epicureanism at Athens – but by his death in 180 AD, Platonism in varying forms had again taken over and begun a curious amalgamating of much Aristotelianism resulting in the Neoplatonised Aristotle who was to dominate the High Middle

Ages in the Christian West, as well as among Jewish and Muslim thinkers.

This Platonic revival seems to have begun in Alexandria in the late first century BC with the little-known Eudorus. It increasingly dominated the philosophical schools until the end of antiquity, though a few Aristotelian commentators (such as Alexander of Aphrodisias in the second century and Themistius in the fourth century) tried to keep a more historically verifiable Aristotle alive: not without inevitable distortions.

The first stage of the Platonic revival – now known to scholars as 'Middle Platonism' – lasted from Eudorus till the advent of what we know of as 'Neoplatonism' with Plotinus in the mid-third century. It is to be noted that these terms are modern characterisations representing scholarly interpretation of the changing styles of Platonism, for all ancient followers of Plato thought of themselves simply as 'Platonists' and believed themselves either to be teaching the historical Plato or carrying on – as is the case with Plotinus – where Plato had left off. Thus they might see themselves as being in the same relationship to Plato as Plato was to Socrates: a stance that would nevertheless render the Plato of succeeding centuries a restricted, even at times a seriously distorted image of the historical original: *Plato dimidiatus* – a Plato halved – as one scholar has put it.

The 'Middle Platonists' – those with whom early Christian thinkers like Justin Martyr in the second century AD and Origen in the third century were familiar – adopted a semi-scholarly stance toward Plato's writings, producing more or less adequate representations of some of the Master's views, which only inexactly represented his thought at any particular period of his life. The 'Plato' of whom they gave their systematised accounts would depend upon which dialogues they chose to emphasise, the most popular being *Phaedo*, *Phaedrus*, *Parmenides* (usually misinterpreted), the middle books of the *Republic* and *Timaeus*. From these was compiled a 'Plato' roughly based on the writings of the middle years of his life, with little perception of how he had worked through his ethical reflections to arrive at the inevitability of a metaphysic. In common with almost all commentators down to the nineteenth century, these Platonists assume 'one head, one philosophy' – as though a thinker as intelligent as Plato would have the same ideas from ages thirty to seventy. While one needs to look out for continuity as well as change, this assumption we now find hard to comprehend.

'Middle-Platonic' accounts usually presented a World-Organising God (the Demiurge of the *Timaeus*) who is identified both with the Good of the *Republic* and as efficient, formal and final Cause of the universe – in this appropriating the terminology of Aristotle, together with his claim that thought is the identifying of the mind with the form of its object. In addition to the supreme Form or God, Middle Platonists offered a World-Soul and an account of matter far from Plato's obscure biological proposals in the *Timaeus*; rather it is to be understood in terms of Aristotle's 'material cause'.

The tendency was thus toward cosmology, with little opening on metaphysical innovation: all Middle Platonic theories of the cosmos were attempts to explain what the world has always been like. Though a few interpreted Plato's *Timaeus* as teaching the origin in time of the informed universe, the dominant understanding was of God as its sustaining, rather than its temporally originating cause: God as organiser of a universe assumed to be eternal. Nor was much attention paid to Platonic theories of love, though these were never entirely lost to sight, being recalled and analysed, especially by the second-century Platonist and historian Plutarch.

*

With the third-century Plotinus (204–270), Platonism would be radically reconstructed into a programme supposed, down to the nineteenth century, to represent the authentic metaphysics of Plato himself – predominantly the metaphysics, for Neoplatonism neglects many important features of Plato's writings. We can thus treat Plotinus as the founder of 'Neoplatonism', though not its most typical exponent; that dubious title must be bestowed on Proclus, whose fifth-century vision of Plato would in the succeeding century beget the unnamed author known to later ages as 'The Divine Denys', and to us as Pseudo-Dionysius – and in the fifteenth century the late Platonism of Marsilio Ficino, translator of the whole of both Plato and Plotinus into Latin. In the seventeenth century, Proclus' 'Neoplatonism' would still be finding partisans in the Cambridge Platonists. Independent, however, of this long deviation, Plotinus' version had commanded the attention of the two most influential Christian Platonists of late antiquity: the Latin Church Father Augustine and his Greek speaking near contemporary, Gregory of Nyssa.

Plotinus held that the universe could be explained in terms of three 'Platonic' 'hypostases'; these he called: the One (or the Good), the Divine Mind and the World-Soul. Derived primarily from book six of Plato's *Republic* and an eccentric (albeit philosophically interesting) reading of the *Parmenides*, we have the One, source of all things (thus overcoming Plato's duality of gods and Forms): the dynamic first principle 'beyond being', not to be identified with anything finite. From that first principle flows ('descends') the 'Divine Mind' and from that the 'Soul'; these lesser 'hypostases', being derived from the One, 'desire to return to it' as their 'father'. Plotinus' universe is thus characterised by what will come to be called '*exitus*' (the outflow of all from the One) and '*reditus*', the longing of all living things to return to their source so far as they are capable of so doing.

This last basic Plotinian tenet issues from his recovery of the cosmic (as well as the personal) significance of *eros* as introduced by Plato in his *Symposium* and *Phaedrus*, but largely ignored by the more 'academic' Middle Platonists. Yet, while thus emphasising the radical distinction of the One from all else (which is to say the engendered universe), Plotinus fails adequately to develop the monotheistic implications of that distinction.

According to Plotinus, human souls, presently incarnated in the bodies of individuals, share in 'the desire to return' (that is, to the One) that lies yet within their power since the soul is not entirely 'fallen': we are not totally corrupt – not, that is, totally committed to bodily, let alone to materialistic life but can, as it were, pull ourselves up by our spiritual bootstraps. Most Platonists after Plotinus were less optimistic, supposing that our unaided 'love' (that *eros* on which Plotinus placed renewed emphasis) will not suffice but we must be helped by the gods via what they called 'theurgy', a kind of pagan sacramentalism. If we ask why we have 'fallen' into our present alienated condition, Plotinus replies that nothing other than the One can be defect-free; moral and spiritual insufficiency is inseparable from our finite existence – necessarily finite since God, being unique, could not produce another God (a logical, not ontological point).

Plotinus had been influenced by Stoic criticism of Plato's failure to account for humans except as members of a set, with a resulting inability to account for the uniqueness each of us exhibits; yet as a good Platonist, he is arguably too little concerned about this. Furthermore he, like other ancient philosophers, thinks of human beings as to be understood in metaphysical and physical terms alone, without attention to an approach via biography, personal and cultural, such as his admirer, the Church Father Augustine, would later emphasise.

For we are not mere members of a human set – so we at least suppose, unless we succumb to a despairing longing to submerge our painful and troubling differences in some hoped-for homogeneous whole. To this we shall return. Plotinus, understanding as he did that reality is inseparable from creativity, might have gone on to investigate our individual natures in more personalised historical contexts. For creativity his One is the supreme exemplar and insofar as we can 'return' to it and be identified with it (that is, literally made one with it, for it is a false reading of Plotinus to regard this identification as a 'submerging' of the self), we can share in that creativity. Indeed our business 'here-below' is to impose structure and order on the world by making ourselves One-like – even though in not *being* the One, we shall always run up against the deadening force of our finite existence. Matter, being 'formless' and inert, is as far from the One as anything can be; the body is for Plotinus 'a corpse adorned'. (As if in illustration of this, Plotinus seems to have died of leprosy.)

According to his pupil, editor and biographer Porphyry, Plotinus had mastered the major philosophical traditions of his day, meaning Platonism, Aristotelianism and Stoicism. Reading Plotinus' *Enneads*, we can recognise the justice of that observation and note how he has carried much further a project already in sight among his Middle Platonist predecessors: namely to set the best of Aristotle and of the Stoics upon Platonic philosophical foundations. Nonetheless, whatever the success of various Neoplatonists, their tendency to believe that Plato and Aristotle were saying much the same thing, and hence Aristotle could be used as an introduction to Plato, had an immense historical impact. Many of the so-called Aristotelian commentators in late antiquity were Neoplatonic philosophers who handed Aristotle down to Medieval Christian successors as a blend of Platonic transcendentalism, providence and *eros*-theory, together with Aristotle's more 'scientific' analysis of cosmos and human nature. From this would emerge the comparatively well developed account of the human person (*persona*) that would dominate Western thought until the seventeenth century and in some quarters yet survives.

*

By the time Porphyry published Plotinus' *Enneads*, a new and radically distinct challenger had appeared on the philosophical scene. The Christians, already recognisable as a group to Plotinus, would be more distinctly noted by Porphyry, who may have been a consultant to Diocletian on the last official persecution. Not yet in control of society, they could be viewed as a threat to ancient culture, dangerous not only intellectually but to the stability of a political order which emperors for nearly a hundred years had tried to unite in a restricted monotheism, with themselves as God's representative on earth, if not its actual god: '*Vae, puto deus fieri!*'': 'Alas, I think I'm becoming a god!' are reputed the mocking last words of the Emperor Vespasian. As this saying implies, the imperial cult allowed polytheism to survive in a subordinate role, often in late antiquity with some overarching form of Sun-worship.

Even before Constantine would authorise the Christian cult throughout his Empire, many Christian intellectuals preferred to think of themselves as purifying and completing the ancient culture with theology *(theo-logia* meaning 'reasoning about the divine') added to philosophy. The more 'fundamentalist' supposed theology would, could and should simply replace philosophy: a dispute foreshadowing the European 'Reformation'.

Which brings us to our third 'foundational' city after Athens and Rome, namely Jerusalem, and that Hebrew culture whose archaic age came to an end in about 400 BC with the formalisation of the worship of Yahweh by the Prophet Ezra after the return from Babylon – and which would provide the roots of a later Christian priestly sacramentalism.

More than 400 years later, after the execution of Jesus, many of his followers in that same city of Jerusalem believed that the Son of Man would return 'in glory' within their lifetime, while others held that the 'time of the Gentiles', in which the Gospel should be preached to all nations, must precede that final Day. Some, such as the author of the *Apocalypse*, believed that following the Neronian persecution and the 'Year of the Four Emperors' (69 AD), when the city of Rome was grievously battered by the competing legions of those who sought to replace the Julio-Claudian dynasty, a new Jerusalem would arise and the Last Day would be close at hand. In the event, Jerusalem, with its Temple and Temple-cult, was destroyed by the Roman armies and the remaining Christians in the city fled to Pella, in what is now Jordan. Imperial Rome was destined to last another 400 years – to be succeeded by the 'New Rome', Constantinople.

The sack of Jerusalem and destruction of the Temple thus proved decisive for both Jews and Christians. Probably in the early days of the 'Jesus-movement' many adherents thought that Judaism would simply morph into Christianity. That did not happen. Temple worship would be succeeded by the Pharisees' careful construction of the rabbinic Judaism we know today, retaining the majority of Jews in a worship of Yahweh more straightforwardly monotheistic than the evolving trinitarianism of Christianised preachers. With the Churches becoming ever increasingly 'Gentile', Christian thinkers began to turn their attention to Graeco-Roman thought and culture, realising that if they were to convert Gentiles, they needed to understand how Gentiles had learned to think. Warned by that outstanding converted Jew to be known as Paul against 'vain philosophies' as peddled by the sophists, yet confident that God's Truth must be one wherever and however found and that the Gentiles too had had – conspicuously in Socrates – their wise men, Christians set themselves to investigate the philosophical schools in quest of a rational basis for their Judaeo-Christian faith.

The immediate task facing these first Christian thinkers was twofold. Their Old Testament roots were largely unknown in the Gentile world, and the Jewish monotheism they had adopted – and, as they held, completed – was alien to pagans: no classical philosopher is in any strict sense a monotheist, though in Neoplatonism in particular we have noted significant moves in that direction. The earliest preoccupation of Christian teachers had been to explain to Jews how their own readings of the Hebrew Bible (usually, including within Palestine, in the Greek Septuagint translation) were validated in that the Prophets had predicted the coming of the Messiah, which prophesies were verified in the person of Jesus.

Yet while polemics with Jews – represented in the writings of Justin in the second century – continued, often with increasing bitterness on both sides, the fundamental task facing Christians became to expound for their Gentile hearers the culture of 'The Law and the Prophets' within which Jesus had lived his earthly life and taught. This led to lengthy and at times fanciful commentaries on what they now denoted the 'Old' Testament or Covenant with God: a tradition persisting down the ages until, in more recent times, historical analysis has generally replaced allegorisation and the search for the 'spiritual' sense of the Jewish Scriptures.

So it was that the Samaritan Justin ('Martyr' as he eventually became), in addition to combating Judaism – in this largely arguing with the past – also pointed to the future, being the first Christian convert who we know sought to 'cover his Christianity with the philosopher's cloak'. Visiting various philosophical schools, he found the Platonists the most edifying and to his purpose; others were to prefer Stoicism as seeming better to support a moral rigorism. Epicureans and Aristotelians were written off as 'atheists', meaning not that they disbelieved in a god or gods, but that they denied providence: that is divine concern with humanity. Scepticism, with its discipline of doubt, was, until Augustine, a non-starter.

Justin is important less as himself a philosopher than as a Christian convinced that Christianity and philosophy, especially Platonism, are compatible. Like all his Christian successors, he would need the proverbial 'long spoon' if he was to 'sup' with those pagans whom many of his co-religionists would regard as diabolical: he needed, that is, painstakingly to sort out which features of (in particular) Platonic philosophy could provide the underpinnings of a Christian metaphysic, and which to discard as alien to it.

Justin understood that though the transcendentalism of the Middle Platonists might seem to serve his turn, unacceptable must be their attitude to the relationship between soul and body, along with their assumption of the soul's 'natural' immortality. For a Christian, as he realised, the soul must be immortal not by nature but solely by grace: otherwise there could have been no beginning of the universe as *Genesis* taught and Christians believed. Nor could survival after death be viewed simply as the immortality of the soul: Christ's resurrection meant that the body must be so integrally wedded to the soul that it too will somehow survive physical death. Indeed, that the human being is composed of (ultimately) separable soul and body was alien to Christianity's Jewish heritage; Platonism, however – as philosophical discussion more generally – assumed their separability in some sort. Justin (and others) had to strive to express a Hebrew understanding in Greek terms.

That pointed to a future in which an Aristotelian account of the soul-body relationship would be needed to replace the Platonic vision. How to square that with Plato's transcendentalism would pose a problem. While pagan intellectuals, as Justin knew, might have room for the immortality of the soul, the resurrection of the body would be, to them, an absurdity. Later Christian thinkers would face such similar dilemmas as: If I want to be a Christian Platonist, what aspects of Platonism must I discard if I am to avoid heresy (the word is from the Greek '*hairesis*', meaning Choice)? Around the year 180, Theophilus, Bishop of Antioch, had warned his readers that they must reject Plato's claim in *Timaeus* that the Maker of the cosmos worked on pre-existing matter. Here we see an early sign of a coming intellectual revolution.

Then could Stoicism, as being also a 'providentialist' creed, serve the inquiring Christian better? Its moral rigor – especially its hostility to distracting erotic emotion – might seem to favour what right religion should demand. Moreover, if the soul is 'material', as the Stoics taught, might that make the resurrection easier to explain, perhaps as a restoration to our original divine (though material) state? Might the Stoic Theory of Action, emphasising willed assent, make more acceptable God holding us responsible?

Yet in a related respect, Stoicism could seem problematic, its world-picture being suggestive of a determinism opposed to free will, so incompatible with orthodox Christianity's account of the just judgments of God. Hence was a Stoicising Christianity, like Stoicism itself, on the way out by the end of the second century, though its teachings about *apatheia* – the extirpation of all irrational feeling – might linger as incentive to ascetic excess. Amid all these Stoic possibilities, and decisive in Christian thought, especially as it was going to develop in ensuing centuries, would be a concept with part-Stoic roots: Tertullian's explanation of the Christian Trinity in terms of 'persons'.

We read in Cicero that according to the Stoic Panaetius our individual nature can be analysed in terms of four *personae* (the

Latin word derives from Etruscan and begins by meaning 'masks'): each one 'inside' the other and each in turn supplying a more detailed picture of the life to which we are best suited. Thus the first and 'outer' *persona* shows our common nature as human beings, the second our individual characteristics (*propria natura*), the third our particular situation in society, the fourth the individual aptitudes for which we may find openings in our life situations – as that one may be apt for politics or for horticulture. If we take all these *personae* together, we shall have a grasp on our *overall* persona and hence what role we may rationally adopt among the opportunities available to us. We 'persons' are thus the 'blends' – to include our blend of soul and body – which render us more or less able to take on and perform our individual roles.

In this wise would Tertullian, in late second century Carthage, expound to his hearers that there are three 'persons' in God and that the second of these 'persons' had united ('been blended') with the man Jesus. Once the concept had become established in Latin theology, it was inevitable that person-language would be used not only to describe the nature and actions of the Christian God, but also of human beings understood as created in His image. As persons, we must be some combination of soul and body and designed for some particular role – and that regardless of whether we be viewed in terms of the all-material blending of the Stoics or as the immaterial soul blended with the material body as proposed by Aristotle. With the growing recognition by Christians that God cannot be material (the 'materialist' view was still alive in fourth-century North Africa where Augustine grew up), it was inevitable that eventually something like the Aristotelian account would prevail: how then to combine it – as we have seen the Neoplatonists (though for different reasons) already trying to combine it – with Platonic transcendentalism?

Though Tertullian would be the future of Trinitarian speculation, in the third century the principal Christian thinkers – often located, like Clement and Origen, in Alexandria and writing in Greek – became more seriously Platonic. In Clement this would produce a certain confused fusion of a lingering Stoicism with a Platonism more learned than Justin's. Origen would settle for a more single-minded Platonism, leading him to combine the soul's pre-existence with the notion ('platonic' and much favoured by so-called Gnostics of his times) that it had fallen into its body as a punishment – to be freed, when eventually purified, to live in godlike immateriality. With both the non-providentialist Aristotle and Stoic divine materialism discredited, Origen's Platonism might seem logical; the correction needed was to emphasise the role of the body. It was to take three full-scale Church Councils (Nicaea, Ephesus and Chalcedon) to indicate the solution in the human completeness of Christ as 'fully Man' while also 'fully God'.

Origen not only failed to disentangle himself from a number of Platonising 'errors'; he fell foul of the seductions of the Greek language in the ambiguities of its word *logos*. John's Gospel famously opens with Christ as the Logos: what could that mean? Plotinus, Origen's near contemporary, held that the Divine Mind is the Logos of the One: meaning by that an inferior manifestation of the One. In Christian terms, that would mean that Christ as Logos is inferior to the Father. Origen, relying on this Platonic, rather than on the Stoic understanding of the word, fails to adequately dispose of that implied inferiority.

Nevertheless, and despite his logos-theory's 'Arian' form being implicitly condemned by the Council of Nicaea in AD 325, the Platonising influence of Origen on the Christianity – especially the Christian mysticism – of the next centuries would be immense. But Origen had to be followed with an eye to avoiding both his 'subordinationist' account of Christ and his Stoically influenced 'encratism': that is, an ultra-asceticism accompanying Platonising accounts of the soul-body relationship. Notoriously he is said to have castrated himself to escape from the temptations of the flesh. In the view of some (and of one of his writings), this story is a canard.

Be all that as it might, Origen's take on creation would prove a 'game-changer'. As we have noted, it had been axiomatic at least since

Parmenides in the fifth century BC that 'nothing comes from nothing' – from which was concluded that the universe is eternal. Yet Christians as early as the late second century had come to realise that the implication of their Scriptures was unambiguously that God is omnipotent and has created the universe *ex nihilo* (from nothing). Negation of the Parmenidean axiom was thus intrinsic to Christianity.

An omnipotent God – though tentatively approached by Plotinus – had been inconceivable to classical Greek metaphysics as implying a radical difference between the Creator and everything created. To Origen it fell to lay down that to deny creation from nothing as an act of God's omnipotence implied an inadequate and irrational concept of the God of Revelation. It nonetheless would for centuries provide Christians with a metaphysical challenge to defend this new axiom, until, in the medieval period, the problem would be reformulated as whether Being is 'univocal': that is, whether or not it applies identically to God the Creator and to created things. We shall come up against this question again.

Origen also made a serious attempt to clarify the necessary Christian assumption that man's will must be 'free' if the justice of God's rewards and punishments is to be intelligible. Observing that neither Platonists nor Stoics had been able to solve the problem of the origin of moral evil, even though the Stoic Chrysippus had made a particularly praiseworthy attempt, he argued that the Scriptures – a source of data unavailable to pagans – reveal that the problem of evil, and hence of free will, can only be resolved if we factor in the fall of the angels: in them a pure case of gratuitous malice. Angels would figure prominently in the coming difficulties for medieval thinkers on this same issue.

Thus despite his 'subordinationist' heresy, Origen must be recognised as the most able representative in pagan times of the coming new order of understanding. Even in his lifetime he was grudgingly identified as such by Porphyry who, deeply hostile to Christianity as he was, could not but admire Origen's great learning, while remaining astonished at how able he was in adapting Greek philosophy to 'barbarian' (i.e. Christian) 'myths' (by which he meant fantasies).

*

The cultural structure of the Graeco-Roman world was soon to change with the providential-seeming success of Constantine over his rivals to become not only sole Emperor but a Christian of sorts. His predecessors had failed to unify the known world under the banner of the Sun-God with themselves as his representative; Constantine found the new 'sun' of the Christians a more plausible option. And we, having arrived at what is a turning point in European and indeed world history, may pause to review, from fifth century BC Athens to early fourth century AD Rome, those features of the coming intellectual vision of man and God which were to dominate Western European thought in those 'Ages of Faith' – our 'Original Tradition' – which might appear in our time to have run its course.

Thus, in summary:

> The universe has been created from nothing by an omnipotent and immaterial God, source of the moral law in his own person and being (and importantly *not* in his 'will' viewed abstractly). Man is best viewed as a conjunction of soul and body, possessed of self-awareness together with powers of discursive reason, intuition and an 'erotic' charge capable of raising him 'by grace' – that is, with divine assistance – spiritually above the level of his otherwise now 'fallen' state. Being possessed of dignity as an image of the divine and able to recognise himself as part of a 'transcendent' cosmos preserved under the eye of its providential creator-deity, man organises himself best in communities based on the laws of nature – to include human nature. The contents of the 'moral space' he inhabits, however, were massively disputed and the later widely used designation 'person' is as yet only sketchily understood. Agreed on all sides was that for the world to be intelligible must

depend on the existence both of the God Whose nature gives us the 'natural law' and of the immaterial human soul. Without these we are reduced to an Epicurean 'atheism' or a corrosive scepticism, while the ghost of a Thrasymachean nihilism lurks – and will reappear with the waning of the Ages of Faith.

3 From Constantine to Henry VIII

You are now a great man; you have restored the ancient Church, and what is a mark of even greater glory, all heretics detest you.

Jerome writing to Augustine

Constantine did not outlaw paganism in the Roman Empire; that would take the best part of a century to come about under Theodosius I. It was as self-styled 'Bishop of the Pagans' that Constantine intervened in ecclesiastical affairs well before he, in 325 AD, summoned his 'fellow' bishops to a Council at Nicaea, allowing them to travel there in imperial style at government expense. His purpose was to ensure that the newly state-supported religion should be unified and he had decided to back what was to become orthodoxy against those dissidents (called 'Arians' after Arius, a preacher of the diocese of Alexandria) who held the Son to be subordinate to the Father. The Emperor did not chair the Council meetings himself, these being placed under the presidency of bishop Ossius of Cordoba in his *de facto* role as court chaplain. The proceedings were governed by rules similar to those of the Roman Senate, with the president controlling the agenda; hence all motions had to pass through Ossius' hands, no motion from the floor being permitted. As a result – and whether or not under the guidance of the Holy Spirit – imperial policy became the prevailing orthodoxy.

Then the Emperor changed his mind, it seems finding Arianism more to his unifying purpose. Soon the principal anti-Arians were in exile and Constantine (having disposed of various uncooperative relatives) was eventually baptised on his deathbed by the Arian bishop of

Nicomedia. Thus were fought out the first battles in a war between Church and State: to continue for centuries, accompanied by an increasing cultural divergence among Christians that would in time yield a divided Empire with distinct Western and Eastern Churches based respectively on Rome and on the new and ever pagan-free imperial capital, Constantinople.

Already before Constantine there had been signs of an East-West split in the growing Church, as in the Empire more generally. Since the time of Hadrian in the second century, the eastern part of the Roman world had been governed by a largely Greek speaking bureaucracy. (The army persisted in using Latin.) In general, Eastern bishops were better educated, with clear theological patterns emerging among them, deriving above all from the work of Origen and to be further developed after the Council of Nicaea – any ('Platonising') subordination of Christ having been ruled out by the 'Nicene' Creed there agreed and promulgated. After the death of Theodosius in 395, the Roman world became permanently divided under his two Emperor sons, rulers respectively of the now Eastern and Western (both claimed to be 'Roman') Empires.

Eastern bishops were now in control of the theological agenda; indeed, at Nicaea most of the participants were Easterners, the bishop of Rome – though afforded a notional precedence in honour of the Primacy of Peter – being represented by legates. Western theology, largely deriving from the dubiously orthodox Tertullian and from Cyprian, must have looked decidedly backward to Easterners and been little noticed by them. However, prospects for theology in the East and West were to be decisively affected by political change outside Church control. Whereas the last Western Emperor would be deposed in 476, his domains being parcelled out among variously developing 'barbarian' kingdoms, in the East the Empire was to last until Constantinople would fall to the (Muslim) Ottoman Turks in 1453. By this time Caesaropapism – the blending of much civil and religious power in a supreme ruler – had been there long and definitively established.

The Eastern bishops most intellectually influential in the century after Nicaea were the 'Cappadocians': Basil, his younger brother Gregory of Nyssa and Gregory Nazianzen. These persisted with the 'Platonising' tradition in mystical and philosophical theology while devoting themselves to ever more elaborate reflection on the mysteries of the Trinity and the so-called hypostatic union of the God-man Jesus Christ. In exaggeratedly Neoplatonic mode, they were followed by a sixth-century Syrian who, claiming to be Dionysius the convert of St Paul, secured huge respect and despite his false credentials remains of interest today as 'Pseudo-Dionysius' – whose 'take' on Christianity, as the Easterners read him, could be summed up as liturgical mysticism with virtually no moral theology.

The Cappadocians' emphasis was pastoral rather than theoretical; they inveighed – to little effect – against poverty, prostitution and slavery. An exception was that Gregory of Nyssa would develop, out of his Trinitarian and Christological speculations, a major theme of Christian metaphysics (for which Origen had prepared the way) in recognising the radical disjunction between the One God and all else as being between the infinite and the finite. Plotinus, with whom Gregory was familiar, had acknowledged this distinction but not its crucial importance: for him it is marginal, whereas for Gregory it became central. Subsequent generations – especially, as we shall see, among the Latins – would draw out further implications.

After Gregory, perhaps the most intellectually distinguished figure to appear in the East would be a seventh-century independent-minded monk-theologian, Maximus 'the Confessor', who combined insights from a variety of philosophical schools with detailed investigation of the Christological teachings of the Council of Chalcedon (451). Maximus' account of human personhood (even today insufficiently clarified) broke new ground but provoked little further development in the East; however, with parts of his work translated into Latin, he would influence thirteenth-century Scholasticism.

After Maximus, the Byzantines would produce rather little that would impact upon what was by now a purely Latin culture in the West, resorting rather to the canonising of their fourth-century theological past. Their influential teacher Gregory Palamas (1296–1359) was virtually unknown outside the shrinking borders of the Byzantine Empire itself, and the more 'Aristotelian' theology of John of Damascus, composed in early Islamic times, had only limited influence in the West. Translated into Latin, and by 1220 increasingly known in the schools, it would play its part in inaugurating the coming Aristotelian era, though it was to prove a mixed blessing, introducing Stoic concepts into Aristotle's account of human action.

'Orthodox' theology remained largely the property of a state church such as Constantine might have dreamed of, albeit from time to time the Emperor's religious authority was challenged; indeed, he might be 'heretically' inclined, especially when seeking the elusive religious uniformity so desired from Constantine's time. When the Empire finally collapsed, its one Church would be gradually replaced by national churches, Caesaropapism persisting not least in the rapidly developing Church of a Moscow styling itself 'The Third Rome'.

Thus in post-seventh-century Byzantium, while there was plenty of theological controversy, much of it concerning icons, there was little intellectual movement – despite the availability of potentially helpful pre-Christian philosophical writings beyond the dreams of contemporary Westerners. Nor did any single thinker emerge in the East who was at all comparable with the Romanised North African Augustine – who would dominate to the extent that even contemporary Western society is unintelligible without some understanding of the Augustinian Middle Ages. Neither the Cappadocians, Maximus, John Damascene nor Gregory Palamas secured an equivalent authority in the East, nor would they substantially influence our present Western culture either positively or by provoking negative reactions. They remain possible sources of future enrichment.

What, however, Byzantium did provide for a Western world growing ever more distant from the Byzantine culture was a gift beyond price. In holding back for more than 900 years the 'holy warriors' of Islam, it would play a major role in saving Western Christianity from the fate of the once Christian lands of the Near East and North Africa – including the early centres of Christian thought and culture at Alexandria and Antioch. Only the defeat of the Turks, first in the crucial sea battle of Lepanto in 1571, then before the gates of Vienna in 1683, would mark effective resistance to Islam having devolved from the Byzantines to the Latins. Meantime, mainstream European culture was free to evolve – in whatever direction.

*

For by then in the West things had worked out very differently, both politically and culturally. Whereas in the East the inevitable church-state wars resulted in national churches, that solution only became an intelligible option in the West with the 'Reformation', some 1,200 years after Constantine. For most of the intervening period, though 'Holy Roman' emperors would continue to claim a 'Roman' authority (while, as Voltaire would remark, being 'neither holy nor Roman'), no secular leader would venture to view the Church as essentially his Ministry of Religious Affairs.

Despite localised disputes from time to time, the ongoing primacy of the papacy rendered minimal any risk that the Church might be subordinated to State; indeed, the doctrine of 'the two swords' (civil and ecclesiastical) had been formally pronounced by Pope Gelasius in 474. In the eighth century the papacy would be materially strengthened by the grant of an Italian principality backed by the Catholic rulers of France and thereafter, rather than the State intruding on the Church, popes such as Gregory VII and Innocent III would be happy (if rash) enough to claim a higher authority for the religious 'sword' even in such political matters as the deposition of princes: this on the grounds that bishops were appointed by and directly answerable only to God.

Nevertheless, and although in the West the political situation in the early Middle Ages was becoming more fluid than in the comparatively static Byzantine Empire, by Constantine's time Westerners had still not adopted an unambiguous theological direction. Though the Great Council of Nicaea had determined orthodoxy for West as for East, nothing analogous to the semi-Platonic theology adopted by Clement of Alexandria, Origen, the Cappadocians and among the Byzantine monks and bishops, had as yet been firmly established there.

At the end of the fourth century, however, an alternative version of this was in the making, due in part to three authorities. Ambrose of Milan was an ecclesiastical paladin able to put even the Emperor Theodosius to penance for ordering a massacre; Ambrose had a certain familiarity with Greek theology and affirmed God's 'spiritual' and immaterial nature in the Platonic and Neoplatonic tradition. Jerome (Hieronymus) is the stalwart translator of the Bible from Hebrew and Greek into respectable Latin. Over these two eminences towers Augustine, soon to become bishop of Hippo in North Africa, whose mark on Western cultural traditions – if not always for the better – would remain unparalleled.

Born in 354 AD in an especially secure part of the Roman Empire, Augustine might well have assumed that his world would last forever; yet when he died in 430, his see of Hippo was under siege by the Vandals and he was writing letters to his fellow bishops urging them to remain unflinching at their posts, even if risking torture for moneys they did not possess. Four years earlier he had completed his book of 'Reconsiderations' (or 'Re-treatments': '*Retractationes*'), in which he catalogued large parts of his writings and corrected whatever errors he found. He had realised that in the impending situation he was about to become an oracle.

At the time when, still a young man, Augustine left Africa for Milan, he was well read in the Latin Classics: Vergil, Cicero, Terence, Sallust, Varro. In Milan the 'spiritualising' Christianity of Archbishop Ambrose was a revelation; previously Augustine seems to have assumed, with many of his North African fellows, that God is material. In Milan he read parts of Plotinus' *Enneads* translated into Latin – much later tackling Porphyry's onslaught *Against the Christians*, along with the exegetical writings of the biblical scholar Tyconius and such Latin Christian authorities as Tertullian, Hilary of Poitiers and Cyprian.

Eventually he would read a certain amount of theological writing in Greek, of which he had limited knowledge; however, his Western successors would normally know none, hence being cut off from theology and philosophy of the remote past except where individual texts had been translated into Latin – when they were at the mercy of the translator and liable to miss differing nuances of words, thus distorting the original sense.

This situation would have an effect on Augustine's 'after-life', that while he himself was widely read in pagan and Christian authors, most of his successors knew little more – the Scriptures apart – than some of his own Latin writings and those of Ambrose, Jerome, Boethius and later Pope Gregory the Great. As a result, Augustine would become the largely unchallenged authority for over a thousand years, his writings conveying into the Medieval period almost all that would be known of the wider Graeco-Roman culture. In effect, he had become the new starting point. Yet his works were not read in anything like their entirety and it is difficult with many of his medieval followers to determine which works they knew first-hand, which they erroneously believed to be by Augustine and which were only read in selected extracts taken out of context – as from the *Sentences* of Peter Lombard, for centuries a foundational text for students of theology.

Augustine had himself warned his readers that his thoughts on major matters of theology or philosophy (he did not view them as separate, holding that theology grounded the intelligibility of philosophy) had changed radically over time, but this warning, even where known, was ignored; 'one head, one philosophy' was again the assumption and on this basis a somewhat variable but always systematic Augustine would be constructed by each and every medieval 'Augustinian'.

What, then, was the outlook of this 'medieval' Augustine who refounded what we have called the Original Tradition of Western thought – to be expounded most fully, in enriched though still imperfect formulation, by Thomas Aquinas in the thirteenth century? It can be summed up as: before all, belief in the Trinitarian God, then that souls created by God are immortal, though each needs purification since damaged by Adam's fall, further that we look forward to bodily resurrection at the end of time.

Augustine believed that God's existence can be demonstrated, since if we conceive of anything superior to our minds, yet eternal and unchangeable, that must deserve the name 'God': must actually *be* God. Such an entity could only be Truth, which Augustine identifies with the person and teaching of Christ. Unlike later ages, he was under no great pressure to demonstrate God's existence, since hardly any were to be found who denied it – as distinct from those who, like the Epicureans, denied Providence or God's concern for humanity. What mattered was to show, against the pagans, something of God's nature, and that Christ's nature and acts, when pondered, add human flesh to metaphysical commonplaces, such as that God is great or just or good. One of Augustine's most influential books would be *On the Trinity*, in which he sets out a theological account of the Scriptural information about God, with an explanation of how we are created in a likeness of the Three Persons in having the capacities of memory, intelligence and love. With Tertullian and others pointing the way, much of Augustine's most important psychological analysis develops from reflection on the Trinity.

As has been demonstrated at various times, unaided human reason cannot come up with the Christian understanding of the Trinity. In offering a Scripturally-based but essentially rational account, Augustine was carrying on the work of Gregory of Nyssa (though he probably had not read him). For Gregory, as we have noticed, the Christian God must be radically distinct from the universe He has created: a difference best appreciated in the distinction between the infinite and the finite. While that is a metaphysical rather than a theological distinction, Augustine's discussion of the Trinity aims to establish how revelation shows metaphysics turned into theology. His description of God as the greatest possible object of thought was to be further expounded in the twelfth century by Anselm.

Augustine came to renounce the Platonic and Neoplatonic view that we 'are' our souls but would never find a satisfactory way of explaining the relationship between soul and body, leaving his account seriously incomplete and being reduced to relying on 'marital' metaphors. Nevertheless, he thought that as 'persons' – his term – we are a mysterious mixture of soul and body and that the resurrection of the body (for which we long) is the essentially Christian corollary of the soul's immortality.

Augustine tells us in *The Soliloquies* that all he wants to know is the truth about God and the soul, for – and as he states elsewhere – he finds himself a mystery. Thus in *On the Trinity* he remarks that 'I want to know what I am, because I do not know myself; yet if I do not know myself, how could I understand that I have come to know myself? I seem both to know and not to know myself.' Although (as first in *Against the Sceptics*, to whom, under Cicero's influence, he paid unusual attention) he can demonstrate his own existence, he cannot know what he will be like tomorrow, nor how he will react to any coming moral challenge; he is unstable and unpredictable. Much of this mystery of himself on which he ponders is due to the fact that, as a member of the human race, he has been stricken – we might now think of this as 'genetic' – by the 'Fall': that is, by the 'original' sin of Adam. For under one aspect we are 'one in Adam' in sharing a common humanity and inheriting its weaknesses, both individual and social.

Inherited sin can, by virtue of Christ's Incarnation, be washed away in baptism, which hence is (for Augustine, as for most in antiquity) now indispensable for all with the sole exception of martyrs, and to be administered as early as possible, hence to infants. Still, the inherited weaknesses of intellect and of our *voluntas* (this Latin word, which for Augustine denoted the expression of our loves and hates, would come to be misleadingly translated as our 'will') remain throughout our earthly lives: a 'genetic' flaw afflicting us as members of the human race, the weaknesses it entrains being at the root of our personal and individual errors (Greek *hamartiai*) or sins (Latin *peccata*).

It is easy, Augustine holds, to forget about the Fall and believe that we can lead good lives without God's assistance, as powered by arrogance, we view ourselves as masters of our own moral destiny, even self-creators. That for Augustine is both theologically and empirically absurd; we can see in ordinary human behaviour the need always to be vigilant as to our moral weaknesses and so dependent on God's assistance. Those who deny this are in effect followers not of Christ but of the deviant monk Pelagius: a Briton, and 'Pelagianism' in various versions becomes an important part of the 'Western' – and not least British – cultural story. Though the Original Tradition ruled against it, it would rebound into favour as the 'West's' characteristic drive for autonomy picked up speed after the Reformation.

Human pride thus identified is cured by the specifically Christian virtue of humility – construed not as the snivelling humbug of a Uriah Heep, but as the recognition that we are created beings and liable to sin. Put more theoretically, Augustine would deny the oft-cited Kantian maxim that 'ought' implies 'can', for it is his view that for us as unaided moral agents following the Fall (for as man was originally conceived by God, Augustine holds that it would have been otherwise), 'ought' will rather imply 'cannot'. In that alone we recognise a fundamental difference between classical ethics and an Augustinian account of Christianity; hence when Aristotle's *Nicomachean Ethics* turned up in the West, medieval thinkers would find a challenge in the reconciling of the two rival accounts of the virtuous life.

Yet mankind is not totally corrupt and the 'elect' – seen by Augustine as a small portion of us (though he disclaims any ability to know who they are) – will be 'saved' by a faith formed upon God's love. Human love of the Good and hence desire for a good life are not abolished by the Fall, but we see their weakness in our moral and spiritual dependence: we are a wounded race and will only be healed by divine assistance ('grace') and so enabled to live a morally better life whereby to advance towards the 'heaven' that is God. 'Salvation' is thus unambiguously connected with moral improvement (by Augustine and others even called a process of 'divinisation': a being made like God). As we shall see, this compactness of salvation with morality (characteristic of all ancient thought) would fade in the later Middle Ages, giving way to purely secular attempts to construct an intelligible ethics.

Thus arises Augustine's view of us as living in two 'cities': the City of God and that of the devil towards which the communities of men will always tend. Inhabitants of the City of God will love God in 'contempt' of the 'world' and their worldly selves: that is, their very self-respect resides in dependence on God and involves loving our neighbour as we love ourselves. Citizens of the city of the devil, driven by pride and lust – for sex or for power – 'love' themselves to the point of contempt for others, for God and God's rational laws. These opposing 'cities' exist side by side in our earthly life, both in individuals and in collectivities. They are the 'wheat and tares' of Christ's parable, to be finally separated only at the Last Judgment.

Despite early 'Constantinian' longings for the construction of a Christian polity as part of a Roman eschatological history, Augustine came to see that political regimes, whether Christian or pagan, will in themselves play no part in the process of salvation – except that a Christian regime will (unless the rulers are heretical) favour the preaching of the Gospel and practice of the Faith. In any case, and whether or not encouraged in a Christian state, human perfection is not to be achieved in the present life: a claim that rejects all theories about perfectibility through any merely human 'care of the self'.

Even Peter and Paul, says Augustine, were not 'free' during their personal lives from the damage wrought by original sin, though like all the saints they will have longed for the 'desired necessity' of goodness that is in the perfection of 'heaven'.

And lest that might seem to deprive human beings of freedom of will, Augustine – like almost all ancient thinkers (Epicurus being a major exception) – held that to be truly 'free' is not to have the option between one course and another (today referred to as the Principle of Alternative Possibilities) but to be able – free – to choose only the Good. This principle had been identified as far back as Plato's *Republic*, where Plato imagines a man in possession of the ring of Gyges, with the aid of which he can become invisible, and asks his hearers whether the man will take advantage to rob, rape, murder. The good man will decline any such suggestions; if pressed he may eventually say that he is just not that kind of person, that 'I could not do that sort of thing' – where 'could not' denotes not physical incapacity but moral repugnance. Augustine calls this disposition 'desired necessity' and indicative of the godlike state to which we can attain only in the presence of God: that 'heaven' where His 'elect', having become like to Him, *cannot* do evil, nor have they even the (earthly) option of *deciding* to reject it.

Nor does God's foreknowledge – a necessary attribute of his divinity – imply that nothing is 'up to us', since that God knows what we shall do does not imply that he compels us to do it. Indeed, that God wishes our perfection must entail that he allows us to sin, ever in hope that we learn from our mistakes and 'repent' (which means to turn back with sorrow); otherwise we would be diminished as not being 'free' agents. What we call 'Predestination' is another matter, and though Augustine's more extreme misreadings of the Pauline epistles (to be further misinterpreted by Calvin) failed to find their place in medieval theology, they would leave behind a confusion perhaps having its root in his indecision. This was to prove disturbing even when the eventual appearance in print of most of what we now know of his writings would replace a partial earlier acquaintance.

Yet even with Augustine's warnings about the development of his thought now readily to hand, the 'one head, one philosophy' mentality would still prevail among his readers.

Though without apparent reference to the efforts of the Stoics and Plotinus, Augustine comes to take seriously the question of how we are to understand 'persons': that is, unique human individuals created in the image and likeness of (the Three-Person'd) God – albeit he apparently remained ignorant of a helpful sense of the Greek theological term *asungchutos*, meaning 'unconfused', used by an earlier bishop-philosopher, Nemesius, to describe that special 'blend' of soul and body of which the person is formed. This term was intended to make explicit something of which Augustine was certainly aware: that each individual human 'person' exhibits a unique 'mixture': that (as Aristotle had realised) he or she cannot be adequately recognised by a metaphysical analysis of soul and body that accounts for each only as a quantifiably distinct member of the human 'set'.

Hence the great breakthrough whereby Augustine understood that there is a non-metaphysical way to approach the 'unconfused' person, by recording the unique experiences of each individual life: that is, by biography or autobiography. He spent much time in the pulpit, not only teaching his congregations dogmatic theology – he had a huge gift for explaining complicated theological ideas in simple language – but also expounding Christian morality; he knew that the virtues and vices of each and every individual are different and that a successful moral teacher must understand individual motivations. We can discover a great deal about his theory of human action from his sermons, many of which have been preserved for us. In his autobiography, the *Confessions*, he points to his own moral weakness, which was for sexual activity, as different from that of his friend Alypius for gladiatorial violence in the arena.

Augustine also recognised that history could play a role in explaining the behaviour of whole societies, exhibiting their weaknesses and their strengths. His *City of God* is in effect the spiritual biography of the Roman Empire and its 'lust for domination' (*libido dominandi*). Unfortunately, though the *Confessions* and the *City of God* were – and are still – widely read, the illustrative implication of writing personal and societal biographies has largely eluded their readers, with the supplement they offer to more metaphysical accounts of humanity passing unnoticed. Indeed, Augustine himself could fail to recognise – as in his particular appreciation for the poetry of Vergil – that what we denote more purely literary works can also be philosophically thought-enriching.

That neglect would continue. As we shall see, only in the eighteenth century would philosophers come to appreciate how, for example, fiction can help us understand people by putting us 'into others' shoes'. We rather observe in ensuing centuries the attempt to exclude 'immoral' literature – too broadly so defined – from Christian reading: leaving such overexuberant authors as Boccaccio and Chaucer the only final recourse of a deathbed repentance!

*

While Augustine becomes a protagonist of the medieval intellectual drama – we have already noted distinguished actors Ambrose, Jerome, Boethius and Gregory the Great – we now turn to Boethius, the Gothic King Theodoric's astonishingly learned official and ultimately (in 526 as is probable) his murder victim. The still-bilingual Boethius seems to have intended to supply his Latin readership with translations of the complete writings of Plato and Aristotle, in addition to his own logical treatises and his death-cell masterpiece: *The Consolation of Philosophy*. Had his translation project come to fruition, the subsequent growth of European thought would have benefited immeasurably; thus, did Theodoric and his club-wielding executioners significantly impoverish the succeeding Western Middle Ages and, more broadly, the developing Original Tradition. A loss truly to be mourned.

On the side of gain, however, is that it fell to Boethius – a semi-Aristotelian Platonist who, like Augustine, feels challenged to understand what he is – to offer the first formal definition of the person, namely that (in the language of Aristotelian categories) a person is 'an individual substance of a rational nature' – or 'qualified by reason': distinguished, that is, by the quality of rationality. This definition – though still incomplete in that it makes no direct reference to human agency, let alone individual human biography – would serve as the basis to which further qualifications could be added – even though under one aspect, the incompleteness would be unfortunately influential in a way unintended by Boethius, who certainly held that man's dignity results from his being created 'in the image and likeness' of God. The Aristotelian aridity of his definition could not but affect future understanding of persons, encouraging the elaboration of increasingly detailed descriptions of man as an item, with only limited attention paid to his dignity and god-likeness. It thus pointed to the coming High Middle Ages when Aristotle (substantially Neoplatonised) would increasingly replace Plato and challenge the authority of Augustine as the major philosophical Master for Christians.

Boethius' Aristotelian definition of the person would in the twelfth century be further developed by Richard of Saint Victor, according to whom a person is a 'sole self-standing existent in a certain singular mode of rational existence'. Significantly, that existence is 'incommunicable': that is, the experience of each person (as Augustine had emphasised) is unique. Thus to the question, 'What is it like to be Richard of St Victor?', no complete answer can be given. Also in the steps of Augustine, Richard's theologising on persons is to be found in his treatise *On the Trinity*, and although he pays no attention to Augustine's emphasis on history and biography, nor to persons as active agents, he emphasises that they are relational beings, reflecting the 'relationality' of the Trinity and, in authentic love, reflecting the Trinity's inner life.

Richard's associating of persons with the Trinitarian Three guarantees that human dignity is assumed. And since, especially since Augustine, the Holy Spirit is understood as the Love proceeding from the Two (Father and Son) and binding the Three, so are Richard's persons properly related to one another by a love expressed in true friendship. Such a theological approach to persons shows us that Richard – despite an approved measure of Aristotelianism – is still living in the Platonic-Augustinian world: perhaps one of its last inhabitants before the accession of Aristotle to centre stage.

*

Before the twelfth century, nothing more than parts of Aristotle's logical works were known in the West. That changed in the thirteenth century when most of his major treatises had been rendered into Latin. Philosophers could now ponder the *Metaphysics*, the *Physics*, *On the Soul*, and – perhaps the most fateful newcomer – the *Nicomachean Ethics*, which reached the Dominican *studium* in Cologne in its entirety in 1248. The arrival of Dante's 'Master of those who know' – if somewhat coloured by the Neoplatonism imposed on him since late antiquity – meant that Augustine's authority, though normally paid at least lip service, no longer went unchallenged. Now the task was to square the two masters.

Prominent earlier thinkers – who, from Anselm and Aelred of Rievaulx through Bernard and Richard of Saint Victor, still lived largely in a world of Cathedral Schools usually staffed by 'secular' clerics (though with a monastic ethos) – had in some respects 'interpreted' Augustine to suit their own interests. Thus they might, as Aelred, emphasise 'spiritual friendship' rather than *eros*; or uphold the more Kantian-sounding suggestions of Abelard and others that Augustine's account of love was too 'eudaimonist' – that is, self-serving; they might, as Bernard, view God as more voluntarist than does Augustine and try to soften the eudaimonism by distinguishing grades of love; they might, as Richard, further develop Boethius' Aristotelian definition to explain the mysteries of the person. These pre-university thinkers, living and working in the Benedictine tradition, still recognised no alternative authority to Augustine. Some scholars view the twelfth century, in its basic 'Platonism' (strikingly displayed in Bernard's writings on the *Song of Songs*) as the last flowering of the Patristic Age.

Before leaving it, however, we should look a little more at Anselm and at his treatment of the radical distinction between the Creator and all that is created. Following in the footsteps of Origen and then of Gregory of Nyssa – neither of whom he could have read – Anselm was at least in a position to consider the progress made by Augustine, who in proof for the existence of God had pointed to 'the highest possible object of thought'. Anselm carried Augustine's intention to account rationally for his faith (as he put it, *fides quaerens intellectum*) into his so-called ontological argument for God's existence.

It is by no means certain that Anselm's primary concern was to argue against the 'fool' (of Psalms 14 and 53) who denies God's existence; rather his argument (like Augustine's) seems intended to show what the highest object of thought must be like: to emphasise, that is, the Christian and proper distinction between God and all else, while keeping open the possibility of giving a rational (not only a scriptural) account of God's nature. To do that – and thus defend the intelligibility of theological speculation – it seemed to Anselm necessary to claim that 'being' is 'univocal': that is, that it includes both God and (similarly) God's creatures. To claim this might, as we have noted, seem to contradict God's radical otherness, even his ability to create *ex nihilo*: Anselm, of course, is still working within the Platonic orbit – albeit 'univocity' is hardly 'Platonic'. We must await Aquinas to find a more successful attempt to explain *meta*physically the divine nature and the implications of the distinction infinite-finite.

In other respects too, Anselm points to the less coherent intellectual world of the *fourteenth* century. He was among the first to misinterpret Augustine's account of the relationship between love and 'will' in treating the will as some sort of faculty pitted against the faculty of intellect in the theatre of the soul. Further, the 'will' thus viewed – in effect as the reification of a concept – has to be free enough to guarantee that our misbehaviour, like that of the fallen angels, can, with justice, be held reprehensible by God. The introduction into the Augustinian tradition of these 'faculties' (will and intellect) gives the impression that not I but my 'will' – alternatively, not I but my intellect, viewed as 'determined' by its object – is agent. This misunderstanding of Augustine's 'classical' sense of the 'will' would afflict debates from Anselm on, seemingly coming to worry Aquinas himself at the end of his life – and illustrating the thesis of the Introduction to this book, namely that to set about answering a question already wrongly posed will only end in multiplying confusion.

In all this, Augustine's pervasive emphasis on will as the expression of love had been elbowed aside, while from the mid-thirteenth century philosophical theologians concerned themselves less with problems about how grace restored human freedom than with philosophical analysis – according to various readings and misreadings of Aristotle – of how 'freedom' is possible at all.

*

When the 'new' Aristotle appeared on the thirteenth century stage, the philosophical world of the Cathedral schools with their dominant 'Platonism' was radically affected. Now appeared the possibility of a more wide-ranging metaphysics, a full account of the cosmos and its contents, living and non-living, without resort to Platonising imaginings: in particular, a better explanation of the relationship of soul and body, which, characterised as 'marital' by Augustine, had significantly eluded him.

The recently formed religious orders, Franciscan and Dominican, who challenged the role of the secular clergy in the now rapidly developing universities – Paris and Oxford in particular – exulted in the new Aristotelian learning: first wave, as it was to turn out, of a recovery of ancient thought to put Augustine's limited knowledge in the shade. It would be followed in the fifteenth century by Latin versions of the whole of Plato and Plotinus and soon after that by the rediscovery of not only Stoicism but of the Epicureanism of Lucretius and the Scepticism of Sextus Empiricus – this last providing a more powerful version of scepticism than that which Augustine had worked to turn to his own purposes and, where he found it misused, to refute.

However, just as in antiquity, Christians attracted to Platonism needed, in accepting what could be compatible with traditional Christianity and its 'rule of faith', to be discriminating of that which could not; so did Aristotle pose the same problem? Perhaps most serious was that his account of moral action needed to be squared with Augustine's teaching that not only is God's assistance (*gratia*, 'grace') a pre-requisite for living the good life but more specifically that recognition of the Christian God is a necessary condition for the performance of every strictly virtuous act: meaning an act both right in its intended object and wholly pure in its motivation. That such recognition might need to be implicit rather than explicit was to prove a major source of the late medieval reconstruction of Augustine's position on baptism by affirmation of a 'baptism of desire'. Such a teaching might appear as a revival – if unwitting – of a claim by Justin Martyr that persons already behaving in a sufficiently Christian way are to be accounted under the influence of saving grace: Justin himself had so identified Heraclitus and Socrates – 'Saint Socrates' as he would become known to some.

Traditional-minded critics of the new Aristotelianism, such as the Spiritual Franciscan Peter John Olivi (ca.1248–1298), Thomas Bradwardine (ca.1290–1349, sometime archbishop of Canterbury) and Gregory of Rimini (ca.1300–1358, General of the Augustinian Order), would be quick to spot the 'Aristotelian problem' (in this at least being forerunners of Luther). As Olivi put it, attacking those members of the Paris Arts Faculty we now call the Latin Averroists (after the Arab commentator on Aristotle) as well as Aristotle himself: 'I am astonished to see that Aristotle the pagan and the Arab Averroes, as well as other unbelieving philosophers, are held by some in so great esteem and veneration and allowed so great an authority, especially in discussions or writings about sacred theology.' Bradwardine more explicitly complains that 'there is nothing about grace in the schools'; and that, for our present theologians, 'it is in our power to do good and bad'. He means *entirely* in our power after baptism: the Pelagian option.

Debate over the role of logic in theology was not new when Olivi wrote, for already in the twelfth century Peter Abelard had run into trouble over it. But with the new universities – and not least because of an un-Augustinian separation of philosophy and theology as institutionalised in distinct Arts and Theology faculties – the situation became more urgent. In Paris, the 'Averroists' thought of themselves as secure in the Arts Faculty; like the later Descartes, they claimed that their speculations – as about Aristotle's ideas on the possibility of perfect virtue – could be ring-fenced against ecclesiastical censure. This view would prove mistaken; yet their time was to come, and we may look back on them as a first step toward the undoing of the link between theology – hence eventually salvation – and ethics.

*

Thomas Aquinas (1225–1274), apart from providing the most complete account of the 'Original Tradition' of Western philosophical thought as it had developed up to his time, is generally credited as the thinker who best unified Augustine with Aristotle. A number of his contemporaries, probably to include Bishop Tempier of Paris, were less than convinced, and indeed though he had a fair degree of success, the assimilation was not complete – as Peter John Olivi would not be the only contemporary to maintain: and to do the saintly Thomas justice, we should bear in mind that before he died at the age of forty-nine, he himself declared that all he had written of God and His ways was 'as straw'. Before looking at the problems which remained unsettled – and which were often made worse by his immediate successors – we need to sketch his account of man, God and the cosmos in what he regarded as an advanced Augustinian synthesis: as the sum (he titled it *Summa*) of more than a thousand years of pre-Christian and Christian thought: in effect our 'Original Tradition'.

First, then, God. Aquinas, dissatisfied with what he takes – as have most, but not all Anselm's readers – to be intended by Anselm as 'proof' of God's existence, offered his Five Ways to demonstrate (rather than 'prove') this more effectively. More important than the details of these 'Ways' is that Aquinas develops a metaphysical account of the Christian distinction between Creator and creation: the Creator's 'essence' is existence itself, whereas creatures have only a dependent existence, inasmuch as their essence (or nature), being finite, exists only secondarily and for limited periods of time.

Then to the cosmos: created *ex nihilo* (out of nothing) by God, Aristotle has shown how its natural laws can be investigated by human reason. Although we cannot determine philosophically whether or not it is eternal (as Aristotle thought), by revelation we know that it was created in and with time. Indeed, since its very existence is good, we must accept it to be God's handiwork.

As for human societies, they are best explained in Aristotelian terms, and although Augustine has not advised us as to any preferred regime, we can rely on the axiom of Pope Gelasius that the spiritual and political realms are distinct. Ultimate authority rests with the Church, which through the duly appointed descendent of Peter has, by the 'power of the keys' (Matt. 16:19), the right to excommunicate and depose religion-defying kings and emperors. (This would work so long as the kings remained Catholic!)

Finally, persons are 'individual singulars' created in God's image. In Aquinas' own words: 'As [John] Damascene says, a human being is said to be made in the image of God, insofar as by "image" is meant something with understanding, free in its judgment and with power in itself.' As persons, we are not only possessed of a divine 'dignity' as images of God but are the source of our own actions, for which we are thus responsible. Going into further detail: we possess cognitive capacities, broadly understood to include self-awareness; we are capable of deliberated actions; we deploy various skills, especially the use of language. In sum, we are 'in act', the first of our acts being that 'act of existence' by which we are distinguished from mere essences or natures. I, that is, am more than a mere thought experiment of humanity, being an existent example of my genus and species.

Aquinas, however, fails to account for the uniqueness of my personal existence. *Qua* metaphysician, and neglecting Augustine's approach through biography, he represents individuality solely in quantitative terms, identifying us as individual substances differentiated materially. He thus accounts (as does Aristotle) for our plurality but not for our distinctiveness – which he of course recognises when thinking of our moral and political selves. Nor – as Olivi would object – has he succeeded in reconciling Augustine's account of the necessity of grace with Aristotle's characteristically 'classical' view that we are ourselves capable of moral perfection: unaided, that is, by God – though inevitably dependent on the society in which we find ourselves.

Aquinas attempts to resolve this difficulty – so mediating between Augustine and Aristotle – by evoking two 'ends' of life: a natural end as the perfection of the human virtues understood largely as Aristotle understood them, and a supernatural perfection possible only for Christians, whose 'Aristotelian' virtues may themselves become 'infused' by virtue of the more immediately 'infused virtues' of Faith, Hope and Charity. Yet, and as the Christian knows, this distinction of 'ends' must remain conceptual: for even if a solely classical perfection were attainable without God's 'grace', it cannot be the proper end or limit for us humans.

We recognise the difficulty when we watch Aquinas' analysis of the peculiarly striking Augustinian claim that pagan virtues are not real virtues: that indeed they are vices rather than virtues, for real virtue must be driven by the love of God and its pure and unmixed motives. This Aquinas 'interprets' to mean that although pagan virtues are 'real', they are imperfect; and that though good, they are not meritorious, being only the possible achievement of unaided man in his fallen state. Underlying his interpretation is a *separation* of moral (in this case Aristotelian) virtues from true virtues. Augustine would reply that an imperfect virtue is an attempted virtue, not a virtue, and that the implied separation of the 'moral' from the 'Christian and meritorious' life is unacceptable and dangerous – as indeed it would increasingly turn out to be from Scotus on. Human excellence, that is, cannot be allowed to be parted from the process of salvation, and Aquinas is clearer than Augustine that God wants all men to be saved by his working in them: that is, by grace.

A further change in the mentality of the newly 'Aristotelian' age from that of its more 'Platonic' predecessor – though we hold in mind Aelred on 'spiritual friendship' – is the increasing replacement of the language of erotic love by that of friendship with God: this perhaps in reaction against the ambiguously carnal, even un-Christian understanding of love in the poetry of the troubadours of the circle of the wife sequentially to Louis VII of France and Henry II of England, Eleanor of Aquitaine. Aristotle in the *Nicomachean Ethics* seems surprisingly uninterested in *eros*, viewing it as merely a more intense version of friendship; but Christian mystics held – though increasingly the more Aristotelian-minded did not – that the language of friendship may apply to aspects of the Christian life, but is inadequate to express the response to the divine love. Yet for Aquinas – personally a man given even to ecstasies – love is defined in coldly Aristotelian terms as 'willing good to someone'.

This development in the understanding of love points to a further and more basic problem. Augustine's account of *voluntas*, as we have already noted in Anselm, was widely misinterpreted, since 'will' for Augustine, is the expression of our loves and hates: hence, in the perfect exemplar of love, the Holy Spirit, love and will are identical. But because of increasingly 'voluntarist' accounts of God in Anselm, Abelard, Bernard and others – some of whom considered Augustine's account of love to be egocentric – the connection between loving and willing tends ever more to disappear. In Augustine this indispensable connection is dependent ultimately on the Platonic axiom that it is impossible to know the Good without loving it, nor possible to love the Good without knowing it.

And as love is moved backstage (so to speak), the soul – as we have noted in Anselm – becomes a theatre in which the two faculties of willing and thinking are seen as rivals: this to the detriment of any serious account of the person. Aquinas himself tried, unsuccessfully, to find a solution whereby thinking and willing could be reconciled and human responsibility thus protected. But the model of warfare in the theatre of the soul persisted – to be resolved differently in Duns Scotus and other post-Thomists.

What Aquinas offers is a more or less complete synthesis of what was possible in his day: a major achievement – and for centuries his writings (though at times inaccurately read – as was partially recognised by Pope Leo XIII) presided over our Original Tradition. He was, though, reliant on only limited support from classical philosophy and often in distorted form. After his death, substantial challenges begin to appear, though still (unlike what was to be the case in the sixteenth century) within existing parameters of Christian thought. They thus indicate less a change of approach than a premonition of change to come.

*

With the fourteen and fifteenth centuries we can already see the next thought-revolution on the horizon; by the beginning of the sixteenth century, it had arrived. The change can be understood as developing in three waves: first the voluntarism of the Franciscan Duns Scotus and of his confrère William of Ockham; then the revival of Platonism in humanist form with Marsilio Ficino and Pico della Mirandola; thirdly, the reconstruction of political and religious society theorised by Machiavelli, of which Henry VIII of England would be the first successful institutor.

Culturally too the fourteenth and succeeding centuries began to differ significantly from earlier times: the Church, still in her 'Avignon Captivity' for most of the century, would often appear both morally corrupt and prisoner of the king of France. The Franciscans in particular would acquire a reputation as lazy and debauched beggars trading on their religious status. In 1348 the Black Death (dramatically depicted by Boccaccio) wiped out at least a quarter of Europe's inhabitants, including William of Ockham (supplying later wits with the line: 'Things were worse in the fourteenth century!'). That the dispute among the learned between the two great Masters, Augustine and Aristotle, had not been resolved, encouraged a growing emphasis on God's omnipotence and the sheer unintelligibility of his apparently arbitrary dispensation of grace.

In many regions the older world-picture still prevailed (not least in England), yet the hierarchical, domineering and increasingly out-of-touch Church – principal upholder of the 'Original Tradition' – was losing her grip as the New Learning came to be desirous of a New (and often ultra-Augustinian) Theology, while there arose in many quarters movements seeking a more personal, less 'second-hand' relationship with God. When the religious Reformation eventually came – and prescinding from the political version which was imposed in England – there was a deep-seated longing for radical change, not least involving a radical revision of the relationship between the Church and the newly-developing nation-states. Few could place their finger on what precisely had gone wrong culturally and intellectually, while the more obvious abuses of the clericalised version of the Original Tradition could readily be exaggerated by radicals. These were unhappy centuries in much of Europe.

*

Duns Scotus (1265–1308) a younger contemporary of Aquinas whose name associates him with the town of Duns in Scotland, has long been recognised as pushing philosophy and theology in a direction which would prove destructive of older ways. Unlike his fellow Franciscan Olivi, however, he was a convinced Aristotelian, always ready to use (or, as might appear, misuse) Aristotle when this seemed to him acceptable. His challenge to much earlier tradition can be summarised under three heads, and firstly in his revival of the concept of univocity as developed by the Muslim philosopher Avicenna (ca. 980–1037). According to Scotus, 'being' is predicated similarly of all that is: that is of both God and creatures; if that were not the case, intelligible talk about God would be impossible. Nevertheless, Scotus' proposal – a revised version of that advanced by Anselm – pointed toward either pantheism or at least a diminishing of the 'ontological gap': that is, between the existence of God and the derivative existence of God's creation as established by Christian thinkers at least since Gregory of Nyssa.

Secondly, Scotus – seemingly to correct other problems raised by univocity – put greater emphasis than was customary on God's omnipotence: this was always a source of logical confusion. Again, the thesis Scotus – and later more extremely Ockham – expounded was not entirely new; rather its apparent implications were pushed more into view. God was held to have created the order of the world by his 'ordained power': that power which gives us nature in a form we can investigate rationally. God's 'absolute power' is wholly unknown because unknowable by us, being, according to Ockham, only limited by God's nature being Truth itself and therefore 'unable' to contradict itself.

Hence and thirdly, the universe in which we live, including our moral space, depends not on God's nature and generosity, but directly on his 'will'. One effect of this move – which again is not entirely original – is that morality begins to look like mere obedience. Scotus starts with a strong distinction between nature and will: all that is in nature is determined (thus stones naturally fall downwards) whereas the mark of willing is that it is 'free'. Scotus and Ockham identify 'freedom' as the most informative aspect of our likeness to God, only that 'freedom' is no longer construed, with the tradition deriving primarily from Augustine, as directed only to the Good (which is to say ultimately to God) but – again reflecting the view of Anselm – as that 'freedom of indifference' which supersedes it down to our own day.

Scotus – developing the thought of voluntarists of an earlier generation – defines the will not (with Henry of Ghent) as rational appetite but as a self-moving rational and determining power. In contrast to the intellect, which is determined by its objects, the faculty of the will, to be 'free', must, according to this view, be able to choose the opposite to what it chooses: thus even in heaven the saints must have the 'capacity', however understood, to act badly, even though they presumably do not exercise it. In effect, the absolute power of choice which views God as able to replace even his own commandments – specifically those of the Decalogue's Second Table – is mirrored in human 'freedom' to choose the inferior or the downright bad, this 'freedom' being viewed as an ideal, not merely a perverse possibility.

And here we recognise a significantly revised emphasis on that voluntarism in theological accounts of God which would dominate the theological scene until the eighteenth century – by which time it had helped to discredit theism itself. When divorced from religion in the West (it would persist in Islam), it became an important source of that purely secular, usually atheist notion which would find expression in the nineteenth century and perverse instantiation in the twentieth: namely that human beings are primarily characterised by their Will to create and assert. (Who says that the history of theology is irrelevant?!)

By our day, secular morality has developed well beyond its original association with religion; that too is foreshadowed in Scotus and Ockham. Scotus raises the question of whether morality is possible without God. His famous *etsi Deus non daretur*, is still for him only a theoretical question but will produce a more powerful challenge some 200 years later with Grotius and his successors. Plus that the possibility of a religion-free road is enhanced with Scotus' offering of a moderated account of original sin and its effects. Though he does not deny them altogether, in this many were to follow him – and further. So was Aquinas' attempted blend of Aristotelian virtue and Christian perfection wrenched ever further apart.

According to Scotus, pagan virtue is real virtue and can be attained without grace, though it is not meritorious ('Protestants' were soon to convict such an account of virtue as a new version of Pelagianism). Salvation, however, following the 'infusion' of grace, is less recognisable in the quality of perfected human acts than as God's raw acceptation. Such may indeed be a necessary corollary of a further Scotist theme to which we have already alluded: namely that we have no natural inclination to the Good, but only to the good of our species. Ockham went further, arguing that freedom is not to be located in actions having an objectively good end (as both traditional Aristotelians and Augustinians held), but in the intention and character of agents (a revised version of the views of Peter Abelard). At the same time, he is more aware than most thinkers of his age that the 'contest-in-the-soul' thesis about human action is inadequate, arguing rather that there is a real identity between intellect and will, which identity is the 'substance' of the soul in its cognitive aspect.

Scotus opens the way for Ockham to argue that it is possible for human beings to choose evil for its own sake. This 'radicalisation' of human godlessness again pointed to a purely secular road to perfect virtue, from which Original Sin would eventually be banished. Among the more religiously-minded (and in line with the by now assumed voluntarism) it would further encourage the thesis that God's salvific action is 'extrinsic': that is, it depends not on our God-guided moral improvement but on God's 'arbitrary' exercise of power to save or to convict. (In the case of God's absolute power, the concept of arbitrariness of course becomes irrelevant – as normally in Islam.)

The interest of much of the story up to this point might seem to lie in the dismantling – even if inadvertent – of the theological and cultural world to which Scotus and Ockham both assumed they still belonged. Scotus, however, also offered one important proposal which, had it been taken up, would have illuminated the philosophical and cultural heritage. Motivated by some of the concerns of the Stoics and Plotinus and – less directly – Augustine, he rejects the

Thomist interpretation of Aristotle whereby matter, 'designated by quantity', determines individuality. For while the simple plurality of individuals (understood as within the human set) might be thus explained, the Thomist account fails to differentiate the unique individual: fails to distinguish Jack from Jill – or Jim.

Scotus holds that the 'form of humanity' cannot account for the uniqueness of the individual, since matter is in each individual case differentiated and we would need a ('Plotinian') 'form of the individual' to account for what he names the 'thisness', the *haecceitas* of things; readers of Gerard Manley Hopkins will be aware of the term. Yet Scotus, while recognising the problem, seems, in a concern for wider questions, to have missed its special significance for those individuals created, and thus dignified, in the image and likeness of God. Rather, while expounding – with an excessive amount of jargon – how our common human nature appears in each individual, he leaves the relationship between our 'contracted' (that is individual) being and our common nature rephrased rather than illuminated. To leave the question of the relationship between the 'form' of humanity (representing our common nature) and our individual 'form' (identifying our 'thisness') parked in philosophic limbo, is to leave our unitary nature as human beings unintelligible. It would be for Edith Stein, in the twentieth century, to expound Scotus' insight further.

*

A full-scale Aristotle had arrived in the West in the thirteenth century, enabling a blend of Aristotelianism and Augustinianism to replace the earlier, more Platonising culture that preceded it and to flower in the universities of the High Middle Ages. But by the end of the fourteenth century, scholasticism had, in the eyes of its critics, degenerated into an abstract logic-chopping dressed up as theology: in the eyes of some, into new forms of Pelagianism. 'Renaissance man' began to respond by emphasising artistic and literary creativity among God's gifts.

This 'new humanism' had begun in Italy with Petrarch (1304–1374) and Boccaccio (1313–1375) and been primarily concerned with reviving Latin literature and the use of classical Latin as distinct from what they considered the pig-Latin which had become the dreary jargon of the schools. Petrarch preferred his Augustine 'neat' rather than as transmitted through scholastic channels; the time seemed ripe for a new foundation for philosophical as well as literary and artistic inspiration to replace what many held to be the decadent curricula of the Universities. Nor was this movement, at least in its origins, in any way an *anti-Christian* reaction.

That new approach would in the first instance take shape with the 1484 translation of the entire works of Plato into Latin – together with the compiling of commentaries and Neoplatonic monographs – by Marsilio Ficino, head of the newly founded Platonic Academy in Florence. In 1495 Ficino would add a Latin translation of Plotinus: unknown in the West since ancient times but recovered early in the century in a single manuscript brought from Byzantium by Ambrogio Traversari. The Platonic revival had already been augmented by Greek speaking refugees who flocked to Italy after the fall of Byzantium to the Ottoman Turks in 1453 and were welcomed enthusiastically (not least for their sometimes even pagan exposition of Platonism) in Florence especially. Nor did this second and 'Platonic' phase of the new Renaissance culture remain limited to Italy; before long Erasmus, the Spaniard Vivès, Thomas More and many others were welcoming it as proffering a more artistic as well as more philosophically inspiring culture to replace Scholastic aridity.

By the late fifteenth century, medieval culture had for many become synonymous with an over pessimistic, even self-abasing, account of humanity, summed up by such works as Pope Innocent III's *De Contemptu Mundi*. This view, coupled as it was with a supposedly needed correction of what seemed philistine contempt for works of human genius, would deem those past centuries a 'Middle Age' intervening between classical achievements and the 'Rebirth' of civilisation now being ushered in. (This 'take' on

European history is officially maintained in our own day in the Preface to the European Union Charter's leap from antiquity to modernity, with glaring omission of reference to these 'middle' centuries!) While Plato, Plotinus and lesser Platonising authorities might have restored balance, in retrospect the eclipse of the Catholic culture as developed since Augustine – and with it the whole Original Tradition – might look inevitable.

In fact, what emerged as the new Platonism was in many respects different from the old and through being expressly associated with the achievements of human beings as artistic and literary creators quickly developed a 'Promethean' character. Nearly 2,000 years earlier it had been noted on the gravestone of the Athenian playwright Aeschylus only that he had fought for Athens: no mention of his place in literature, of his so powerful tragedies: no hint, that is, of a cult of the creative artist. Likewise would Plotinus, and before him Plato, have found in the Ficino-style glorification of man a loss of touch with reality; it indeed smacks of the Gnosticism latent in Pico's *Oration on the Dignity of Man*, exalting humanity as, in Ficino's words, 'a divine race dressed in mortal clothing'. Soon the more traditionally religious, followed by the more Protestant, would be fearing a new Pelagianism to be added to the version they claimed to identify among the late Scholastics. Yet Pico himself still had one foot planted firmly in the Middle Ages. Combining a dedication to the new mystical Platonism with the rigorous religious revivalism of his fellow Florentine, the Dominican preacher Savonarola, he would be murdered, apparently by libertine upholders of a new-fangled anti-Christian hedonism.

A developing cult of the creative artist was not the only feature to distinguish the new Florentine Platonism from earlier versions. Misreading Augustine's (as Cicero's) emphasis on the 'heart' as representing the whole human being, these new Christian Platonists held it up as the symbolic repository of a more complete humanity than the merely logical 'head' privileged (it was claimed) by the scholastics. That in turn led to a far higher evaluation of rhetoric than among classical Platonists – from the time of Plato himself aware of its misleading and rabble-rousing capacities – the Florentines lightly ignoring how the rational enquiry they admired and valued could be subverted by appeal to the emotions. Within a few years the effect of this failure would become apparent, as self-styled 'humanist' followers of Luther would have recourse to a sophistic rhetoric, sweeping aside rational criticism of their new version of Christianity and now assisted by the uncritical acceptance of late scholastic moves viewing 'freedom' not – as Augustine had viewed it – as the true 'freedom of the sons of God' but as that 'freedom of indifference' which rhetoric could manipulate.

*

Along with the new Platonism, the fifteenth century saw a revival of interest in the largely forgotten philosophical school of Epicurus, when in 1417 Poggio Bracciolini discovered a manuscript of Lucretius's Epicurean poem 'On the Nature of Things' (*De Rerum Natura*). In an age on the lookout for novelty, the intellectual excitement that aroused can be gauged from the surviving copy once owned by Niccolò Machiavelli and containing his annotations. From these it appears it was not the Epicurean aversion from politics that attracted him, but one of its most important themes: the 'indeterminism' of a world notionally constituted by the random collision of atoms in empty space. For Machiavelli that well represented the randomness of the life we experience day by day: life as governed by a 'Lady Fortune' who needs to be manhandled.

Randomness and indeterminism signal a different world from that governed by the divinely constituted teleological laws of the medieval cosmos; hence the problem Machiavelli addresses is how best to survive in unpredictable circumstances. Claiming in *The Prince* – as also in the *Discourses on Livy* – to offer an entirely new approach to the study of politics by placing it in its proper historical setting, his solution is that castigated by Plato in the *Laws* so many centuries before: namely that political societies have nothing to do with what is natural, let alone divinely ordained, but are the random constructs of human artifice.

For Machiavelli, a competent ruler of any political stripe, living in the Augustinian world of strife and fierce competition – driven by hate rather than love, by fear, greed and envy, not least of the glory of others – must calculate his survival with ruthless attention. And even beyond that he must hope for good luck, for even the most able politicking can go terribly wrong: Machiavelli's exemplar is to hand in Cesare Borgia, who in aiming to increase his power provided for every possibility – except that he would himself be gravely ill when his father, Pope Alexander VI, lay dying, thus could not influence the succession, the 'surd' factor in man and cosmos destroying his hopes!

For Machiavelli, human beings are of two sorts: one sort wants only to survive in peace; the other are those with *virtù* (this word, like the Greek *aretê*, is used, amorally, to mean a skill in handling situations), who want to rule over others – but in that desire may be hindered by Christian teachings. Religion may be useful as social glue (we shall see this view of it expressed in the nineteenth century) but humility as preached in Christianity allows us to be trampled on by 'wicked men': so in Machiavelli's time had Italy been trampled on by the 'barbarians': that is, chiefly the French.

Machiavelli – his politics in some way paralleling Scotus' metaphysics – thus stands at a *political* crossroads: the man of *virtù* must choose between God and secure earthly power; he is naive if he does not choose security and for this he must be prepared to resort to politically motivated lying, defaming, cruelty and killing, as may be necessary to control the minds of others and use them for his own purposes. Sometimes, of course, it will pay to appear virtuous in the Christian sense; either way, it is better to be feared than loved: summed up in the words of the old Latin poet Accius, adopted as motto by Caligula: *oderint dum metuant* ('Let them hate so long as they fear').

The problem with this is not whether Machiavelli's evocations of political life are accurate – as in many respects they are – but that pointing to 'political' behaviour as 'evil' (as does Aristotle) is very different from suggesting its necessity, let alone its desirability. Whether Machiavelli is merely doing value-free political science or recommending 'immoral' activities as common sense (which must seem more likely), the world he promotes is quite other than anything advocated by medieval thinkers. Machiavelli wants a political scene realistically constructed by shrewd, hard-nosed political planners: a very different project from that of, for example, Marsilius of Padua, who wants to change his society but within traditional parameters, substituting the ultimate authority of king and state for that of pope and Church.

For Machiavelli the Church is, like any institution, a means to the construction of a secure society: that is, for men of *virtù*, a society governed by themselves. Within that project, of course, it might be found convenient to allow for a Church in subordination to the State: an outcome already under way in England in Machiavelli's lifetime. But Machiavelli's project involves much more than such a reversal of roles: not only the institutional Church but Christian morality itself becomes a means to an end; thus man has replaced nature or God as the social rule-maker *par excellence*. The teachers of the Florentine Academy will have hardly anticipated this conclusion to their theorisings on the loftiness of man!

In politics as in ethics, Machiavelli favours a return to the style of ancient pagan government, specifically that of Imperial Rome – founded, as he duly notes, on the necessary murder of his brother Remus by the 'eponymous' Romulus. Neopaganism was making a comeback elsewhere too: one of the Greek refugees from Byzantium, George Gemistos Plethon by name, was, according to some, a worshipper of the ancient gods. By the mid-sixteenth century, as we have noted, we find a scenario not unreminiscent of our contemporary European Union – with even the Dominican friar Giordano Bruno wishing to jettison the barbarous and 'unscientific' Christian centuries. Clearly anti the Roman Church – and it seems, while living in Elizabethan England, prepared as an agent of Sir Francis Walsingham to inform on Catholics – Giordano was eventually burnt at the stake in a desperate ecclesiastical move to cut off the encroaching world of modernity: his specific offence was Eucharistc heresy, but his wider hostility to the prevailing culture was well recognised.

*

Combine Marsilius of Padua and Machiavelli, add lust for a scheming woman with hope of a son to continue the dynasty and you get Henry VIII of England. Henry Tudor marks the end of an era; hence we leave to the next chapter the theological and philosophical effects of the Reformation, to concentrate on the political and social scene generated in England (but with wider ramifications) by Henry's more local fulfilment – now at a time of rapid advance politically and economically towards early modernity – of Constantine's hoped-for amalgamation of civil and ecclesiastical power. Henry indeed went beyond Constantine, inasmuch as – and by what would later be asserted as 'divine right' – he was to be no mere 'bishop of the pagans' but Supreme Head of the Church in England. He thus secured control both of cult practice and of Christian doctrine itself, though his nationalist version of Christianity would be finally shaped by his daughter Elizabeth and her Counsellors.

Ironically, Henry had been granted the title 'Defender of the Faith' by Pope Leo X for his writings (probably 'ghosted' by Thomas More) against Luther, and though no Lutheran himself – indeed he burned the occasional Lutheran, such as Friar Robert Barnes – found it convenient to promote to Archbishop of Canterbury the Lutheran-inclined Thomas Cranmer, who could be enlisted to promote his divorce from Katharine of Aragon and marriage to Anne Boleyn, already pregnant, it might be with the hoped-for son. A later Irish missioning ditty, cited by Brendan Behan in *Borstal Boy*, would put it all more crudely:

> 'Pay no heed to the alien preacher,
> to his Church without reason or faith,
> for the foundation stone of his temple
> is the bollocks of Henry the Eighth.'

If the world-historical significance of Henry's self-proclamation as Supreme Head of the Church in England more than fulfilled the dreams of not only Constantine, but also Marsilius, certainly the skills of his principal adviser, Thomas Cromwell, in this first stage of the destruction of the Catholic Church in England, would have elicited the admiration of Machiavelli himself. Cromwell may have known Machiavelli's writings – indeed may have met Machiavelli; in any case it can reasonably be concluded that his aim – to establish the power of the king as representing the state and secondarily the state church – would have won the Florentine's approval. As a result of Cromwell's machinations, in England the State, represented by the king in Parliament, would henceforth be in control of official religion, with Catholic observance banned under dire penalties, Catholic priests exiled or executed and convent-dwellers turned out on the world (to the great detriment of provision for the poor and the sick). Protestant groups other than the State Church continued for now only on sufferance.

There would follow an extreme Calvinist period under Henry's eventually acquired but short-lived son, Edward, after which even the brief Catholic restoration under Katherine of Aragon's daughter, Mary Tudor, made little real difference to the new setting of the stage. Though it is likely that had Mary lived longer, Catholicism would have returned at least for some time, its legitimacy too now depended – as had Christianity as available under her father and brother – on the will of the monarch. This implied that those who opposed Mary's restoration of a now increasingly Tridentine Catholicism could be condemned not only as heretics but also as traitors: the recourse adopted for dealing with those Catholics who would continue to defy the monarch into the reign of Mary's half-sister, Elizabeth.

The successes of the first generation of Reformers in Germany, as also in England, had depended on the will of kings and princes, but the more extreme version of Protestantism ushered in by Calvin threatened monarchs as well as prelates. Both versions would be rephrased in seventeenth-century England as the creed of the national Church of England, Henry VIII thus inaugurating a new European world in which religion would never again exert the authority, political or spiritual, it had in the previous age. The decisions of Constantine had led to the Christianisation of the Roman Empire and eventually of many lands beyond that empire's borders; Henry, the bullying petty Constantine, may be almost without exaggeration said to have been – if unwittingly – the architect of the politico-religious transformation of Europe from Christendom into its latter-day post-Christian condition.

4 Man Enlightened

Montaigne to Kant

Nature and Nature's Laws lay hid in Night.

God said, 'Let Newton be!' and all was light!

Alexander Pope

'Modern Man' can be used to distinguish the European of roughly the seventeenth century from the 'Enlightened Man' of the eighteenth; however, we shall treat the two as synonymous insofar as it was 'Modern' man who took the crucial steps towards 'Enlightenment'. If we ask, 'Enlightenment from what?', the ostensible answer will be 'From the Middle Ages', while understood – at least by the most 'enlightened' – will be 'From Christianity'.

That 'enlightenment' was never completed. We have shown how Augustine and others reconstructed intellectual life in post-Constantinian Western 'Christendom' into a form that reflected much, but by no means all, of its Graeco-Roman heritage. The ending of the Middle Ages varied in time from country to country, with Italy leading the way – to be succeeded by that 'early modern' period which would reach its catastrophic ending with the French Revolution of 1789. Significant aspects of the older Christian mentality continued to characterise 'modern man' – some of whose distinctive features (plus some surviving still from his remoter Constantinian ancestors) similarly will persist when 'totalitarian man' will bid to take over the reins of state.

That is important because, as Constantinian man, modern man and totalitarian man are funnelled into one another in varying doses with each succeeding generation, hope must fade that the 'common man', that is, the individual with his (in Socrates' phrase) 'unexamined life', will be able to identify who or what he is. In effect he or she has turned into one of a great zoo of intellectual hybrids who have lost sight of their mixed origins while still assuming they have a more or less coherent mental outlook, 'obviously': hence are liable to solve intellectual and emotional puzzles without recognising how these have been infected by a series of incompatible past conditions, each having left its own confusions unresolved. Of this more anon.

The principal characteristics of 'modern man', as he begins to emerge, are rationalism and scepticism; among them we include such 'moral sense theorists' as Hutchison, Hume and Adam Smith, who argue on rational grounds that morality is not generated by reason but from 'moral sentiments'. And despite those forerunners of 'modern' thinkers we find in the late Middle Ages – despite Scotus and Ockham and even despite Machiavelli, who still lived in part in a Christendom he was busy subverting – we have specified Henry VIII as signalling the end of the post-Constantinian world-picture: not just because he replaced Catholic Christendom in England with a 'Catholicism' fashioned to his own diktat, but because in so doing he was able to employ those who looked to new versions of Christianity. Henry's national church, if not their ideal, was for them a start, and by retaining the king's favour, what more might not be achieved?

Luther may have hoped at first that his reforming proposals would be accepted within the older Christendom; if so, he soon understood that this was not to be – to be next puzzled as to why other reformers failed to recognise his chosen road as the right one to follow. Alternative Christian roads – already plural – were available when Henry broke from Rome, but Henry was intent on a Catholicism without the Pope. Thus in Henry, surrounded by pliant enough Lutheran chaplains (the less pliant he might burn) and jumped-up Machiavellian counsellors – Thomas Cromwell in chief – we greet the political face of modern man. Henry's soon-to-be-eliminated Chancellor, Thomas More – who resembles Machiavelli in his realistic view of man's moral character – again had one foot in the older world and one in the new, more optimistic humanism.

But Henry himself – after a stab at being a chivalric medieval knight on the Field of the Cloth of Gold – had turned modern tyrant, determined that old religious ways should be emended in the pragmatic manner of 'modern' statecraft and of man looking out on a newly expanded world.

For, philosophy and theology apart, that world was changing rapidly, providing new opportunities for wealth and power. First to note is the invention of printing. Lutheran Protestantism might well have been suppressed, as had heresies in the past, if it had not been able to rely not only on the marital, dynastic or wider aims of King Henry or the Elector of Saxony, but also on the inability of potentates to suppress, even when they wished to, the flow of new essays in theological variety. Even while that earlier Henry, 'Defender of the Faith', was putting about the tract against Luther that earned him that title, his kingdom was being deluged with a flood of Lutheran propaganda he could not block. Indeed, the intellectual world had been awash with books for more than fifty years, while the geographic world too was expanding beyond those largely Muslim territories that might have represented its limits. America had been discovered and knowledge of non-European societies was gaining ground, with even China on the horizon since Marco Polo. All this on top of widespread hostility to traditional patterns of thought – and not only among the new 'Protestants', for More, Colet and Erasmus, all Catholics and almost in despite of themselves, were as keen on change as Luther – though in theological method, not doctrine: that is, on a more integral reform.

In philosophy, further new material for thought seeped into the West in 1562 with the Latin translation of Sextus Empiricus providing a more radical and coherent 'Pyrrhonist' version of Scepticism than that found in Cicero and debated by Augustine; meanwhile the Stoics – in antiquity rivals of the Sceptics – also seemed to offer a metaphysical alternative to both the older Aristotelianism of the Schools and the new Neoplatonism of the humanists. Among those attracted to Scepticism, the most immediately influential (including on Shakespeare) was Montaigne. Widely thought of now as a Christian fideist rather than a philosopher, Montaigne agreed with the Pyrrhonists that neither the mind nor the senses guarantee certain knowledge, concluding (strangely) that only suspension of judgment could secure peace of mind. In that spirit he urged on his French compatriots a willingness to go along with the religious authority available – in France the Catholic Church – as the only hope of restricting sectarian violence. This would prove prescient, Montaigne's admonition holding good for another century and not only in France: until, that is, Montaignian Scepticism would itself convince many 'modern' men that the growing numbers of deists (and even atheists) might talk more sense and restore more peace – in mind as in society – than brawling religious partisans.

While Montaigne's scepticism was reinforced by an increasing knowledge of the New World beyond the Atlantic, Spanish conquests there also spawned an important and persisting set of philosophical problems. Teaching in Salamanca, the Dominican friar Francesco de Vitoria (1483–1546), though not opposed to slavery as such, challenged the standard interpretation of Aristotle's account of *natural* slaves, paving the way for a more radical re-evaluation of slavery by arguing in a series of pamphlets that the 'Indians' too were human beings, persons in the full sense, formed in the image and likeness of God. Further moves to rethink slavery in Christian terms were developed by his Dominican confrère, Bartholomé de Las Casas (1484–1566), who as formerly a landowner in the Islands had concluded there was no need to import black slaves from Africa as the Indians would do as well, but became persuaded – influentially when appointed bishop of Chiapas – that all slavery was an offence against God.

This Las Casas expressed philosophically, in terms of justice and in a significantly new way: the Indians, indeed all human beings, had the *right* not to be enslaved, and to be allowed to live as freely as their new Spanish overlords; they were even to enjoy a freedom of religion until preachers could induce them to give up barbarism and convert to Christianity. Famously Las Casas debated the rights and wrongs of slavery with a traditional 'Aristotelian' defender of it, Juan de Sepúlveda. Both sides claimed victory and the debate made little practical impact at the time. The future would lie with Las Casas – but only much later and effected not by Spanish Dominicans but by English Evangelicals of the early nineteenth century 'Clapham sect'.

The 'subjective' right not to be enslaved because of the human dignity claimed for the Indians by Las Casas brings into focus the strengths and weaknesses of theories of rights more generally. There had been a shift in late medieval times – building on the canon law – from recognising the objective rights of various groups against one another (bishops against kings, burghers against feudal lords, etc.) in the direction of Las Casas' wider claim that human dignity demands specific 'subjective' rights for all as a matter of justice. But what rights, and from whom can they be claimed?

Las Casas demanded respect for 'natural' rights: these were neither the later 'rights of man' nor 'human rights' in our contemporary secular understanding. Some of the difficulties of these later developments, however, are already implicit in the version derived by Las Casas from traditional accounts of the dignity of man: above all, who – originally it would be God and those who fear God – are to recognise which rights are accorded? Then, what kinds of rights claims *are* acceptable (I may have a right to life; have I the right to own a house?). Finally, what to do when apparently reasonable rights-claims conflict with one another?

Two further difficulties arise, the first being, Who is properly possessed of a right? For Las Casas, it would be all persons as traditionally understood – but what if the definition of the person and his (and her) dignity be less than all-embracing? Might some humans not be persons, thus possessed of no rights. So, notoriously, the Nazis would hold? Secondly, though a tradition dating back to Augustine identified all the virtues as modes of love, Las Casas, as we have seen, made rights a matter of justice – perhaps because love, being by the scholastics defined as an 'infused' virtue, might not seem relevant in dealings with non-Christians. But the move was to prove risky; soon, according to Samuel Pufendorf (1632–1694), justice and rights are matters for lawyers, not theologians, and whereas among Christians an appeal to God's love should determine which rights are appropriately defended, in a non-theistic society it will become a matter for human lawgivers depending on variable public opinion or their own 'moral compass' – or on whether they have been (directly or indirectly) suborned.

Even before Pufendorf, we find in the thought of Hugo Grotius (1583–1645) that rights theory has moved into a context already more modern than the world of Las Casas. Grotius takes much more seriously the case of there being no God, at least as understood by Christians: the scenario offered as a thought experiment by Scotus but rejected by Grotius' neo-scholastic near contemporary, Francesco Suarez (1548–1617), as rendering unintelligible any 'voluntarist' account of morality as dependent on the will of God as lawgiver.

More generally, Suarez's interminable attempts to combine Aquinas not only with voluntarism (and hence an Ockhamist 'freedom of indifference') but also with a 'nominalism' reminiscent of Abelard, betrays the growing incoherence of later scholasticism. As perhaps does an already recognisable tendency in the new Jesuit Order to which he belonged – and who in England were to show a true utility and heroism in ministering to the persecuted Catholics – to think that being 'all things to all men' requires jumping on intellectual bandwagons. Yet even a trendier version of scholasticism was to run into trouble with the new 'scientific' determinists like Hobbes, as well as those more Calvinistic 'Augustinian' Catholics who would eventually be condemned as Jansenists.

Grotius may have thought the Christian God, as received, no longer fit for new purposes. A Dutch Protestant of the Arminian persuasion who thus abandoned Calvin's 'double predestination' – conclusion widely rejected in Holland and Scotland but accepted into the evolving Church of England – he held that an expanded commercial universe required revision of the foundations of natural law, since Muslims and other unbelievers could not be expected to recognise the authority of the Christian Gospel. To resolve the problem he adopted two apparently conflicting strategies. On the one hand he holds – as already in the fourteenth century had Gregory of Rimini – that, Suarez notwithstanding, natural law is binding even in the 'absence' of God. Hence, thinking presumably of the old Roman *ius gentium*, he offers an account which will transcend the now divergent versions of Christianity and also be acceptable in that non-Christian wider world within which natural law would provide the basis for commercial agreements acceptable to all parties.

However, since Grotius also supposes there to be a binding force more than merely pragmatic behind such achievable agreements, and since, as a good voluntarist, he finds moral obligation to depend upon the will of a superior, that binding force can only be supplied either by Nature (This some of his neo-Stoic contemporaries might hold, but it would come to seem less plausible in a demythologised, 'scientific' universe.) or by a God not necessarily assumed to be the God of the Christians.

And this God seems to be active, for he has given everyone 'rights' as a means of self-protection: here we have a wholly different account of the origin of rights from the human dignity invoked by Las Casas. If we ask why God has thus benevolently granted these rights to us (it is unclear who the 'us' would include, except that it includes all traders), Grotius' answer is that human nature is both aggressive and sociable, and that rights enable us to make profitable use of our sociability while protecting ourselves against the aggressiveness of others: rights are thus prerequisite for deal-making. Even when 'passive' (that is, protecting us from being *treated* unjustly), they can be legitimately claimed from those, however identified, who should respect them. But though they still depend on an extra-human authority, they will clearly require legal arbitrators – meaning that rights advocates will forever be with us and forever litigious.

Grotius' proposals are radical and their novelty can be clearly recognised in that he has scrapped the older more or less Aristotelian account of virtue – now to be defined as acceptance of the rights of others. Whereas medieval thinkers could have constructed an account of rights dependent on the traditional virtues – thus if it is *just* for me to treat someone in a particular way, he will have a right to be treated in that way – now for Grotius the situation is reversed: I am virtuous if and only if I respect another's primary rights, defined as to life, body, freedom and honour. That indeed would seem to assume – and Grotius does assume – that there is something more than human convenience behind such rights: some metaphysical power or at least metaphysics substitute. Grotius himself determines they should be attributed to the protective generosity of God, yet his theory opens the possibility that – God or no God (Scotus' *etsi deus non daretur*) – respecting rights (*however* derived) constitutes virtue.

Grotius further decides that rights come in two kinds: perfect and imperfect. A perfect right – above all else the right to self-preservation – provides the basis for justice. An imperfect right, while not imposing strict obligation, is a recognition of human sociability and is both commercially helpful and adds a further element of protection: Grotius views it as the instantiation of the Christian law of love – which stands only as an 'imperfect' obligation; thus a pragmatic justice, accounted obedience to the will of a superior God, trumps traditional Christian Charity.

That Grotius has nothing traditional to say about sin, let alone the Fall, shows (as was soon recognised) how different his understanding of 'natural law' is from that of his medieval predecessors. We enjoy the (by now standard) 'freedom of indifference' and Grotius' theory of rights will enable us to use that freedom to everyone's advantage – ruling out, in particular, commercial fraud, at least theoretically. Still uniting Grotius and Las Casas, however, is that 'rights' are not recognised empirically but are a rational deduction dependent on the existence of a voluntarist God, however incoherently understood. What is to become of them when God, or at least God's Providence, is removed from the equation?

*

That might bring us conveniently to Thomas Hobbes, except that we must first return to the second feature of modern man we have identified, namely that he is not merely a rationalist but a sceptic. We can view the two instructively combined in the man who, under King James of Scotland and England, would fill Thomas More's old position as Lord Chancellor: Francis Bacon, who further spiced the blend with doses of empiricism and political Machiavellianism. Bacon regularly campaigned for the abandonment of all questioning of final causality in the new scientific cosmos 'discovered' by Copernicus and championed by his contemporary, Galileo Galilei (1564–1642). Indeed, much of the scientistic (as distinct from properly scientific) mentality of modern man is summed up by Bacon's comment that 'Inquiries into nature have the best result when they begin with physics and end in mathematics'. Nature is not to be viewed as indicating the greater glory of God, nor for the beauty of, say, landscapes or flowers, but to be mastered for the practical purposes of men.

Though Bacon's writings summarise many of the ideals of modern man, his Machiavellian political career ended in disaster when he fell from King James's favour. While in office he had strongly supported the harshly repressive measures which characterised the Elizabethan and post-Elizabethan treatment of religious opponents, aligning himself with the Cecils, father and son, who – in contradiction of Elizabeth's profession that she had no wish to 'make windows into men's souls' – operated more standard principles of *Realpolitik*, to include institutionalised (though in theory illegal) torture – it being the stated conclusion of Sir Francis Walsingham that 'without torture we shall not prevail'. Bacon thus appears in many ways no mere sceptic but a proto-totalitarian whom Machiavelli himself might have compared – both in his rise and in his fall – to Cesare Borgia: undone by an unforeseen blow of Lady Fortune. It is perhaps another 'urban myth' – albeit *ben trovato* – that on hearing of his death, his widow exclaimed: 'My Lord Bacon is dead. The world will never see his like again. Thanks be to God!'

*

Contemporaneous are, in France, Descartes, founder of modern sceptical philosophy, and in England Hobbes – in youth a friend of Bacon – the unabashed authoritarian whose vision of society is in many, though decidedly not in all ways, reflected in our contemporary world – even if few of our gurus might admit the comparison. Descartes, though slightly the younger, however, shall come first because he claimed to be a Catholic Christian, while wanting to start again in metaphysics. With his further claim that his philosophical speculations had no bearing on Christian truth, the Roman Inquisition, reasonably enough, would disagree.

Until comparatively recently, many philosophy departments in the Anglo-American world gave up on the history of philosophy after Aristotle, to resume it with Descartes. Some still do – and though the aim of contemporary philosophers is more often to refute Descartes than to profess discipleship, that nonetheless indicates how successfully he rewrote the philosophical curriculum to his own composing – with its predominating *ostinato* of 'systematic doubt' or scepticism. Viewed more 'world-historically', this change of tune signals a retreat from metaphysics, to be recast as epistemology.

Like many others in his age, Descartes was convinced both that scholastic philosophy had failed and that Aristotle's account of physical nature needed to be jettisoned in light of the new Copernican cosmology and mechanics. Aristotelian metaphysics, moreover, were too abstract, too little empirical, too embroiled in hypothetical speculation about final causes; therefore, in thinking about the contents of the world, physical or mental, we must start from the beginning – but where is that? Descartes' answer lay in demonstrating first his own existence and from that the existence of God; that much given, the world would be open to scientific investigation. Hence his famous *cogito*, 'I think, therefore I am' – which some have found to be insufficiently sceptical, arguing that to start with the assumption of one's own identity is already to beg the question.

Descartes, though, was satisfied that his argument as it stood gave him what he wanted: the self-conscious mind – forerunner of that 'self' soon to be identified with consciousness: not much connection there with the medieval Aristotelian soul as the principle of living things, nor with the soul as somehow blended with the 'spirit', whether holy or otherwise, whether moral or aesthetic. We should be careful, however, not to confuse Descartes' project with that of later 'subjectivists'. Descartes is an epistemologist, his aim is not to create his own 'subjective' world but to examine and understand – and so be able to manipulate – the actual 'demythologised' world in which he finds himself.

Having fixed his own existence as the existence of his thinking mind, Descartes 'secures' the existence of God by positing that he could not have created himself – further that it would be contradictory for God to be a deceiver. Granted, too, other minds, all that remains is to investigate matter in all its manifestations and in accordance with the best available rational and scientific principles. Some considered that his demonstration of his own existence sounded like Augustine; this, while denying direct influence, Descartes welcomed insofar as it exonerated him from ultimate scepticism, but he claimed to differ from Augustine in that his own purpose was merely to establish the thinking self as an 'immaterial substance'.

However, while part of Descartes' purpose in 'proving' his own existence was to find a rational basis for the existence of the cosmos, he does seem to have hoped that some sort of reconstructed Augustinianism could provide the theoretical groundwork for the anti-Aristotelian physics now under rapid development: that the new mechanics (with perhaps some input from Plato's *Timaeus*) might be combined with Augustinian rather than with scholastic theology.

Be that as it may, given the existence of minds (human and divine), Descartes was left with the problem of what is to be said about matter and bodies. Being devoid of mind, these must be inert substances – leaving no room for any ancient 'vitalism' – and to be manipulated for whatever purposes minds have 'in mind'. And since among those bits of inert matter are our own bodies – apparently only fortuitously connected to our minds – Descartes is driven back to something like the view that Augustine had come to reject, namely that *we* are merely souls. (Descartes prefers to speak of the 'mind' (*mens*), the soul (*anima*) with its religious associations being for him a mere survival and playing no significant part in his thought.)

We seem, then, to be conceived rather as self-conscious calculators: devoid of affections, erotic or other. Yet our mind must somehow be identified with our will, with its freedom – that is, the 'freedom of indifference', not freedom in the Augustinian sense as the unrestricted ability to recognise God and the Good; for Descartes has blended these two medieval 'faculties' rather than explicating their relationship or even separating their functions. Later, Hume would propose a possible solution, separating the mind, which distinguishes similarities and differences, from the will and the passions which possess the power to promote action.

For Descartes we are bisected into minds and bodies, though he avoids drawing the 'Platonic' (but unchristian) conclusion that only the soul can survive. Although he claims that his work is philosophical rather than theological, yet given that he fails dismally to explain any necessary connection between soul and body, the ecclesiastical authorities would have had reason besides his seeming determinism to be disturbed.

About both God and man Descartes is yet another voluntarist, viewing God's will as unrestricted in the absolute manner espoused since Ockham; that is, such that He could have commanded us to hate him, while His ways (the Christian Scriptures being apparently to be ignored) are entirely beyond our knowledge. As with Bacon, final causes cannot be invoked either in physics or in ethics (where, as with Grotius, both grace and original sin have disappeared). All we can know of God's plans is that they are consistent. For religion, as with Montaigne, all we can do is follow the customs and laws of the society to which we belong; this pre-empts that slogan which would bring the wars of religion to a merciful though philosophically incoherent close: *cuius regio, eius religio*: follow the religion of the local ruler. As for the goal of ethics – though this can only be established provisionally – it is no longer the older Aristotelian 'activity of man in accordance with the virtues', but contentment: a conclusion suited to times dangerous for a too unconventional philosopher.

For all his concern with mathematics and the mechanical laws of nature as empirically observable, Descartes is usually regarded as a rationalist rather than an empiricist, on account of his theory of innate ideas. This seemingly Platonic notion is actually radically unplatonic in that Descartes' 'clear and distinct ideas' are not reflections of an eternal and unchanging world but refined constructions of our innate – 'hard-wired' – capacity to see in the universe patterns of ordered structures which thinking can further clarify. Yet – and prescinding from a Christian faith that God is no deceiver – these patterns have to be merely provisional, indeed, little better than more or less coherent dreams.

*

And so we come to Thomas Hobbes: no uncertain empiricist, mechanist and determinist, and widely reputed an atheist: perhaps wrongly if by atheist we mean (as now) a denier of God's existence rather than of his providential concern for human beings and the universe in general. Certainly for Hobbes, knowable about God – assuming Him to exist – is only that His power must be immeasurable.

That Hobbes does constantly refer to God and the Christian Scriptures may indicate a surviving, though hardly nostalgic, memory of earlier (in Hobbes' case presumably Calvinist) habits – no doubt not discouraged by the fact that, at least for most of his life, professed atheism was still punishable by death. Yet his claim that the phrase 'immaterial substance' is a contradiction in terms certainly implies that, if there is a God, he must be material, leaving closet pantheism as a possible explanation of his religious views. And if God is material, so is the soul, which will therefore perish with the body and have to be brought back to life at the (hypothetical) General Resurrection. In the absence of love, grace, original sin (indeed sin altogether in natural man), predestination and other trappings of Christianity as preached, Hobbes can certainly assume – if not assert – with the scientifically-minded, that we can forget about God – unless when convenient not to.

Atheists, however, had already popped up: Christopher Marlowe was reputed to have been one, and his membership for a time of the circle round Sir Walter Raleigh – the possible author of 'hellish verses' emanating from the group – might seem to confirm it. Like Bacon, Raleigh and Marlowe were keen readers of Machiavelli. For the arguably more Machiavellian Hobbes, religion was a useful social glue – and social glue was urgently needed to prevent England lurching again into civil wars whipped up by religious partisans, both Catholic and Puritan. Queen Elizabeth and her counsellors had the right idea: a new and English church in which both liturgy and eventually dogma is placed (as Constantine might have wished) in the safe hands of the Sovereign. It may not even matter which religion we have; in Muslim countries one presumably should obey the Sultan. In England both Catholics and Puritans are potentially traitors, but some form of organised religion may be a necessary evil.

Apart from the political aspect of religion, what are Hobbes' views of his fellow human beings who seem to require it? How can they be tamed? He concludes they are best to be thought of not as psychological egoists who pursue their basic desires instinctively but as rational egoists who understand that a prudent *indirect* pursuit of what we really want is better than a risky assertion of 'liberties'. Humans have no inherent dignity; their 'value' – note the term – depends on their Price, on 'how much would be given for the use of their Power': not, that is, on God or on being in God's image but 'on the needs and judgment of others'. It is for the commonwealth to determine who counts as a human being.

By way of example, there may be cases where the death of a newborn seems desirable; his or (perhaps more likely) her fate would then depend on whether he or she is classed as a human being (that is, a person acceptable in society) or not. In sum, for Hobbes, modern man will be accounted a full human being, a person, as the state decides; and has responsibilities if it is judged convenient for him to be held responsible for his behaviour. Individuals are to be determined forensically to be or not to be citizens.

According to Hobbes, we have emerged from a state of nature in which we must endure 'a war of all against all'. He hardly distinguishes between whether some version of this has existed historically or whether it is a thought experiment in imagining the chaos that will ensue if society relapses into the anarchy (well known to his age) of a civil war. Because of the actuality or dread of primitive conditions in which life is (in his well-known words) 'solitary, poore, nasty, brutish and short', human beings will naturally bond together to establish a set of moral and political rules under which they can live in comparative safety: thus the desire for self-preservation – and if possible the maintenance of a 'commodious' lifestyle – are the marks of civic society. In pre-civic societies there are no rights such as Grotius proposed, not least because God, even if he exists, has no known desire to bestow them and because one man's right must, in a pre-civic situation, infringe on the rights of others. Grotius' so-called natural rights are no more than 'liberties'; rights in any stronger sense could only emerge as legal fictions in a society organised under some form of supreme power.

Theoretically it does not matter whether sovereignty resides in a king, an aristocracy or a controlled democracy; what matters is that absolute power be taken as granted by covenant by the citizenry in return for protection against force or fraud. However, a monarch is more likely to perform this required task efficiently – and if he does not, he (as any other short-falling sovereign power) can be properly deposed as having offended against the 'natural law' in virtue of which the office is held with the sole and rational responsibility of looking after the lives and material possessions of the subjects. By the time

Hobbes writes his major work, *Leviathan*, he makes no requirement of the ruler to provide any nonmaterial benefits.

Hobbes has thus stood all traditional accounts of natural law on their heads, as having nothing to do with God, nor with Nature personified: the nature in 'natural law' refers simply to human nature as observed with an unblinkered eye. An appeal to nature is an appeal to how things, and not least human nature, just *are*: not what they should be or could be. That account recalls the view of Machiavelli, not to speak of Thomas More or even Augustine: men are by nature vicious, better controlled by fear than by love and willing to kill if their honour and status (let alone their lives) are threatened.

Some scholars think Hobbes has identified the conditions of the growing mercantilist society of his age and claimed – fallaciously – that the human nature he recognises around him can be universalised. Hobbes would reject that and insist that – while he has indeed extrapolated from his own society's move from a post-feudal, national tyranny to rule by a protocapitalist middle class of those who hold the purse strings – yet similar traits in human nature can be observed in all societies. Admittedly the mix of horrors would vary from place to place. The English Civil War, he tells us, had been won by those who cared little for the rights and wrongs of either side, but could be induced to fight for whoever offered the best opportunities for looting and violence. The Puritan Parliamentarians had simply bought enough soldiers to secure, eventually, the king's execution.

In some respects Hobbes can be thought of as picking up his account of modern man where Machiavelli left off. Machiavelli still has one foot in the old religious world where a would-be Prince (of whatever ideological stripe) must choose between God and the Church on the one hand and necessary force and fraud – coupled as required with the pretence of 'virtue' – on the other. Hobbes no longer thinks there is any such choice, at least for the clear headed. We no longer live in a spiritual world peopled by scholastic clergy and popes but – if we will but face it – in a world governed by the determining forces of matter in motion, where all those who do not recognise the risks they run are naive and may be used.

Yet Hobbes' world still is not that of Plato's Thrasymachus, where the wiser like to maintain belief in morality as a device to keep the fools in order and bend them to their own purposes. For Hobbes, though in their natural state men are vicious, cowardly and brutal, they recognise that a well-run society is better for themselves as for their sovereign – provided, that is, that he acts rationally. Hence, they will be happy if they find a Sovereign to ensure their protection while allowing that whatever is not ruled illegal – and hence 'immoral', since morality is identified with political prudence – is a permitted 'liberty': again we have a potential litigants' and lawyers' paradise!

It might seem Hobbes would approve of at least some features of the current Chinese regime, with elimination or re-education for troublemakers, a chance to live a more 'commodious' life for those not bothered about political freedom. Like our Chinese leaders, he is prone to discount the risks of the abuse of autocratic power. Nevertheless, and unlike Thrasymachus – who wants to exploit the weaker to the advantage of the strong, who are by nature 'rulers in the strict sense' – Hobbes hopes to benefit humanity by telling it as it is: offering his bleak remedy as realistically the best available.

*

Hobbes, like Machiavelli, values religion as social glue: acceptance of doctrine and obedience to the law is all the Sovereign need insist on in a Christian polity. Neither Hobbes nor Machiavelli avows himself an atheist, though both come close to it, with Hobbes leaving his possible, but certainly inscrutable and nonprovidential God no other function than that of Cause (in some sense) of the world in which we live. Nevertheless to retain, but by options less frightening and shocking than the proposals of Hobbes, religion as social glue, while dispensing with such awkward features as Original Sin, grace and more or less independent ecclesiastical structures, would be open to other seventeenth century men.

Thus Christianity might be reduced to the proto-deism of Lord Herbert of Cherbury (1583–1648) who – in contrast to his relation, the poet George Herbert – held that, stripped of revelation, all religions are reducible to a simple theism though in forms appropriate to various cultures. Recognition of this will rid us of the curse of sectarian strife and allow for a rational, scientific and 'natural' theology, purged of claims to final causes discoverable in nature. Reason will tell us what to believe, possible belief being limited only by logical coherence. In effect, religion is reduced to an assertive moralism.

Later in the seventeenth century, the Cambridge Platonists – hostile to Calvinist theories of double predestination and to voluntarism, whether divine or human – proposed a strong account of the freedom of the will, rejecting both determinism and indifferentism. Abandoning the Augustinian axiom that in our fallen state 'ought' regularly implies not 'can' but 'cannot', they come close to claims to human autonomy as later developed. At the same time – and platonically – they reject the normal medieval distinction between will and intellect, uniting them in what Henry More (translating Plotinus) calls a single 'boniform faculty': that is, a capacity for the intellectual love of goodness.

Fearful of the mechanist determinism of Hobbes, the Cambridge group were yet fervent advocates of the new anti-Aristotelian science, while associating contemporary scientific discoveries with Platonic theories largely derived from Plotinus and Proclus. They hold the universe to reveal the divine spirit forming inert matter atomically viewed, rendering it intelligible and where appropriate bestowing life: all this somewhat in the manner of Plato's World Soul, with the anti-voluntarist proviso that not God's will but his nature is the first principle of the universe.

Yet along with a metaphysic imbued with Christian and Platonist theories of love, these new Platonists explain their denial of voluntarism and divine inscrutability in terms of the old (Scotist) account of being as univocal. (Univocity, a radically unplatonic idea, has recurred in this history and we have noticed the metaphysical anomalies it entails in Anselm and Scotus.) This, plus these Platonists' by now fashionable rejection of Original Sin – implying a diminished need for grace – narrowed the gap between God and an increasingly autonomous view of human nature. That in turn encouraged a move in the same direction as Lord Herbert to find the essential of religion in moral behaviour. Such they apparently judged the best weapon to hand, given the increasingly 'scientific', post-voluntarist world-picture they yet themselves underwrote, with its encroaching atheism. Against this two of their members argued (Henry More in 1662, Ralph Cudworth in 1678). The hope was that a more tolerant, less dogmatic, albeit still moralising creed would obtain greater purchase on those intellects bent, in the 'libertine' reign of Charles II, on obliterating the theological excesses of the reign of the godly, whether Presbyterian or 'Independent'.

Bishop Berkeley, some half century later, was to find such optimism misplaced, myopically tracing the by now patent decline in Christianity to the reign of the Merry Monarch. Where he was right was in recognising how the autonomy now transparent in 'Platonist' man marks another stage – after the 'Prometheanism' of Ficino and his circle in Florence – in the substituting of human autonomy for God's more inscrutable sovereignty.

*

It took more than Hobbes' effective atheism and determinism to arouse fear and resentment; there was also his rejection of any natural rights except for the (far from inalienable) 'liberties' of the savage in a primitive state of nature. In the revolutionary world of mid-seventeenth century England, the destruction of Christian unity was, many hoped, to be followed not by Henrician style Caesaropapism (now widely appearing in less blatant guises elsewhere in Europe) but by implementation – if short of Las Casas' interpretation of human dignity – at least of a more Grotian support for the 'natural' rights of mercantilists of the middle class.

Exemplary of the ensuing discussion were the 'Army Debates' held at Putney shortly before the execution of Charles I and which determined the form of freedom to be attained. Controversy centred not only on the end of royal autocracy but, among the Independents, on the abolition of any uniformity of religion: privileged Anglicanism must go, along with its founding monarchy. All these demands, though still comparatively limited, were couched in the language of those rights that Hobbes had considered dangerous to social stability: not yet the 'rights of man', let alone our 'human rights': that phrase, of its very wording, implying a godlessness absent from the official Europe of 1648. As the Levellers put it at Putney, concern was for the inalienable rights of 'the Natives of this Land'. That did not include women, far less the slaves living in British owned plantations in the Caribbean or the American colonies.

Nor indeed did it include more than about half the male population of England itself, those who worked for others being judged to have no independent stake in the country and to be incapable of making free decisions – whether on account of their state of life or rather resulting from the absence as yet of a secret ballot – and so being excluded from the franchise (which word implies a 'free' man). In retrospect, Levellers, Diggers and other seventeenth-century radicals had a rather limited practical agenda and in the longer run obtained little of what they demanded; still, theirs was a first step and – though still under God's auspices rather than in contempt of a god whose existence is questioned or is irrelevant, as for Hobbes – the door opened a little wider to contemporary man's claiming for himself variety of rights. For now the rallying cry was, 'When Adam delved and Eve span, Who was then the gentleman?' So the Levellers chanted, in hope of constructing a less unequal society purged of hierarchically organised religion.

*

It would fall to John Locke to formulate modern man's nature, rights and duties in a free state with comparatively free choice of religions – with Catholicism specifically ruled out as seditious, as by Hobbes. Indeed, Locke had more in common with Hobbes than he would want to admit: first, his radical empiricism coupled with rejection of Descartes' 'innate ideas'; then his agreement that we naturally seek only our own good. Yet it was empiricism of a new metaphysical stamp, for we cannot, as Aristotle and the scholastics had supposed, grasp the 'real' essences of things but only, in Locke's view, their *nominal* essences: this entails, for example, that we cannot describe persons as even partially 'substantial' (in the Aristotelian sense of 'substance'), because we do not know what substances *are*, only how they appear and are *named*.

Persons, though, are recognisable 'selves', to be viewed as bundles of qualities and experiences held together by memory. If we are conscious of our memory chains we are persons; if the connection is broken or never established, we are human beings but not persons. Persons are thus (as for Hobbes) defined forensically as those judged capable of being held responsible for their actions; those not so enabled are merely humans, with none of the rights to which a person is entitled. Earlier metaphysical accounts of persons are thus to be recast, with persons becoming rather the subject matter for psychological research (or as Locke might have called it, 'mental philosophy'). As he puts it himself in his *Essay on Human Understanding*, 'Consciousness always accompanies thinking, and it is that that makes everyone to be what he calls *self*, and thereby distinguishes himself from all other thinking things: in this alone consists *personal identity*, i.e. the sameness of a rational being'.

Locke's original emphasis on responsibility arose from a need to justify – forensically – our fate at the General Resurrection: if we are not responsible for our actions, we can be neither rewarded nor punished by a just God. Of course it must be the same person who is judged as who performed the action in question; therefore our 'serial selves' must be coherent and the atomic composite that is our body unified by a diachronic continuity that only memory guarantees.

Persons have bodies, but Locke no longer views these as integral to the 'self' (the word he normally prefers to 'soul') nor to our 'personal identity'. Rather they are owned as property, though it is a strange sort of ownership since if I own a house and it is destroyed I may survive, but if my body is destroyed, I no longer exist (at least in the present and known world). And ownership has a wider role in Locke's account of society: as good mercantilists, we shall include the right to *absolute* ownership among our attributes as persons; gone is the medieval notion that we are stewards of God's property.

Whence come those rights that Locke, in then current terminology a 'Whig', is desperate to defend? According to him, they are bestowed on us by God, but for what purpose is not so clear: they point to a certain social value and respect that is not the dignity traditionally accorded persons; nor do they simply play the protective function they have assumed in Grotius. Be that as it may, they would not subsist if there were no (still voluntarist) God to bestow them, since according to Locke, modern man has rights by God's command; without that his theory of rights would have to be abandoned. If any godless individuals wanted to claim rights – and such were rarely to be found in Locke's time – they would have to find some other justification for proposing such gratuitous metaphysical entities: otherwise must, with Hobbes, scrap them altogether. Only if man in some sense *is* God – but again, in what helpful sense? – will such justification be available.

Moreover, if our personal identity depends on memory, how are we to understand the relationship between the soul (or mind) and the body that makes memory possible? Locke has in effect bisected the person – not, as did Descartes, into immaterial mind and inert bodily matter, but into the conscious self and its material matrix. Which leaves the problem: how do we think? Locke hesitates, sometimes seeming to suppose that the conscious self is to be understood rather as an epiphenomenon of the body in which it originates – a view long rejected by Plato, Aristotle and the subsequent Aristotelian tradition – sometimes that matter itself may be able to think (perhaps a revised and anachronistic version of Stoic vitalism). As he notes, 'It is not much more remote from our comprehension to conceive that God can, if he pleases, superadd to matter a faculty of thinking, than that he should superadd to it another substance with a faculty of thinking'. (Among our own contemporaries we find a similar toying with that idea, though usually with a more resilient admission that matter as understood by physicists lends it small support.)

What then are Locke's contributions to the wisdom of 'enlightened' man, his contemporaries? That a voluntarist God is required to keep us in order; that we cannot grasp real things but only their 'nominal' essences (that is, as we speak of or name them); that some humans are not persons and therefore have no rights either to property or presumably to respect; that we 'own' our bodies; that property (like our bodies) must be understood as an individual, not a communal possession; that original sin (again) must be dismissed, for Adam's guilt could not be handed down to his descendants, most of whom have never heard of him (!); that we – our personal identity once forensically established – are responsible to God for our behaviour since we can 'suspend the execution and satisfaction of any of its [i.e. the mind's] desires'. Theologians might find this last claim Pelagian; historians of the development of European culture can recognise in it another step toward the coming Enlightenment thesis that we are essentially autonomous agents.

Since for Locke, as for Hobbes, we have no special instinct for the good or for virtue, this has to be an imprint to be inscribed on the *tabula rasa* (the 'clean slate') with which we are born. For we have (again as with Hobbes) a natural tendency to (psychological) egoism, which must be corrected by sanctions ultimately justified by their divine origin. In sum, Locke may look more respectable than Hobbes – and in his own day was certainly so regarded – but there are many similarities. As his former pupil and later severe critic, the third Earl of Shaftesbury put it in a letter to Michael Ainsworth: "Twas Mr Locke that struck the home blow (for Mr Hobb's character and base slavish principles in Government took off the poison of his philosophy). 'Twas Mr Locke that struck at all Fundamentals, threw all Order and Virtue out of the world, and made the very ideas of these … unnatural and without foundation in our minds.'

*

What then had the noble Earl to do? Firstly, repudiate Locke's insistence that only God's big stick would suffice to inhibit wickedness and hedonism; as he observed, an animal tamed by fear is not really gentle. Following in the footsteps of the Cambridge Platonists, Shaftesbury held that we are capable of self-determination and self-control: and (in defiance of Aristotle's distinction between self-control and virtue) that this and not simple obedience must be at the heart of morality. As for Descartes, he is no help in psychology: we are not mere calculators, but possess an innate capacity to distinguish right from wrong: a *moral sense*. Shaftesbury may not have been the first to use that phrase, but he certainly brought it to attention as that which distinguishes our humanity and hence is the source of our worth.

Shaftesbury is old-fashioned, being more interested in virtue than in rights, and he strongly objects to Hobbes's view (to which Locke would be eventually converted) that goods are simply what we want: objecting too to the contention that at the bottom we are only concerned with survival, the 'virtue' of benevolence being little more than a pleasing veneer. For Shaftesbury we, in respect of our moral sense, are sharers in some sort of cosmic harmony, though we must develop a capacity for it, moral sense functioning rather like the acquired appreciation of works of art. According to Shaftesbury – in this typical of his aristocratic status and Whiggish age – the capacity of moral sense can only be recognised in people of 'liberal education'. Not only does this leave uncertain the state of the rest of humanity, but it remains unclear why such a sense should point even the elite to what are *objective* cosmic harmonies. Nevertheless, Shaftesbury and his followers were right to draw attention to affect as – for better or for worse – no mere accessory to the human condition; we do seem to need to *experience* the rightness of a thing we are doing or see others doing.

Nor is it entirely clear how the 'moral sense' works. While its function is to induce us to reflect on our passions and desires and hence, to evaluate them, it is that evaluation that generates secondary affections for rightful experiences and aversions from the wrongful. Thus, though standing at the origins of moral sense theories, Shaftesbury has not fully jettisoned the role of the judging intellect, this being for him – as distinct from 'moral sense' successors such as Francis Hutcheson – an active power: not inert and merely receptive as in Locke. Even so, for Shaftesbury its activity is apparently limited to consideration of feelings proposed to it by the moral sense, which remains the sole source of moral concern, as also of the power to decide whether or not to proceed to action on the feelings the intellect has evaluated.

In all this there seems rather little place for revealed Christian theology, though as a social (but not political) conservative Shaftesbury is able to draw on the Christian capital he inherits. What this cashes out as is deism, understood as a belief in divine benevolence with for ethics a Stoic-sounding appeal to self-control, for metaphysics a vaguely Platonist notion of cosmic harmonies vouched for by God's existence and nature. Understandably, Bishop Berkeley fingered Shaftesbury alongside Bernard Mandeville as enemies to Christianity: the former as *de facto* deist, the latter *de facto* atheist. Auguste Comte would later come along to claim that humanity (in the first instance the intellectuals: his *avant-garde*) has moved from religion via metaphysics to science. For now Shaftesbury, at the very point when metaphysics was being discarded as unscientific, has moved to uphold fragments of the earlier tradition as supposedly rejuvenated by his 'moral sense' ethics.

*

Whither hence? Bishop Cumberland of Peterborough would go one way, Mandeville (notoriously) another, Hutcheson a third, while Leibniz would attempt – more effectively than Shaftesbury – to stem the anti-metaphysical flow.

First then Cumberland, who saw his main task in his *De Legibus Naturae* (*On the Laws of Nature*) as to refute 'the wicked doctrines of Mr Hobbes'. Unfortunately part of his response was based on claims which Hobbes would hold unproven, namely that God not merely exists and is powerful, but functions through a rational morality akin to ours and that His will, being that of a superior, renders the rational demands of 'natural law' obligatory. Cumberland lays down that 'God will determine the same End and Means to be best, which the Reason of any Man truly judges to be so'; this, recalling Scotus' account of Being as univocal, sounds like a trial run for Kantianism in raising the question why God is needed if man is so well resourced.

More cogent is Cumberland's claim that Hobbes' account of human nature is in part misguided: that though Hobbes was right to emphasise human aggressiveness and egoism, that is not the whole story; Grotius' 'sociability' is not to be omitted. Our benevolence (which mirrors God's) cannot be overlooked or dismissed as of secondary importance. By benevolence, Cumberland means active love – though he also believes motivation to be as telling as actions. Predictably for an Anglican bishop of his time, he sounds conservative, echoing Aquinas and Hooker as to our rationality and indicating that neither God's action nor man's can be viewed in crudely voluntarist terms: basically, he reverts to an Augustinian view that love is the fount of the virtues, which he supposes makes them obligatory. For Hobbes – dying in 1679, seven years after Cumberland's *De Legibus Naturae* was published – Cumberland will have begged many questions.

According to Cumberland, Hobbes is wrong about 'good' as merely a name for what we want, and yet more wrong about language being merely a code whereby each of us ultimately seeks his own preservation; for were that the case, we should not be intelligible to one another. However inadvertently, he agrees with Hobbes that we should envisage the 'common good' as a mere aggregate of individual goods which can thus be quantified and – as with their attendant 'felicity' – maximised: clear precursor of approaching Utilitarianism.

We could conclude that Cumberland's heart is in the right place, but that he appeals too uncritically to that rationalism that (as we noted at the beginning of this chapter) marks his age's offering as an alternative to both Hobbesian 'realism' and theological voluntarism; indeed, like Hobbes he thought that the goal of natural law should be the certainty and precision of mathematics, since ethics, like mathematics, is in the business of determining necessary and eternal truths. Like Shaftesbury, he prates of cosmic concord.

Aware though he was that it little availed to introduce Cartesian innate ideas or other dubiously acceptable bits of metaphysics, Cumberland failed adequately to recognise that to defeat Hobbes he would have to show him either incoherent on his own terms or too selective in his empiricism. In his account of benevolence, he scores hits later to be approved as corrections by Hume – but overall Hobbes would have had little reason for concern; indeed, some might conclude from Cumberland's 'proto-Kantianism' and 'proto-utilitarianism' that he was being pushed where he should not – and basically did not – want to go. We may think of his ambiguous position as an early prototype of those further confusions (to be discussed in later chapters) which arise from attempts to blend parts of the Original Tradition with what essentially contradicts it.

*

Bishop Berkeley, writing *Alciphron* in 1731, rightly saw in Shaftesbury's theories a threat to Christianity; he worries that the Anglican Church is full of deists and has one speaker report that he has heard a foreigner say the English are 'Good Protestants but no Christians'. He erred, however, in supposing Bernard Mandeville, though an enemy, one less dangerous than Shaftesbury. Mandeville (inevitably dubbed by some 'Man-Devil') was a refugee from Holland, a hater of Catholics but otherwise a more or less secularist advocate of religious toleration. In 1723 he published an updated version of his earlier *Fable of the Bees*, which he entitled *An Enquiry into Moral Virtue*. In this he asserts that private vices promote the public good: thus drunkenness, prostitution and in particular greed, benefit the exchequer and are the engine which enables the circulation of money and development of commerce. Such views procured for their author something of the notoriety of Machiavelli and Hobbes, being widely read, not least in France where their mockery of society earned the esteem of Voltaire, their 'honesty' Rousseau's if ambiguous endorsement.

Defending himself against moralising objections such as Berkeley's, Mandeville, somewhat disingenuously but not entirely inaccurately, claimed merely to depict the society of his day: that rapidly developing mercantilist world which conferred new significance on 'economic man'. He further claims that he himself has always respected traditional virtue – though, and significantly, his 'virtue' has no religious grounding and Mandeville gives rather little indication of how it is to be defended despite its apparent economic disadvantages. His emphasis on the needs of economic man, however mockingly expressed, points to the future.

Though Mandeville would deny a religious foundation to morality, he has a practical, if disingenuous and dubiously moral, reason to claim that morality is desirable: it encourages people to be concerned with prestige, with being of good repute. (Hobbes too, we recall, had upheld the importance of status, noting that people will kill to maintain it.) Although such 'virtue' encourages the hypocrisy with which Shaftesbury already charged the veneer of benevolence he found in Locke, hypocrisy is to civic advantage in functioning as social glue.

'Moral virtues are the political Offspring which Flattery begot upon Pride': so Mandeville sums up his analysis in what is surely a distant and distorted echo of Plato's myth of Poverty and Abundance in his *Symposium*. Mandeville's view of the world is that it is full of hypocrites who, virtue-signalling for fame or merely for (self-)respect, use private vice to create public wealth while promoting as by-product such social inequalities as poor educational provision and so enable society to retain an underclass to satisfy the need for agricultural labour (later, for proletarianised factory workers). Hypocrisy makes the world go round.

Whether or not Mandeville is advocating rather than reporting the social situation, his claim is to be telling it as it is and as it will continue in a society looking for ways to establish at least the veneer of morality to replace a fading Christianity: similarities with the world as painted by Hogarth are too obvious to be missed. Indeed, as we noted, Berkeley had more reason to worry about Mandeville's dystopic vision than Shaftesbury's over-optimistic and sentimental elitism with its beliefs as to basic human goodness: now being dismissed by Mandeville out of hand. Reborn into our own society, Berkeley would surely recognise his mistake, seeing how, with the dismemberment of Christianity which Mandeville is already assuming, a Utilitarian 'calculus' of 'felicity' would present itself, first to Jeremy Bentham, as the recourse to disguise – even though not resolve – the contradictions between mankind's sociability and aggressiveness.

*

Mandeville had his view of life, Francis Hutcheson another. A Presbyterian minister regarded as heretical by many of his brethren, he like Cumberland framed his response to Hobbes around Christian love: though he prefers Shaftesbury's term 'benevolence'. This is the calm and disinterested virtue with which our nature has been adorned by God and which brings happiness, since making others happy affords human beings the greatest pleasure.

Benevolence must be approved by the moral sense, though it remains unclear how such approval could be given, since for Hutcheson the mind – in this differing from the active mind of Shaftesbury – is inert (as Locke held), being merely a recorder of experience. As Hutcheson sees it, however, the moral sense tracks our experiences and induces feelings of approval or disapproval – though why it should induce us to approve of the 'right' things remains mysterious; presumably a properly formed moral sense will provide the right answers, but how is it to be 'properly' formed? An analogous difficulty will arise later for Bishop Butler who, relying – as does Milton – on Conscience to make us know or intuit what is right, neglects the necessity of its proper formation. Rousseau, as we shall see, at least knew better than that in making such formation part of his manipulative armoury; Hutcheson just seems to assume that God gave us a moral sense to work that way. (In more modern terms we might ask him how it is that some people appear to have 'lost their moral compass' to the extent of approving, even enjoying, acts of cruelty.)

Nevertheless, the 'sentimentalist' Hutcheson was on to something important, if rather for an analysis of human psychology than as guide to the good life, and the feelings to which he appeals as indicative of a God-given capacity would be presented in more popular light by a later contemporary. In his 'sentimental' novels *Pamela* (1740) and *Clarissa* (1747–1748), Samuel Richardson would present no longer the picaresque society of libertines, free-thinkers and whores served up by Daniel Defoe, Henry Fielding and Aphra Behn, nor tragic heroes or dashing Renaissance aristocrats, but ordinary people (usually female) into whose bread and butter troubles and moral dilemmas we are admitted and with which we are invited to sympathise. That would be well received, and again not least in France, where Denis Diderot praised Richardson as revealing by the novel our capacity for empathy: for putting ourselves imaginatively into others' shoes.

Thus, were 'sentimentalists' assisted in responding to Hobbes and Mandeville: through illustrating how we really can be affected by the troubles of others and how sympathy can encourage us to try to help more than will a merely intellectual grasp that they are suffering. True, in some circumstances – as with a mob – feelings may promote cruelty rather than kindness; nevertheless, empathy is an aspect of human psychology largely neglected not only by 'realists' like Hobbes but by the great majority of previous philosophers, and to bring it to our attention might help not only Hutcheson but any non-cognitive account of moral experience and obligation. Richardson's English contemporaries, however, were not always impressed, being by now prone to suppose he confused emotion with more hypocritical sentiment: hence Fielding's parodic response, entitled *Shamela*. As for Hutcheson himself, he begins to look like our latter-day clergy: hanging on to Christian institutions and selected teachings after the credal core has been knocked out of them, yet still seeming to believe that they can offer coherent moral advice.

*

Thus Anglican and Calvinist England and Scotland. In Germany, where Lutheranism prevailed, the intellectual world would develop somewhat differently. From the point of view of kings and princes, Luther was preferable to Calvin because his followers, far from seeking a new theocracy, were usually happy to shelter under the protection of existing authority. At the end of the seventeenth century, the increasingly influential Prussian dynasty of the Hohenzollerns – Calvinist rulers of a largely Lutheran population – took advantage of this to encourage a burgeoning Lutheran 'Pietism', not least at their new university foundation at Halle. Their hope was that a more unified Protestantism, state-supported and state-friendly, could be established. In the twentieth century this statal aspect would herald an ominous future for such Christian pliancy.

Furthermore, in Germany, as in politics so in ethics and metaphysics, the ferocious reaction against everything scholastic was – despite Luther himself – more muted than among many of the more radically 'Reformed'; indeed in the figure of Leibniz (1646–1716), we recognise something of a counter-revolutionary: a powerful thinker who becomes very nervous about the way things theologically and philosophically were shaping up. Leibniz would hold back the anti-metaphysical tide in Germany until traditional metaphysics would be more forcefully debunked – or so it would seem – by Kant at the end of the century.

Though a distinguished mathematician and in actual rivalry with Newton as co-discoverer of the calculus, Leibniz wanted to restore final causes in physics as well as in ethics. He also wanted to reconnect morality and religion: the two, in his opinion, had been too widely separated by Pufendorf, whose claim that existence is not good *per se* he repudiated. While agreeing broadly with the rationalism widely accepted since Descartes, and with many of his contemporaries that the concept of original sin was abhorrent, he fiercely opposed a voluntarism, human or divine, that turned God into a mere tyrant, preventing recognition of him as good and lovable. This had been the position of Hobbes, carrying the implication that good and evil are merely so designated by God's decree. For Leibniz, God has created not only a recognisably good world but the best of all possible worlds (claim for which he was to be mocked by Voltaire in *Candide*). As for the so called 'freedom of indifference' – by now the regular companion of voluntarism – it is to be dismissed as unintelligible. Nor – in this like the Cambridge Platonists – has Leibniz any time for the medieval identification of a separate faculty of the will; for him – as for them – the whole soul reasons and decides.

For Leibniz love – or, as with Shaftesbury and Hutcheson he prefers, 'benevolence' – is at the centre of the moral universe. Even self-love (without divine grace and therefore contrary to traditional theology) can be transformed by our increasing understanding into concern for others. Nonetheless, Leibniz is remarkably Catholic – even arguably confused – in his philosophical and theological preferences, appearing happy with many Catholic as well as Lutheran and 'Reformed' authors. Yet, and though he quotes Scripture widely, he can give the impression that Christianity is a bonus: that many of its important tenets (*pace* Hobbes) fall within the range of natural reason; thus, Revelation is not needed to show that there is a 'sole Principle of all things, entirely good and wise'.

Leibniz often prefers scholastic and classical thinkers to those of more recent times, in this showing himself largely devoid of an intellectual myopia afflicting many of his contemporaries (and of ours) about the Middle Ages. Outside of Germany, where his influence remained great, he in many ways resembled the Cambridge

Platonists; indeed, he admired Cudworth in particular and engaged in a philosophical exchange of letters with the latter's daughter, of the resplendent name of Damaris Lady Masham. In Leibniz we find none of the later German insistence that philosophy – indeed culture more widely – has become a German preserve.

Why then did Leibniz's attempt to keep his finger in the dyke while redirecting 'enlightened' man to his traditions have more success in Germany than did the Cambridge group in Britain? Partly because Germany (unlike France) was – despite Pietism – not overwhelmed by the 'sentimentalists', rather retaining more of the intellectualist-rationalist tradition of Descartes; also because it was less inclined, after the Thirty Years War ended in 1648, to opt for the more political – hence highly controverted – aspects of both Catholicism and Calvinism.

Leibniz could hardly be accused of ignorance of the new science; thus, older intellectual paths could be followed more effectively by him and his followers: until, that is, their more theological aspects would be abolished in the thoroughgoing revision of Cartesian rationalism that would replace his morality of love with the morality of duty we associate with Kant: himself from a Pietist background. After Kant, German thought, whether 'Christian' or more secular, would set off in directions that were to prove intellectually exciting, if morally and politically threatening.

*

Of contemporary Anglo-American philosophers, a high percentage are Humeans of some sort, and most would admit to it. Which shows how important Hume is as painter of the desired portrait of modern, enlightened man – quite apart from the effect he had on 'Continental' thinkers, more especially on Kant who, on his own admission, would be woken from his 'Leibnizian slumbers' by Hume's scepticism.

There is a curious paradox about Hume's influence. His professional position seems calculated to render philosophy a mere spectator sport; he claimed he got so bored with it that he needed to refresh himself by playing backgammon. How, then, is his paradoxical importance defensible? The answer is to be found by comparing his attitudes to physics and to philosophical psychology. In physics he argued that it is impossible to demonstrate that the apparent cause of motion is its real cause, though he knew that physicists will continue their investigations, and make significant discoveries, on that assumption and in complete disregard of his sceptical objections. Similarly in philosophical psychology he would claim that what we recognise in sense perception is but the construction of our imagination, and yet we go on living and communicating – and awarding praise and blame – as though a world we imagine were the 'underlying' reality.

Hume contributed substantially to modern man's view of himself. Opening fire on Descartes' view of a 'self' sustaining our various behaviours, he rightly observed that 'when I enter most intimately unto what I call *myself*, I always stumble upon some particular perception or other … I never catch *myself* at any time without a perception …' So much for the inert underlying self of Descartes. Earlier views of the soul might be immune to this kind of attack – but be that as it may, with the Cartesian self discredited, Hume's counterproposal is again that we are (as Hobbes had suggested and Locke had argued) a set of serial selves, an ever-changing bundle of qualities given a common and socially useful name which indicates our identity. In Hume's own words, 'I cannot compare the soul more properly to anything than to a republic or commonwealth … And as the same individual republic may change its members … so in like manner the same person may vary his character and dispositions without losing his identity'. Identity thus again becomes forensic, though now, in contrast to Locke, Hume seems to have greater difficulty explaining in what this continuing identity consists: it seems, however, again to lie in persisting consciousness – which might raise problems such as whether I am murdered when I am stabbed in the heart as I sleep …

But if that be a disadvantage of the theory, an arguable 'advantage' (not always recognised at the time) is that when I come round to consciousness, it might seem I am no longer responsible for my past actions (as, for example, repaying debts or remaining married – for in that latter case the two who married are now different people). Apparently when I wake up, I remember that someone did various things and normally, if mistakenly, I assume that someone to be 'myself' – though why I regularly assume that remains unexplained.

Forensically, of course, at least some of 'my' actions *must* be attributed to myself, whether I am to be taken to be a set of serial selves or not; otherwise no ongoing society would be possible. Presumably which actions are to be so attributed will be determined by the customs of differing societies, though this can be helped by the evidence of those who recognise my continuing bodily self, not to speak of my past and largely continuing attitudes or claims to ownership of 'my' property. Such an account of the 'self' seemed (and seems) to win a certain respect, many philosophers assuming the only alternative to be the Cartesian view that our 'personal identity' is an inert substrate rather than the traditional dynamic soul. For Hume is right that he cannot 'capture' the apparent Cartesian self – and if Descartes is wrong, then Hume must be right (or so 'enlightened' man will be inclined to suppose).

Hume treats the moral thinker as an 'impartial observer' of human psychology, though that term is not his but his friend Adam Smith's. Hume's problem then is why the signpost should go in the direction to which it points! What we observe (though why should we be taken as impartial observers?) is that we feel the effects of what happens around us and evaluate them through our moral sense. Our mind, being merely instrumental – and Hume calls it the 'slave of the passions' – is thus 'instructed' and looks for the means to bring about what the 'passions' propose. In the first instance it only records what is the case (here we can recognise Hume's famous distinction between facts and values, between 'is' and 'ought') while we, governed by feelings and desires, determine what we 'ought' to do and so are impelled into action. No amount of knowledge of mere fact will in and of itself motivate us to act as we think we 'ought'.

What then has happened to the virtues? Hume's account of them is remarkably conventional. They can be divided, as Grotius distinguished perfect and imperfect duties, into the natural and the artificial, justice being (as in Hobbes) artificial: a social construct. The most important of the natural feelings is (again) benevolence, for Hume will not accept Hobbes' tendency to treat this as mere veneer. We naturally sympathise with people; we put ourselves into their shoes (being in this like the reader of a Richardsonian novel) and this sympathy tells us to reconcile the 'Grotian' characteristics of sociability and aggressiveness not, as with Hobbes, by handing our fate over to an authoritarian Sovereign, but by applying our developed sense of justice to conflict-resolution. That is how we survive, how we have constructed the various societies in which we live, the conventions which we should normally follow. 'Virtues' will tend to vary with differing social conditions; Hume (a Scot) seems to assume that the norms of eighteenth-century English polite society are the best on offer.

What about God? He has disappeared (though for Adam Smith still necessary as 'the great Superintendent of the universe'). For Hume, 'God' is the product of ignorance and such 'monkish' virtues as humility, asceticism, celibacy. Nonetheless, and though he regards atheism as common scientific sense, his concerns to erase God are 'academic' and dismissive, lacking the virulent, ideological hostility to Christianity in particular which characterises French *philosophes* of his day – many of whom regarded him (as also his English predecessor Locke) as an oracle of an enlightenment they longed to transfer to their own soil. As for miracles (so essential to revealed religion), since they cannot happen in a world governed by Newtonian mechanics, they don't happen. And Hume is equally hostile to the natural theology which deists had tried to substitute for the revealed, more properly Christian version, dismissing it as mere poor thinking.

As for the divine voluntarism, assumed to be religious, which Hume himself had learned in his Presbyterian childhood, it is philosophically confused and morally unedifying. Hume would surely have appreciated the 'Mandevillian' hypocrisy of 'Holy Willie's Prayer' by Robert Burns, his younger contemporary, which opens:

> O thou that in the heavens dost dwell!
> Wha, as it pleases best thysel,
> Sends ane to heaven and ten to hell,
> A' for thy glory!
> And no for any gude or ill
> They've done before thee ...

And the Reverend Willie concludes:

> Yet I am here, a chosen sample,
> To show thy grace is great and ample.
> I'm here, a pillar o' thy temple
> Strong as a rock,
> A guide, a ruler and example
> To a' thy flock.

Did his friend Adam Smith add anything to Hume's moral world? Apart from retention of God as *deus ex machina* in the manner of Hutcheson, little except a Stoic-seeming confidence about self mastery which will engulf Smith in the old problem as to who masters whom; plus new emphasis on Hutcheson's further claim that we *just like* being benevolent. Smith, clearly an optimist about human capabilities, was soon to transfer his optimism to economic theory, teaching that in a mercantilist society a 'hidden hand' – that of 'the Superintendent of the Universe'? – ensures that the prosperity of rich entrepreneurs 'trickles down' to the poor. It might seem as though philosophical 'sentimentalism' had run its course – as in Kant's view it certainly had: time for modern man to retain the metaphysical scepticism of Hume while returning to a more rationalist, improved Cartesian approach to human psychology and moral capacity in the mechanical world cheerfully delineated by Hobbes and apparently for ever established by Newton.

*

Like so many German thinkers who were to follow in his train, Kant comes from a decidedly Protestant – indeed in his case Pietist – background: from a world in which faith mattered and where Pietists feared Lutheranism was at risk of degenerating into a mere formalism. Hence he claimed that his attack on much traditional metaphysics inherited from Leibniz via Christian Wolff was motivated by a desire 'to do away with knowledge to make way for faith': if not quite Luther's description of reason as 'the Devil's Whore', a subdued version of the same tradition.

Kant claimed that Hume and Rousseau had taught him to give up his earlier ways and Hume to recognise that we live in a world controlled by the laws of Newtonian mechanics: a world interpreted through imagination acting upon sense perception and composed of the raw motion of atoms in their ordained courses. From Hume's misguided account of what is given in sense-perception – there being for him no other foundation of our knowledge – derives Kant's determination to find some non-mechanistic aspect of human nature that will allow for moral choice and such human responsibility as (for example) society will normally assume and require.

Here we turn to Rousseau – and should the reader wonder why, as an older contemporary of Kant, he is not introduced into our story before him, the reason is that Rousseau stands at the origins of an altogether different vision of man from Kantian 'rationality': a newly 'totalitarian' version of humanity of which we shall give a more chronological account in the next chapter. At the same time, Rousseau does profoundly influence Kant's account of Enlightened man, not least in the way Kant comes to view himself. As he writes, 'I at one time thought that the search for truth in which I was engaged "constituted the honour of mankind", but Rousseau set me right ...

I learned to respect humanity. I should consider myself far more useless than the common labourer if I did not believe that one consideration alone gives worth to all others, namely to establish the rights of man.'

Why did respect for humanity and the rights of man (a phrase seemingly first used by Rousseau and to be distinguished from the earlier 'natural rights' and later 'human rights') matter in the mechanist universe from which Kant was trying to escape? The answer is that the single feature of human nature indispensable to that escape must be present in everyone and cannot require any professional or academic skill to be seen in the light of day. Such a characteristic of humanity was already available in Kant's religious background, though it apparently took the rhetoric of the dubiously believing Rousseau to draw to his attention that Lutherans held man's dignity to depend upon our being created 'in the image and likeness' of God.

But what if there is no God, as Hume, Kant's other new mentor, argues more coolly than Voltaire and the French *philosophes* in general. Can human dignity yet be preserved? Locke's defence of rights still had depended on God's decree. In a new and godless context, if human 'value' (Hobbes' word, though Hobbes had reduced it to our social price) is to be defended, we need Locke's conclusions without Locke's theological premise. If rights ('of man') are to be defended, they must depend on some capacity shared by the whole of humanity and explicable without reference to God.

Kant thought he had discovered the answer in the unfolding concept of autonomy – it would seem without realising the term's strongly anti-Christian implication, not least in implying a rejection of humility as in any sense a virtue. Had not the Cambridge Platonists looked to something like autonomy to defend both Christianity and humanity from voluntarism and divine determinism? By Kant's time, however, the threat was less from God than from a mechanistically conceived nature; hence, would Cudworth's 'Platonist' version of autonomy be found still too 'heteronomous' – too other-dependent? What Kant presumably had set himself to prove unnecessary was any specifically Christian version of the escape from determinism – immediately such as that of Leibniz and Wolff.

Kantian autonomy is to be understood as the ability to make decisions with absolute freedom (always within the parameters of logic and physics). Its opposite is heteronomy: dependence on another – in many versions, on God. Thus to be autonomous one has to live in a moral universe under rules where 'ought' implies 'can'. That we are free in that sense is precisely what Christian tradition had denied in its doctrine of 'grace' (given canonical form by Augustine, according to whom 'ought' *outside of* God's grace will rather imply 'cannot'). For Kant this required 'autonomy' must be universal: shared by high and low, whether in birth or in intelligence, and at the least by anyone who can understand Kant's cardinal concept of 'duty' – and here the assumption is that understanding will bring compliance.

How then can we establish that we possess such a capacity? Not, that is, a capacity merely to think that we live in 'moral space', that there is a difference between right and wrong; not such a 'moral sense' as satisfied Hume; not the inert mind offered by Descartes; not Locke's *tabula rasa*: not any of these, but a communal ability to recognise a common principle that in effect is the moral law in accordance with which to conduct our lives. And the first step to that must be to disentangle something of our selves from the Newtonian universe – without which Hobbes and his ilk will never be satisfied, though dignity and responsibility fall together.

Kant's solution is to divide human nature into two aspects which he names 'phenomenal' and 'noumenal' (from the Greek roots *phain* – meaning 'appear', and *nous*, meaning mind). In our 'phenomenal' (or apparent) selves we live in a world of natural determinism to which moral responsibility is irrelevant; in our 'noumenal' (or higher mental) self we live in what Kant – here adapting the language of Lutheran 'two kingdom' theology – calls the 'kingdom of ends'. Nevertheless, though it is easy to see that this distinction is useful to Kant, it is difficult to see how it can be valid, implying as it does that our 'real' self is not a soul-body complex in action but an autonomous mind: an angelic-seeming entity in which we are asked to believe – but why?

Such a theory of the 'person' is now normally dismissed, even by the many Kantians (and some approximation to Kant has become the fall back position for not a few 'intellectuals' deprived, as socially they prefer to think, of a theistic option); it is certainly a desperate move which might seem to reformulate the problem of human freedom rather than resolving it. Kant, however, thinks it necessary as a buttress for our assumed capacity (in a universe where again 'being' applies to man in the same 'univocal' sense as to God) to frame for ourselves the moral law. In so proposing, he takes upon himself the role which earlier voluntarists had attributed to God – even adopting religious language when denoting our autonomous power a 'holy' rational will, thus inaugurating a soon to become frequent appropriation of Christian terminology's emotive force.

And what does our 'holy will' actually do? Kant's answer is that it enables us to formulate moral laws that will apply to all, ourselves included: which laws are, in his language, 'categorical imperatives' requiring all to treat each other with equal respect as 'ends in themselves': no one merely as means to the end of another. Since we all live in the same 'kingdom of ends', we are to 'act only according to that maxim through which you can at the same time will that it should become a universal law'.

If we pursue further the nature of Kant's rational will, we shall find it very Cartesian: not as proposing an inert underlying self so much as in placing reliance on no affective but only on purely cognitive capacities. Thus Kant stresses that moral action must be free from any concern with self-interest and so independent of our desires or inclinations: otherwise we would not only be at least to an extent 'heteronomous' (that is, responding to some rule extraneous to our 'noumenal self': a cardinal sin against Humanity), but also 'eudaimonist' self-seekers who rule themselves out of the moral universe as not simple devotees of duty.

Thus do most previous writers on moral philosophy stand condemned as eudaimonists – more especially those with an eventual eye on heaven, or even on the flourishing of their human nature if that is understood more widely than as simple moral agent. For neither love nor friendship can have moral force; indeed, we have scant need to be improved morally since we already possess the essential sense of duty. It follows that Kant has little interest in character development, except insofar as we may struggle to respect the moral law – and here there is no excuse for ultimate failure, since our 'holy will' underwrites endeavours in which we might suppose it to take (unfallen) angels to succeed!

If all this may seem drily unappetising, it is hard to avoid supposing that Kant, in calling this capacity a rational *will*, implies that mere recognition of our duty to obey the moral law will supply, together with the knowledge of what we ought to do, also the will to do it. Hume would object that merely to know what I ought to do is not to want, let alone intend to do it. And if to that objection Kant would counter that what we ought to do is simply what is rational, then does he imply that, for example, the only thing wrong with the Holocaust was that it seems to make no sense? (Whereas in the view of those who carried it through, the elimination of those they adjudged in some way inferior made at least practical sense.) And does this differ essentially from Hobbes' reduction of the moral to the prudential (even leaving aside differing judgments about what is the prudential course to pursue)? Then if the answer to such questions is 'No', what has become of Kant's absolute – 'categorical' – imperative?

There are further problems: What are the contents of the law that the fulfilment of duty prescribes – apart from the condition that it be accepted by all including oneself? And if we see this law as prescribing rights, what rights does it prescribe? In earlier days of rights theory it might have seemed obvious which 'rights' were being infringed by Church or State and who was being treated unfairly; but such discernment begins to look subjective and too bound to particular circumstances. What if we move from the right not to suffer degrading punishments to the right to kill – or to own a Mercedes?

Kant's account of the moral law has always and rightly been accused of formalism: you – all of you out there – must do what is rational. Yet even someone who intends his decisions to be rational, rather than be dictated by his preferences or passions, may well have difficulty in determining which decision to make and how to prioritise among apparently irreconcilable goals. Shall I never regret having chosen whatever course I follow? What if my ('rationally') chosen course is to do nothing? (We may recall Christ's parable of the man who buried his talent.) We shall find the same problem arising for those who will later be called Utilitarians: like Kant intent on what is best for Humanity, and eventually reduced to maintaining that one should 'maximise the good – whatever that happens to be'. Kant's formalism leaves him with a similar difficulty, apparently only to be resolved by recourse to one's preferences: hard to justify as driven by a pure respect for duty and the moral law, unalloyed by emotional and other inclinations.

Thus and granting – as we should not – that Kant has demonstrated that we should value all humans equally positively and without reference to God, he still leaves us in ignorance of what we should actually do – even if we agree that everyone should do whatever she or he does with unalloyed motives. That will bring us back to the assumption that we have the capacity to act morally without recourse to love, friendship or other passion or incentivising emotion. The noumenal-phenomenal distinction will turn out to be designed merely to give us – But now which of Kant's selves is 'we'? – an assumed means of escape from mechanistic determinism, to be free to respect one another as ends in themselves. Quite simply, Kant has begged the question, in effect claiming that since we would wish to be free from the determinism of the natural world, therefore we must be free of it. Perhaps, indeed, we are, but his phenomenal-noumenal distinction only gets us there by relieving us of the human nature we know experientially that we possess. Our 'noumenal' nature is thus reduced to a will o'the wisp.

And where might God – still there – fit into all this? Kant holds that we do not need Him in order to show that we are all equal in possessing the right to be treated as ends and not as objects of manipulation by others. And yet he holds with God as our Creator – who, it is implicit, has given to him the very power to formulate the categorical imperative, as to us to live in accordance with it if we choose freely so to do! But what if God has not so created us? How then do Kant or we know we have such powers? Are we not victims (again) of a further example of Kant-induced wishful thinking?

Why should we care if some of us – preferably others – are treated unfairly, as so often befalls? What, further, about the man who finds it repellent to be expected to be 'good' and dutiful? Or the one who has an actual preference for the life of a criminal? Why will – or should – such a person accept Kantian principles? And here God will get back into the act: in the end it is (even for Kant) God who will reconcile duty with happiness, as being possible only if He is there. Which solution will imply we are not autonomous after all! A hundred years after Kant, Henry Sidgwick too will be obliged to admit that after a lifetime of (God-freed) meditation on the problem, he had failed to reconcile happiness and duty!

Despite what we have shown to be the ultimate futility of Kant's bleakly formal position on ethics as duty, it is due to him to observe that, while rejecting traditional metaphysics, he yet entitled what is his major work in moral philosophy, *The Groundwork of the* ***Metaphysics*** *of Morals*. In that work he proposes that we look for rescue from materialism and consequent determinism not immediately to arguments about the necessity of God as constructor of the physical universe – classically represented by Aquinas's Five Ways of 'proving' (though better of understanding) God's existence – but to our ability to recognise, even in our very respect for the moral law, a capacity to point ourselves to a nonmaterial target. Though this does not (yet) constitute an argument for God's existence, yet once any such immaterial principle of ethics (or aesthetics) is admitted into our world-picture, God is waiting, as it were in the wings, to supply the missing justification and explanation of the phenomenon.

Before leaving Kant, we turn from ethics to politics – and to a further disturbing feature of his legacy. Kant composed a treatise on universal peace, seemingly in hope that humanity would progressively come to override national boundaries. He thus promoted, if he did not originate, a still widely held belief that large international organisations can be expected to be less corrupt, less inhumane, more enlightened, as well as more effective, than national ones. That can now be seen to be highly doubtful; rather it might seem that a diversity of polities enables more hope of just and democratic laws and customs. Even before our present age, there were differing ideas as to what would constitute 'enlightened' – followed by post-enlightened and international – New Man. In the immediate future Kant's political vision would be neglected, but in an ensuing more totalitarian age we might seem to have returned to it in its original naive form.

It is reasonable to conclude with Kant the European-philosophical age which began with Montaigne, for in his handling of the new science, as in his advocacy of the rights of autonomous rational man, Kant sums our period up, revealing its aspirations but also its radical defects. In a newly 'Enlightened' world, Kant's autonomous man has largely, even though not entirely, replaced God: above all in being expected to prescribe the moral law for himself. It might seem as though Beethoven's 'Creatures of Prometheus' had supplanted their creator.

5 Totalitarian Man

Theory and Practice

I'm finished. I trust no-one, not even myself.

Joseph Stalin in 1952

Totalitarian ideas do not appear first on the streets; rather their appearance on the streets results from their prior appearance in print. What burgeons around some 'ivory tower' may wither unseen by the wider world; escaped, however, into the public domain, it ceases to be of purely 'academic' interest – and once on the streets and disclosing its source may be revised in any number of variants by publicists and demagogues. This is what happened with ideas we call 'totalitarian' and which we proceed to chronicle as they developed in Europe from the mid-eighteenth century to the twentieth.

In 1945 Karl Popper published his influential *The Open Society and Its Enemies*, his targets being Plato, Hegel and Marx. Popper, however, failed to distinguish what are properly regarded as authoritarian regimes from their totalitarian descendants: the very decided difference being that authoritarians may, and often do, believe in such traditional values as goodness and truth (however understood), while totalitarians prefer to assume that the 'bourgeois' account of them demands radical revision. Plato is authoritarian in his politics; Marx is totalitarian.

In order to give a stipulative definition, let us start by looking at 'authoritarian' to see how it differs from its 'totalitarian' rival and – too often – supplanter. To begin with, in authoritarian regimes power is located with a group of individuals who may exercise it without restraint: they may be popular or unpopular and may or may not brook a limited opposition. They may be concerned with the good of their subjects or only with their own perceived good, but generally speaking, they are interested in the control of *public* life. (If of a religious character, they will aim to extend that control further.) An authoritarian regime, rather than 'eliminating' its opponents, may allow them to retire to 'spend more time with their families' – so long as retirement is judged not to provide occasion for plotting further public dissent. An example of a contemporary authoritarian state would be Egypt; of a totalitarian – apart from its most obvious exponent, China – North Korea, perhaps Venezuela.

Authoritarian states rarely possess the means to control every aspect of their subjects' lives; when they do, they will be on the road to totalitarianism. They may resort to terror, though normally to obtain formal obedience rather than control of 'minds and hearts' as does the totalitarian. Thus though totalitarian *features* appeared in authoritarian and Christian governments before the French Revolution, there is reason to assert that only after 1789 did a full-blown totalitarian regime seize power in Europe – and that while not explicitly so, that Revolution bore the hallmarks of violent totalitarianism from the outset.

What then are the basic differences which separate the authoritarian from the totalitarian? First, totalitarianism is a form of substitute religion, with its own adaptation of religious concepts, especially those of dependence and freedom. As the Christian or Jew holds that he or she is dependent on God, the totalitarian subject knows himself to be dependent for his well-being – even his survival – on the State. Christians believe that they enjoy the 'freedom of the children of God': that is, to obey a God Who is simply good, is Goodness Itself; totalitarian subjects are 'free' to obey the Party, the Police and ultimately the Leader. The Leaders themselves may recognise that they do well to parody many of the practices of their suppressed religious rivals; thus Heinrich Himmler, commander-in-chief of the SS, is reported as urging that the manuals of his organisation ape those of the Jesuits, more particularly their demands for absolute submission to General and Pope.

Secondly, and as we shall explain, totalitarianism is a perverted form of egalitarian *democracy*, or of a society which aspires to this. Totalitarian rulers must claim – and may even at times believe – that they are the whole people, even though and temporarily merely the 'vanguard' of that General Will to be accomplished by their 'total' control. Implicit is that in its beginnings total control must be desired or at least accepted, despite its obvious risks, by sufficiently large numbers of citizens – not necessarily a majority – for whom it will follow from a desperation fanned by demagogues. In 1933 thirteen million Germans *voted in* Hitler.

Totalitarian states – as the name implies – require the firmest of grips to enforce the uniform obedience of the governed. The mechanism by which this is achieved is usually three-fold: the ruling oligarchy or 'vanguard' controlling the army, the (single) Party and the police; while Nazi Germany affords the clearest example, more or less similar authority structures are found elsewhere. In the Third Reich, the Army, that once proud and independent militarist caste, was reduced to a subservience which eventually became humiliating, with party hacks occupying the most influential ranks. The police (of various stripes) was placed under the control of 'der treue Heinrich' (loyal Himmler), the Party under that of Martin Bormann, a necessarily more shadowy, more strictly bureaucratic figure who must never give the impression of being more than the servant of the Leader; Bormann remained more or less unknown to the general public, yet by the ending of Nazi rule his power was virtually supreme among Hitler's subordinates. Such hidden power seems prevalent among modern tyrannies more than in antiquity, probably because of vastly expanded bureaucracies. Ancient tyrants – and those who wrote about them – can seem more concerned with the perquisites, and the conspicuous flaunting of their absolute mastery before their victims, than with the raw reality of power: this Seneca already illustrates with Nero and Caligula.

Both totalitarians and authoritarians can take advantage of a striking anomaly in human nature already noted by Plato: a tendency to admire crime on the grand scale – in particular political crime – while deprecating it among petty criminals. That may help to explain why sympathisers with at least some aspects of both authoritarian and totalitarian regimes are willing to overlook obvious atrocities those regimes commit. Saint-Simon reasoned away the barbarities of the Jacobins. Bernard Shaw, in admiring the achievements of Lenin, ignored the darker side, such as the artificially-generated famines. Sartre's expulsion from the French Communist Party will fail to expunge his praise of the regimes of both Stalin and Mao. Heidegger was for a time a paid-up member of the Nazi Party.

*

Having roughly identified totalitarianism, we turn to some of its more obvious intellectual roots – beginning with a specially significant one in the work of Jean-Jacques Rousseau. Rousseau's General Will – envisaged as instantiated in some form of social contract whereby we give up our more personal and parochial desires – aims at allying an apparent autonomy with a uniformity of purpose that avoids 'alienation'. Writing in the mid-eighteenth century, while he was not the first to propound such a theory, he would bring it to prominence.

We have already met Jean-Jacques persuading Kant that the will of each individual is potentially as moral as that of any other: hence that everyone, of whatever intellectual capacity and social conditioning, can respect the moral law. Yet what does that moral law – and thus the General Will – actually lay before us? Clearly that all men – at least all adult males, for women look less certain in Rousseau's case – are equal and have equal rights: already Rousseau writes of the 'Rights of Man' in a way which was to become standard. For more, we must search his account of man's natural and social conditions.

Contrary to the opinion of Hobbes, Rousseau views man in his natural state as reasonably benign – while leaving it unclear (as does

Hobbes) whether such a man is proposed as historical fact or as thought experiment. In either case, Rousseau's man in his native state has a certain love for himself (*amour de soi*) largely limited to a concern for self-preservation, yet though solitary feels pity for other sentient creatures. Neither envious nor worried about status, he does not feel any *socially-driven* obligations to others. Such obligations are a feature of what is now recognisable as the bourgeois character, the fruit of society's transforming of our *amour de soi* into what Rousseau calls *amour propre* with its self-indulgence and self-satisfaction.

Our pre-rational pity survives this transformation but may now take a perverted, heteronomous form whereby we may choose to put ourselves into the shoes not only of the virtuous but also of the vicious. We need to be trained to avoid this pitfall into such vices as competitiveness, possessiveness, greed and the lust for money. In the *present* state of society, we merely try to avoid *revealing* such characteristics, thus becoming (in later terminology) 'inauthentic'. Thus our only real hope of authenticity lies in a radically reconstructed society. Rousseau approves Mandeville's analysis of the hypocrisy of eighteenth-century England and calls for this feature to be overcome. But how? And to what end?

In our normal ('bourgeois') existence, we are, he argues, in effect two selves: our continuing natural self and its social face. Our aim should be to recover and retain our 'authentic' nature in the right kind of society. How 'right' cashes out (other than tautologically as 'authentic') remains obscure. Nor is it easy to see how Rousseau, while claiming to be no advocate of violent political revolution, thinks the right society is to be salvaged out of the cohorts of corrupted individuals we form as adults. He will have far more to say about how the young should be educated in such a way as to preserve the virtues of their 'authentic' selves than about what to do about our adult 'fallen' and apparently irredeemable state.

In his *Confessions* and elsewhere, Rousseau presents himself as paradigm victim of a failure in education; he sincerely desires to do the right thing but the corrupt society around him prevents him.

The 'sincerity' to which he appeals – a debased version of traditional Christian appeals to an educated conscience – is to be applauded as genuine and 'authentic' (self-evidently he had not met 'sincere' Nazis – nor even perhaps 'sincere' slave owners). In writing what he titles his *Confessions*, he presents himself as a passive victim – 'Not my fault, gov!' – and intends to recall and subvert Augustine's book of the same title, but while Augustine confesses his sins to God and asks for grace to repent and reform, Rousseau indulges in self-pity, roughly thus: 'I would not have done all the wrong things I did had I been brought up properly. I would not, for example, have falsely accused a fellow servant of stealing a ribbon I had myself stolen. If only those who accused me had acted differently I would, of course, have told the truth. I would not have had to cause the poor girl to lose her job and probably end up as a prostitute. I much regret all that: I always will!'

Though Rousseau purports to unmask the hypocrisy of others, his own hypocrisy is blatant, not least when accompanied by appeals to sincerity: Mandeville would have applauded the 'double-take'. In line with his patent unwillingness either to accept responsibility for past offences, or to shoulder responsibilities for the future, would be his failure to take responsibility for the children he fathered and left to the tender mercies of the orphanage. He cannot accept his responsibilities – so he wants us to believe – because he is a victim – and here we can note that presenting oneself as a victim is the reverse side of more violent totalitarian tendencies, the totalitarian mind under both aspects – as victim and as aggressor – reappearing in our more contemporary totalitarians of whatever political stripe.

Then how, we may wonder, can we proceed from our obligation-free natural state to a social condition where obligation is 'authentic', untainted by the desire to 'save face'? Rousseau will reply that though some sort of social self is inevitable, it must be conscience-driven, conscience being a developed version of our natural pity, or – as he tells us in more inflated vein in *Emile* – 'a divine instinct, an immortal and celestial voice . . . an infallible judge of good and bad which makes man like unto God'.

Unlike his near-contemporary Voltaire, Rousseau shows no interest in reforming French society: no concern, for example, to improve the criminal law at a time when Frederick the Great of Prussia had abolished judicial torture and the Italian jurist Cesare Beccaria was advocating the ending of capital punishment. The only solution to society's problems, Rousseau believes, is not mere sticking-plaster reforms but a wholly revised scheme of education, starting with young children. In spelling out the curriculum for this project, he provides no clear idea of the intended 'end-product' – only that at least our minds must be taught to conform to the General Will – whatever that is – and thus live a life of 'Spartan' virtue. Albert Camus remarked that 'The Jacobins destroyed the transcendence of a personal God and replaced it by the transcendence of principles' and much the same could be said of Rousseau, who with 'principles' that for him are 'rights' became one of the main inspirers of Jacobinism – though he might have been too naive to recognise the germ of violence embedded in that movement from its inception.

Rousseau had acquired from Locke and Hume – with the latter of whom he was on friendly terms until paranoia struck – that our diachronic selves are held together by memories; hence he is much interested in our acquiring, from the earliest age, a memory properly constituted both intellectually and emotionally. Though he tells us in *Emile* that only with knowledge and self-awareness does the life of the individual really begin, it seems unclear as to whether or in what sense we would have been persons in those times we can no longer remember. Perhaps before that we are only potential people, not people with potential. Be that as it may, Rousseau has a strong sense of what must be done when we reach the 'age of memory'. And firstly, we must be shielded from the wrong kind of literature.

Himself a voluminous author, Rousseau claims to hate books because they induce sympathy with the wrong crowd. Excessive reflection, as encouraged in ordinary society, destroys spontaneity (an intriguing development of moral-sense theorising); hence our aim as educationists is to make our pupils self-sufficient. The model of such self-sufficiency is to be found in Defoe's *Robinson Crusoe*, in which (even if we assume educators must also read Rousseau's own works) properly educated people may find sufficient reading matter. Yet there is a sinister edge to Rousseau's proposals as to how the child's (or adult's) mind is to be programmed: for while the child must be induced to think that he is developing an autonomy, his instructor must ensure that the content of his 'autonomous' mind be only that of the instructor himself. The child is only to *believe* he is autonomous.

In *La Nouvelle Héloise*, Rousseau presents Saint-Preux as a kind of 'natural' Rousseau, sheltered from social corruption, being re-educated by De Wolmar, who happens to be an atheist (Why is that necessary?) and who seems to represent Rousseau himself wearing his other hat as educational *maestro/maitre*, preparing his pupil to re-enter normal society while retaining the virtues of his natural state. That is the programme as set out, but one may wonder whether it will be effective unless some further and totalitarian control can be exerted on Saint-Preux when he leaves the academy. The general aim – to maintain *amour de soi* while inhibiting the growth of *amour propre* – is clear enough, but what further measures are needed if we are to retain the (acquired) 'autonomous' conformity?

One thing certain is that however generated, Rousseau's 'New Man' is no longer to be viewed as created in the image of God, for although Rousseau will allow God to exist, he will not tolerate His omnipotence to impinge on human autonomy – giving us the right, as it were, to rule Him out. In effect the New Man is a repaired version of what Rousseau himself might have been – and though paradoxically it looks as though he will be a homogenised, depersonalised, egalitarian sub-human, he will at least be incapable of real wickedness: or rather – and as Edmund Burke pointed out – he will exhibit a spurious benevolence toward humanity as a whole while lacking fellow feeling for those closest to him – very much, indeed as Rousseau showed himself to be.

One feature of Rousseau's programme is that it appears designed primarily, if not exclusively, for males. Similarly the Jacobins, taking up from him, would conclude that female citizenship must be 'passive'. Not that Rousseau would have identified himself as a Jacobin or as any kind of political revolutionary (since revolution may introduce changes for the worse). Yet how else could his dreams be satisfied? In more recent times a social revolutionary need not be overtly political; the modern propagandist (as we may see in the billionaire George Soros) knows that his goals may be more effectively achieved by deception than by immediate legislation or crude force. In the eighteenth and nineteenth centuries – and beyond – violence might seem the only route whereby to convert the 'liberating' demands of the General Will into concrete political and social structures.

*

The French Revolution was not the first revolution of the late eighteenth century, having been preceded by the American (supported, ironically, by the old French monarchy). It is instructive to compare the two: apparently similar (and often engaging similar groups of foreign onlookers) but radically different, not least in their proclamations of the Rights of Man. Thus although according to Thomas Jefferson's preamble to the Declaration of Independence (1776), 'all men are created equal … endowed by their Creator with certain inalienable rights', when it came to constitution-building, the universal applicability of those rights was diminished and we read of the rights of those *within the new Republic*. Even so had the Levellers at Putney, some 150 years earlier, addressed themselves only to 'the natives of this land'. In both cases large numbers of even male 'natives' were excluded: in England those with no property, in America slaves, whom the Founding Fathers owned in large numbers; Jefferson himself wrote against slavery without freeing more than seven of his own 200 or so slaves (of whom, 'nutmegging' on the side, he impregnated at least one). With similar inconsistency, though a deist, he manages to sound like a Christian praising his Creator.

While in Puritan England women got a poor deal, in America the 'patriot' John Adams exclaims satirically in 1776 that soon they will even be claiming the franchise! In France, as noted, the Jacobins – despite Condorcet, Olympe de Gouge and the 'honorary Jacobin' Tom Paine – eventually settled for women to count only as 'passive' citizens. However, unlike the American 'patriots', revolutionaries in France were not satisfied with rights for their own people; the revolutionary programme and Rights of Man must be extended at least to all Europeans. And many Europeans applauded, seeing in the Revolution a beacon for humanity.

But it is not only in their international expansion of their call for universal 'rights' that the Jacobins mark the coming totalitarian world. It is also in their claim to speak for *all* Frenchmen: they will fight wars by *total* mobilisation of the People; they will determine how *all* 'enemies of the People' – though actually of the vanguard who control politics in Paris – are to be eliminated swiftly, efficiently and systematically by the People's newly-invented instrument, the guillotine.

In warfare, the distinction between combatants and non-combatants, which prevailed down to the dynastic wars of the seventeenth and eighteenth centuries, is now to be abandoned as an inappropriate anachronism and will remain in abeyance when revolutionary 'democracy' turns into revolutionary Empire under Napoleon: this the last straw for a disillusioned Beethoven! The self-appointed Emperor and Leader of 'the People' now walked (though with different pretensions) in the footsteps of his imperial predecessor and model, Augustus, who had proclaimed himself first the tribunician voice of *all* the people of Rome, then of *all* Italy (*tota Italia*), eventually of every Roman citizen of his empire.

*

Although in the American Declaration of Independence Jefferson emphasises that all men are created equal, that slogan – whatever he intended by it – is ambiguous, for in what respect are people 'equal'? In the original Christian formulation, they are equal as possessors of equal dignity in the sight of God, not as actually or desirably identical; thus in Dante's *Paradiso* we find differing types of virtue displayed and ranked. To turn people into identical units becomes the goal (professed or not) of totalitarian states, and the Jacobins moved early toward that assimilation in the abolition of the distinction between combatant and non-combatant. Not yet the abolition of private property or the traditional family; far as the French revolutionaries had advanced towards equality in the sense of indistinguishability, it was possible to go much further – and not only by edict but by social and legal pressure.

In more strictly legal arrangements, the Jacobins were less hesitant, constructing from the outset a further feature of totalitarian democracy: what we recognise as the 'kangaroo-court' would provide a significant precedent for the 'courts' of Nazi Germany and Stalinist Russia. Such courts being 'the voice of the People' (that is of the party viewed as representing the People), there could and can be no appeal against their determinations.

The practices of antiquity were important for the Jacobin leaders. The ancient Athenian courts of law similarly were the voice of the People and allowed of no appeal – as Socrates was well aware when he would pay the ultimate penalty for defying them. Modern totalitarian courts have repeated and improved upon both Athenian and Jacobin practice, following similar theoretical principles. The totalitarians of France had not yet developed the techniques intended to secure ascendancy over the autonomous 'souls' of their victims: were not yet, in George Orwell's words, able to 'persuade people to deny the clear evidence of their senses' – as to admit to being saboteurs, because the all-seeing Party said they were.

All changes in society, whether authoritarian or totalitarian, must involve the dismantling of previous political and social structures, but with totalitarians the destruction must be more effective, more determined, more driven by a hate whipped up by theorists and demagogues. In the case of the Jacobins, this was in fair supply, having been nurtured (though usually without direct calls for violence) by the *philosophes*. The clarion-call by Holbach, Diderot and especially Voltaire (rather than Rousseau), for the obliteration of the Church in France, gave occasion for a stream of obscene falsehoods put out by pamphleteers and satirists. While the *philosophes* were divided between deists and atheists, all agreed that the Church, as a potentially rival institution to the state, must go. Their hatred of the Church was more intense even than of the monarchy, being more immediately ideological, and with the Jacobins already more or less licenced to destroy, a huge wave of vandalism descended upon ecclesiastical properties.

Perhaps most egregious was that visited upon the Abbey just north of Paris whose name of Saint-Denis honoured the author of the theologically important writings of 'Pseudo-Dionysius', the self-styled disciple of St Paul later believed to have become bishop of the French capital. In that great Abbey many kings and queens of France had found their traditional resting place; thus in smashing it up and throwing the royal bones about, the totalitarian mob was able to indulge their hatred of Church and Monarchy in equal measure. Such activity, though organised locally, was brought about by a massive emotional contagion (to use Max Scheler's apt phrase). It is a defining characteristic of totalitarians always to like to destroy: even, in the last resort, to destroy themselves when, their project being itself brought to ruins, they may resort to final and futile killings followed by suicide: a behaviour seen in individuals as well as in collectives.

The emotions and sentiment of Rousseau were thus enabled to form a noxious mix with the anti-religious, and specifically anti-Christian, lusts of the *philosophes*. Important is that this should occur in France, 'eldest daughter of the Church', where an attack on Christianity could be nothing less than an attack on the foundations of European culture. That culture – and not only in France – could not have received its specific form without Christianity: hence the aim of the Jacobins to replace it by a specifically anti-Christian totalitarianism symbolised in that exotic parody of worship, the enthroning, in the very cathedral of *Notre Dame de Paris*, of a whore representing Reason. This dedication of the new anti-Christian state and society (in totalitarian systems the two are identified) to worship of *La Déesse Raison* rather quickly failed the popularity test: however, in rather muted guise would serve as example in 1968, with student revolutionaries hailing a latter-day Jacobin, Simone de Beauvoir, as '*Notre Dame de Sartre*'.

*

In Germany, Reason fared better, at least for a while and as represented by Kant who, as Rousseau's convert to universal moral capacity, made the biggest impact on the intellectuals – albeit there too, as in France and also in Britain, the apparently full-blooded if 'sentimental' Rousseau appealed to nature-loving 'romantics' groping after some form of pantheism. Even so, Kant's attempt to restore reason as guide to the moral life had more than one epistemological flaw – this some of his successors would claim – in that he still recognised 'things in themselves' as beyond our reach and known to us only by inference since they fall beyond the purview of our spatio-temporal spectacles. This, therefore, led to the next question: Do they really exist? and Fichte was soon to think there is no reason to suppose they do, since they seem to have no place in any rational account of what is knowable.

That meant that subjectivist accounts of the cosmos were on the way back – whether as 'imagined' data (as Hume had held), or recalling Bishop Berkeley's 'divine subjectivism' whereby our impressions are underwritten by a God Who – in the words of Ronald Knox's limerick on the good bishop – is 'always about in the quad'. Hegel managed to combine both human and divine approaches, but though the 'I' is now always at the centre of reflection, what it *is* will raise a new version of questions about personal identity already posed by Locke – as, what about other 'I's and how to relate to them, individually or communally. Who then was right? Fichte in disposing of

God – or those who would fire him from his university post at Jena? Before all else the question loomed: Is each of us alone 'in the quad'?

Nor was epistemology the only problem Kant bequeathed to his successors. First, as we have seen, he had separated human nature into his 'phenomenal' and 'noumenal' aspects, thus in a sense separating mind and matter; could they be reunited? Hegel was to think so. Kant, moreover, though not eliminating God altogether, had largely ruled Him out of moral philosophy, reducing him to a mere *deus ex machina* to get rid of awkwardnesses about reconciling duty and happiness. Many would conclude he had not gone far enough, as the irreligion of eighteenth century France spread – eventually to take on a new murderous force in Germany.

What then was to be done about religion in general and Christianity in particular? Many in Germany who thought it should be erased came (like Kant) from Lutheran families and often from Lutheran departments of theology in prestigious universities. In the event, the demolition of intellectual approaches to religion was to be carried out in three stages. The first, primarily associated with Friedrich Schleiermacher, generally recognised founder of a 'liberal' Protestantism hopefully to be freed from state-control, involved reducing religion in general and Christianity in particular to *feeling*: thus doing for theology what the British 'sentimentalists' had done for ethics; for this Pietism had certainly cleared the way. The second stage was to demolish the 'historical Jesus': this in the first instance was the approach of David Strauss. The third was to show that all religions, and Christianity in particular, are projections by the 'I' – now centre-stage – onto the screen of our apparent awareness; this would be the claim of Ludwig Feuerbach. Put all this together and it might appear that a 'search for nothingness' is, as Schopenhauer came to believe, what we are engaged in. We need to examine these three phases before tackling the alternative and anti-personalist ideologies which would be offered as religion substitutes.

*

First, then, we turn to Schleiermacher (1768–1834), a philosophically minded pastor well read in Plato, Spinoza, Kant and many others, and not merely a Protestant clergyman on record as having had an affair with the wife of a clerical colleague, but one unable to believe in the divinity of Christ or accept any of the Christian Creeds. Despite which, his influence has remained and he takes his place as the first figure to be studied in a number of University programmes of 'historical theology'.

Schleiermacher marks the beginning of the end for much Protestant – as later for much Catholic – theology, as too of attempts in the eighteenth century to construct what Kant deemed religion 'within the limits of reason alone'. Reason, it appeared, had failed in that project, as, in the view of our moral sense theorists, it had failed in ethics. Religion needed to be redesigned so as to be properly concerned not with what you know, nor even what you have faith that you know, but as quite simply a feeling of dependence: a ghost of earlier Christianity's recognition of a dependence on God then thought rationally explicable. No place now for dogma, none even for traditional faith: that more or less desperate feeling must suffice. And of what is the feeling? Of God, apparently, for Jesus 'felt' as He evidently did and provides the example for us all. Schleiermacher seems to neglect that some may have no feeling of dependence, or not on anything non-human – though conceivably on the Prussian State, already beginning its nineteenth-century apotheosis in the minds of Fichte and Hegel as well as in those of more apparently Christian figures.

After Schleiermacher came Strauss: like Schleiermacher (though more resolutely) an enthusiast for using in biblical studies the latest 'historical-critical' techniques developed in classical philology after Friedrich Wolff's 1770s *Prolegomena to the Study of Homer*. In 1835 Strauss published a *Life of Christ Critically Examined* in which he argued that we in fact know little of Christ's life, hence is Christian theology in the main mythology. Atheists and deists were of course delighted and one of them, Marion Evans (pen-name George Eliot), translated Strauss' book into English in 1846 – to be requited with a torrent of abuse such as had already been poured over the original author. Too late! Strauss' book proved persuasive, initially to Feuerbach, to be followed by Nietzsche: not in his case unreservedly, yet Strauss is to be presumed one of those he compliments on accomplishing 'the Death of God'.

For Feuerbach, Hegel is a fallen hero – fallen into the same intellectual mire as more orthodox worshippers of Jesus. Neglecting imagination, along with those feelings and longings evoked by Schleiermacher, he has included the Christian God in his eclectic vision of Absolute Spirit. Into this, indeed, are also blended all the individual 'I's of humanity, together with all nature, to yield a glorious pantheist mix of Matter with Spirit as the culmination of European thought since the days of Plato and Aristotle. Yet with God dead, why had we ever thought him alive? Why had any of this happened?

Because, according to Feuerbach, we had misinterpreted our ideals, the objects of our strivings. As in post-Kantian philosophy we may imagine (or project) the existence of 'things in themselves', so in religion we imagine – and reify – our own ideals. Feuerbach claimed not to be an atheist but simply to have repaired the use of the word 'God'. Applying a revised version of Hegel's thesis-antithesis-synthesis to the religious situation, he concluded that from the thesis that we have aspirations, and the antithesis that their non-fulfilment induces alienation, so by synthesis we can relieve that alienation by recognising that man himself is the god. In his prophetic words: 'The turning point in history will be the moment when man becomes aware that the only god of man is man himself'.

Feuerbach declined to draw practical conclusions from this, moving on to ask, 'If God is a projection, what has become of his image?' His book was criticised because, while satisfactorily disposing of Hegel's Absolute Spirit (along with other less novel delusions), he had left the human 'I' intact. That too, he soon came to agree, is a projection and decidedly nothing to do with Absolute Spirit. Eventually, via calling for a return to a Nature determined more or less mechanically (the conclusion Kant had vainly tried to evade), Feuerbach reached the conclusion that human beings are organisms with drives to a contentment viewed as little more than the satisfaction of bodily needs – leaving them with a prospect almost as dismal as that projected by Schopenhauer at his most pessimistic.

The 'I' thus left in limbo, it follows that what remains of it must be a creature of society, leading the hopeful reformer to look for such reform of that as might enable human contentment: for with God and the soul in abeyance and the 'I' on the verge of disappearing with them, some new and hopeful dependency must surely be discerned! Fichte and Hegel had looked to Prussia, and for many nineteenth-century German intellectuals, responding vicariously to the militarism of its army, the solution to the human situation must surely be German: had not Kant shown – in contrast to the internationalist approach of Leibniz – that anything worthwhile in philosophy (as in what was left of theology) must be of German provenance?

Nor even now has that attitude entirely disappeared, as we see as we reflect on the later dismal blind alleys (title of Sartre's play *Huis Clos*) energetically pursued by those we have accepted as guides in the Modern and Post-Modern periods. Even after Heidegger, some may continue to insist on German philosophical superiority, though now seeming mere *revenants* from the Aryan past. We lovingly recall a vignette from not so far back: the scene is a college dining-hall, the occasion lunch, to which we have been invited. At the same table is seated a Professor of Divinity who happens to be German in origin. Introductions are made and on learning our name he remarks, 'Ah, Rist – good German name! Very zuitable for a philosopher!' John swallows the implied compliment without revealing his reservations – nor that he understands his surname may have come from further east, perhaps Estonia where it means Cross. (Did we perchance recall the 'philosophical soccer match' envisaged by 'Monty Python' as between Greeks and Germans, and won by a late – and inevitably disputed – goal by captain Socrates?)

Yet Prussia, being as yet only authoritarian, not yet totalitarian, might seem to serve only as the latest instantiation of Absolute Spirit. As expressed in a 'Declaration to the Cultured World', signed on the eve of the World War I by ninety-three German academics – including the leading Protestant theologian of the age, Adolf von Harnack – the Germans were defending the land of Kant, Goethe and Beethoven against the barbarians. Yet the urge for absolute authority on the one hand, on the other for absolute submission – coupled with absolute abandonment of personal responsibility, that truly totalitarian urge – would find its eventual fulfilment not merely in applauding Bismarck's transformation of the Prussian monarchy into the German Empire but in voting in (the Austrian) Hitler's Third Reich. Perhaps it is not too difficult to see why Feuerbach left to others to draw the practical conclusion that the new task of philosophy was not to learn but to act, not to reflect on society but to change it – now that we had been taught to face 'reality'.

*

Unlike Hegel, Fichte and Feuerbach, Marx and Engels, abandoning nationalism, offered an alternative, though also totalitarian route by which the self could be submerged, 'alienation' relieved. Similarly reductionist – as are all totalitarianisms – that enterprise was to be embarked on through recognition of a new variant of determinism: not Newtonian physics, not militaristic supremacy, but an inexorable history of economic change that can be observed: and such that if one could observe the past sufficiently accurately, one could predict the future with equal accuracy, so join the March of History and help it along. And the goal of that March being societal perfection, all means of obtaining it become allowable: such that, once established, any persons attempting to modify it are by the very fact criminals whose 'elimination' is to become a logical necessity – as it had for the Jacobins. Now all will understand themselves as beings in the grip of an iron determinism whereby their personal fate can turn out well provided the processes of that determinism are accepted with absolute submission.

The Stoics had long ago offered an analogous 'wisdom', albeit in a providentialist rather than an economic context. For them we resemble a dog tied behind a moving cart: if we do not trot along, we shall be dragged along. So too in more recent times ideas about the iron determinism of economic forces were not entirely new: Hobbes had recognised the power of wealth to change societies; Adam Smith maintained that a properly developed capitalism could provide the most prosperous life for all. It was for Marx to point out that this was not happening, for the reason that transition from an agrarian to an industrialised society had left millions of people uprooted and in miserable conditions: still dependant on the 'bosses', yet in theory ripe for revolutionary violence.

Marx's economically based predictions proved only partially correct. When the revolution he had promised came, it was not in the more industrialised countries: Britain, France, Germany or the emerging giant, the United States. It would be in Russia where, although under the last of the tsars industrialisation was well under way (concentrated on the Moscow-Petersburg corridor and including such soon-to-be Communist strongholds as Ekaterinburg, scene of the murder of the Imperial family), society remained largely agrarian – as the Bolsheviks would learn to their dismay in the coming Civil War. Then why was the Revolution there? Why indeed did it befall where expectation of overwhelming popular support for a Marxist dictatorship failed to transpire and where after the end of the tsarist monarchy there seemed a good chance that comparatively democratic structures would be established?

Communism was imposed on Russia not according to textbook Marxist theory but as the result of a *coup d'état* by the originally quite small vanguard group of Lenin's Bolsheviks: another example not of the laws of economic determinism in the form of 'dialectical materialism', but of the more banal norms that all rule is the rule of elites and that in revolutionary situations the most violent and murderously determined are liable to prevail. Uttered in the interim between February and October 1917, Lenin's claim that 'There is such a

Party' (*scil.*, as is ready to take absolute power) was the risky and implausible-seeming challenge of a small group of desperate but determined fanatics who in the ensuing years would show themselves devoid of any restraining capacity for pity. These understood that, in the words of their coming rival totalitarian, Adolf Hitler, in revolutionary politics success requires 'originality plus brutality'.

Yet though communist elites brought about a revolution in Russia in 1917, why did they fail in those countries where Marx expected them to succeed? Not least because the elites of those countries staved off revolution by making concessions – at the same time managing not to move so fast and in such panic as to give the impression that much more could be easily and violently achieved. Thus before and after the fall of Napoleon, the British ruling class feared a Jacobin uprising – not yet, of course, a communist one – but eventually staved it off by extending the franchise and – slowly and often reluctantly – improving working conditions, thus demonstrating that the alienation which Marx assumed would inevitably produce the shift from capitalism to socialism, thence to communism, was less deeply rooted (in his words less 'determined') than he had predicted. What the proletarians in the factories and mines wanted was less the destruction of capitalist society (and with it their jobs) but better conditions for themselves with a larger slice of the national, if capitalist, pie.

Thus, though it might seem there should have been a Communist revolution in the United Kingdom in view of the misery inflicted by the Industrial Revolution, did other factors come into play. The 'alienated' showed themselves in general happy enough if their position in society improved; they in the event lacked that 'solidarity in the class-struggle' which Marxist theory requires, so demonstrating that homogenised cohesion – the totalitarian version of equality – is no natural historical process but the artificial construction of Marxist (or other) political theorists. In more recent times there are obvious examples to show that the claimants to alienation need not be the 'proles', but anyone who, like Rousseau, identifies him or herself as a victim; such a one may or may not be so persuaded by a lying 'propaganda', but more commonly on account of a personal history.

The conclusion which Marx failed to draw but Lenin understood, was that the masses had to be induced, if needful by brute force, to promote the 'inevitably' coming paradise. That inducement might not require any improvement in the conditions of the working classes, but rather the reverse: Marx hoped the Indian Mutiny would be brutally suppressed because that would make a backlash more violent. In promoting the 'inevitable' March of History, any means will do to usher in the desired outcome – but especially the even further depersonalisation of the workforce so as to function as an organised but irresponsible mob: obedient to the Party because the Party is always 'on the right side of History'.

Thus just as in the Russian Revolution the bosses, the 'muck of ages', must, even though themselves victims of the 'system', be 'eliminated' as irredeemable, so when the earthly Paradise comes, the elimination of dissidents must also be approved, since they have nothing to protest about. The key to securing such approval submissively is in the organised lying, called 'propaganda'. As we shall see, Marxism may show itself in this regard only in degree more totalitarian than some purportedly 'liberal' – but equally dogmatic – rivals prepared to lie and to adapt means to pre-determined ends.

That the failure of Marx's prediction as to the arrival of communism did little to discredit the theory itself might suggest that he had got something right but drew wrong conclusions; we need to identify both facts and the unwarranted deductions from them, with firstly the theory of economic determinism itself. For certainly Marx is right – as Hobbes, Adam Smith and others had been right – that earlier thinkers had underestimated economic factors in explaining societal change. His mistake – in mode characteristic of the totalitarian (as similarly of such as University lecturers longing for charismatic fame) – was to over-simplify matters.

Though Marx's predictions have not come to pass, it is not difficult to find societies deeply affected by Marxism displaying in some degree such totalitarian tendencies, in the first instance, as to destroy: this had been already clear enough with the Jacobin exemplar in the years following 1789. By the mid-nineteenth century, Marx and those who followed him would know what they hated; these were largely intelligible facts of society. What they disagreed about – ominously for them and those they would come to govern – was what steps might reduce injustice (rather than merely vary or reverse it. A Polish joke from 'Soviet times' asks, 'What is the difference between capitalism and communism?' and answers, 'Under capitalism one class oppresses the other; under communism it is the other way round'.).

*

Lenin 'improved on' Marx in understanding better how the 'March of History' must work itself out. Both agree that society must be homogenised, ultimately in accordance with some form of 'General Will', meanwhile with the 'March of (economic) History' – as interpreted by the all-knowing Party: that 'Big Brother' who can tell you who is the enemy you hate, or at least envy. Homogenisation, as the Jacobins already understood, means the abandonment of an older authoritarianism which allowed dissenters – but now 'enemies of the people' – to retire into private life. For there is no longer to be a private life; all lives are politicised and society which Hegel clearly distinguished from the state – is to be identified with it, and the state with The Party. To ensure that totalitarian result, an all-prying political police becomes a necessity – carrying the risk that in some circumstances its leaders might pose a threat (as was Beria on Stalin's death) to the Party established.

From a Marxist viewpoint, the Jacobins had lacked the courage of their convictions in permitting the continuation both of private property and of the family. In regard to the unequal right to property, their concept of 'equality' fell far short of identity: that is, of merely numerical differentiation, at least among the subject masses, for the *avant-garde* could always pretend to privileges (or as in the words of the Polish joke, 'It's the other way round'!). In contrast to the Jacobins, Marx held that there are no rights (as in a non-providential because a godless world is only reasonable), the right to property (with most other so-called rights) being essentially a pretext for private greed and vain egoism. Hence must the process of homogenisation, of producing an identical set of New Men, go a lot further than the elaboration of rights claims.

In the family Marx himself took rather little interest, but Engels was well aware that families are serious obstacles to human 'equality' in the sense of homogenisation. Nor – again – is this Marxist 'truth' entirely false: clans, as Plato had understood more than 2,000 years previously, can encourage particular and local interests against wider or national ones: hence their power cannot be allowed to be excessive if a feud-free society is to be maintained. But restrictions are one thing, abolition quite another. Although it is extremely difficult to determine the appropriate limits of family *versus* state power – one man's discipline is another's child-abuse – some pragmatic balance must be found; yet if that balance tips too far toward the state – as for example in dictating what religious or political creed be taught by parents to their children – then totalitarianism has arrived, whether or not a society declares itself to be anti-totalitarian, or views itself as 'liberal' in the (if not deliberate, at least unconscious – and not uncommon) equating of 'liberal' with 'right' or 'acceptable': that is, to me and those who think like me, we the '*bien pensants*'.

We leave further treatment of anti-family doctrines after Engels for a later chapter. We must similarly postpone discussion of the problem – hardly foreseen by Marx, though recognised by his disciples, especially Stalin and Mao – of preventing (especially) the vanguard elite from slipping back into old-fashioned individualist ways and 'bourgeois' corruption. In following up such backsliders, Stalin and Mao would make the achievement of social 'purity' a cyclical rather than 'linear' requirement.

*

Thus far we have treated some more obvious forms of totalitarianism which may take over at times of legitimate discontent: by 'totalitarianism' meaning, the absolute control by a recognisable (even legal) body: such was the Nazi Party; such is the Central Committee of the Communist Party of the People's Republic of China. Yet De Tocqueville, writing about (the United States of) America in the early nineteenth century, was able to identify another totalitarian pattern, one far more relevant to contemporary Western societies as arising not in despotisms but in so-styled 'liberal' democracies, while remaining dependant on the same myth of human 'equality' as rated by the lowest common denominator.

Such a society may arise through a materialism become habitual, though the addictive habit can be worsened by planned deceit. Tocqueville associated the American desire for 'equality' with a perfectionism to be achieved by the dictatorship of majority opinion. He believed that in the United States the desire for a comfortable life – precursor of more recent consumerism – paired with a thesis about this world perfectibility, had generated a set of habits and practices conducive to a banal mediocrity: indeed that such habits grow up more or less instinctively in would-be egalitarian societies – though perhaps we should add if peopled by hard-working immigrants lured by 'the American (or other) dream': easily purveyed as access to a consumerist paradise.

Tocqueville seems to have overlooked that acceptance of a banal mediocrity, occurring 'naturally' enough, can be further manipulated by propaganda – that is, by direct lying as deemed useful – and that the propagandists will be in the first instance representative of minority groups working on the public by deception and insistence ('All propaganda is good propaganda', Goebbels would put it) to secure power to support their own desires and aims. That a minority group may gain the ear of an uncritical populace to transform its conventions into a new and ever more divergent orthodoxy is observable in the twenty-first century 'West' in regard to homosexuality and gender fluidity. Rendered uncritical, the victims are prone to delude themselves that rather than being misled and manipulated, they are being given the invitation to a more enlightened, better-run, less 'divisive' world.

That said, we need to recognise that a banal subservience to mediocrity indicates an important difference between such violent totalitarianisms as those imposed by Hitler and Lenin and those that may arise from liberal materialism. In the former case – in what we specify as 'violently imposed totalitarianisms' – the victims know through the terror that menaces them who their masters are and how they exercise control; in a world of liberal materialism – pointing as it does nevertheless toward ('liberal') totalitarianism – apparently non-violent power-wielders may long remain anonymous and perhaps with little official relationship with those governments whom they nevertheless influence: seducers rather than rapists.

If we wonder why liberal societies are liable to such manipulation, we might recall an observation made long ago by (among others) Herodotus, and revelatory of historical reality in many a time past, namely that those who Herodotus thinks of as 'plains-people' – living, that is, in comparative comfort – are liable to become flaccid and too indolent to defend themselves against hardier dwellers descending upon them from high ground. Comfort, that is, overwhelms defensive precaution and preparedness, inviting servitude. In our present times it is not hard to see how – and along post-Marxist lines – pressure groups 'coming from the high ground', may impose their will by a sheer mediatic insistence. Thus without any but 'soft' force (at least in the first instance), a society – especially if but lightly and uncritically educated – may be enrolled into a new order which will encourage its citizens to appear conscientiously 'up-to-date': apt to flaunt their virtue in new forms of hypocrisy and in due course to suppress 'bigoted' (latterly 'populist') dissenters.

Marx himself might have approved if minority groups, by force of emotional contagion, could achieve a result analogous to what Lenin's Bolsheviks (originally a minority) secured by violence – while still keeping that 'in reserve'. Other vanguard groups may read the

March of History (or of Economic History) very differently from Lenin's Bolshevik Vanguard. These latterly may prefer to call themselves 'liberals', but this designation notwithstanding, their position on 'the right side' of some progressivist cause is remarkably similar to Lenin's – and likewise menacing to those who prize their personal and intellectual integrity.

*

Feuerbach would be succeeded not only by Marx but by a second nineteenth-century figure, equally important in the contemporary West, who pointed to a totalitarianism less of History and Economic Determinism than of the Will – and beyond totalitarianism to nihilism. Meanwhile in Anglo-Saxon countries in particular, the cult of Humanity (rather than of individual human beings) had taken root, offering worship not of the Will but of 'Happiness', so readily converging with Tocqueville's totalitarianism of banality. We will leave this cult of Humanity for another chapter, to turn to the more 'nihilist' approach that leads from the early Romantics through Nietzsche, prime prophet of our contemporary Western age. This road, debouching into a fashionable middle-class nihilism in overtly democratic states, historically will turn, via a perversion of Nietzsche which grew up in Germany, into enhanced admiration for militarist Prussia – found already in Fichte and Hegel – and descending to its murderous depths in the more straightforwardly nihilist cult of the Führer.

Nietzsche is not the product of nineteenth century anti-Christian movements in Germany merely, for what we may dub his 'Prometheanism' is the culmination of the process of dechristianisation in Europe, of a replacement of God by Man-as-God. Such thinkers of the Florentine Academy as Ficino and Pico prate of Man as divine – in reaction against an exaggeratedly wretched portrait of humanity widely (though certainly not universally) preached in the previous age. The *form* in which the thinkers of the Florentine Academy indicate their metaphysical preferences foreshadows what was to come: that is, that Man is greater than the medievals had believed because he, like God, is a creator. God, however, is still in the picture – even literally, as when Michelangelo 'creates' God creating Adam.

With the development of eighteenth century anti-Christianity in France – as distinct from a more academic atheism in Britain – the obvious question arose as to what we propose shall replace God. In Scotland Hume was inclined to say 'feeling and convention'. In France Jacobins settled for anti-Christian political violence that initially – and ironically – took the form of the worship of *La Déesse Raison*: ('Enlightened') Reason. Later in the same country Comte was to develop further the idea of the religion of Humanity (complete with rituals, based on Catholic practice, which even the earnest John Stuart Mill would come to deride as ludicrous). Atheism in its specifically anti-Christian guise, reduced to a still smouldering state in France following the defeat and fall of Napoleon, found a new home in Germany where, as we have seen, Strauss and Schleiermacher attacked the intellectual foundations of Christianity and Feuerbach proclaimed all religion mere 'projection'.

Earlier, in a fit of adolescent hyperbole, Shelley had told a correspondent how he wished he were the anti-Christ, as he would never forgive Christianity and longed that it might be his 'to crush the Demon'. Now Nietzsche found himself in a position where he could fulfil Shelley's wish together with Feuerbach's contention that man is the only God available. But unlike Shelley – let alone Matthew Arnold, writing nostalgically in 'Dover Beach' of the receding tide of faith – Nietzsche's prognosis for Europe was more considered, more like the Christianless Europe identified by Dostoevsky: though provoking very different hopes and fears.

According to Nietzsche, 'God is dead and we have killed him', but what has so far been put in His place is pathetically similar so far as morality is concerned: 'They are rid of the Christian God and now believe all the more firmly that they must cling to Christian morality … When [the English] suppose they no longer require

Christianity as the guarantee of morality, we merely witness the *effects* of the domination of the Christian moral judgments.' Germany is just as bad: 'He [Strauss] proclaims with admirable frankness that he is no longer a Christian . . . Abashed we see that his ethics is quite unchanged.' And again: 'Strauss has not even learned that . . . preaching morals is as easy as giving reasons for morals is difficult; it should rather have been his task seriously to explain and to derive the phenomena of human goodness, mercy, love and self-abnegation from his Darwinistic presuppositions.' Nor, Nietzsche continues, was even Schopenhauer much better who, having identified a vision of the world as bleak, almost absurd in its senselessness, took cowardly refuge in some para-Buddhist nirvana: no way of asserting one of the few things Kant got right, namely human autonomy, or more precisely the autonomy of the Will. (That is, of course, Man's, not God's will: a very different proposition, as for followers of the Original Tradition Augustine in particular had already made plain.)

The truth (as Feuerbach had partly understood) is that the ending of Christian morality (as well as its post-Christian leftovers) is a cosmic event: it is (to quote Nietzsche) as though 'the earth has been uncoupled from the sun which is now beginning to set'. The proper attitude to this cosmic change is a mixture of dread and exaltation at 'That great spectacle in a hundred acts which is reserved for the next two centuries in Europe, the most terrible, most questionable and perhaps the most hopeful of all spectacles'.

We may wonder how far Nietzsche would think we had progressed through this drama by 2022 – and conclude he would probably suppose that we were still not thinking honestly enough, since – as he perspicuously observed – 'I fear we are not getting rid of God because we still believe in grammar'. To 'believe in grammar' is to believe in the ultimate intelligibility of a Universe which can at best be only partially grasped by gnomic (so less than 'grammatical') utterances like those of the 'obscure' Heraclitus – and one might note that Heraclitus, like Nietzsche's German contemporaries and successors, had a high opinion of what Clausewicz would call, 'diplomacy by other means': that is, of warfare. For Heraclitus, war is 'the father of all things'; for the Prussians it was the art of human greatness. Both are right insofar as it promotes scientific (and scientistic) advances – too often at the cost of de-humanisation.

The logic of Nietzsche's final position entails the denial of truth (as instantiated in 'grammar') itself, but he did not reach that conclusion without a struggle. His eventual resolution of how to 'come to terms' with the bleakness of the world did not emerge in his first work, *The Birth of Tragedy*; though already there he sees the defeat of nihilism only in artistic creation – reminding us of the Florentine Academy, but now set in a quite different (because atheist) world-view. And he continued to believe in art as the ultimate value for the enlightened – the human race being divided between the vast majority who look for meaning either to religion or to religion-substitutes and those few 'overmen' (*Übermenschen*) able to view the world as it is and survive heroically.

What then for Nietzsche does it mean to be heroic? Part of the answer lies in his reading of attitudes prevalent among the ancient Greeks: not only in the heroes of the Homeric poems but in the pitiless, 'realistic' tone which he finds in the writings of ancient historians, especially Thucydides. The 'overman' discards the snivelling, hypocritical Christian and post-Christian virtue of pity – so much for Rousseau – as well as mercy and humility, for he is above the banal world of good and evil. Nor has Nietzsche regard for the rationalism of more recent European thought: least of all for that of the Utilitarians. Nor, in his ferocious hostility to Christianity, does he find (as Schopenhauer in his flirting with Buddhism) time for other religions. True, in *The Antichrist* he indicates a certain approval of the Hindu caste system, though hardly as religious but because it keeps the herd in their place.

Although in his earlier years Nietzsche was prepared to accept even saints among the class of 'overmen', his mature position identifies these last not with any race or class – notably he is not an anti-Semite – but most obviously with the great creators of beauty. Thus

Goethe, Shakespeare, Beethoven were men, Nietzsche believes, capable of fighting through great suffering to become 'themselves': that is, fully autonomous, living out what their Will propels them to create. The role of this their creativity is to 'cast a veil of beauty over the horror and absurdity' of the universe: the influence of Plato is here apparent, though the difference is great, for whereas for Plato art derives from representation of transcendental realities, for Nietzsche it flows from a pure Will to create.

Eventually Nietzsche will identify creativity as the superior application of a Will to Power which underlies all human activity. Thus while the herd may resort to procreation or (better) to morality to relieve their alienation – insofar as these enable them to exert a form of predominance over others – the overman achieves something infinitely more valuable. Famously Nietzsche connects suffering with creativity in his striking observation on Shakespeare: 'I know no more heart-rending reading than Shakespeare: what must a man have suffered to have such a need of being a buffoon!' He presumably is thinking here of such Shakespearean characters as (pre-eminently) Falstaff (by some said, like other of his characters and in some respects, to stand in for Shakespeare himself). Did Nietzsche note Shakespeare's frequent (in his Sonnets) playing on his own name as 'Will' – though with very different implications from his own evocation of the Will's determining force?

In any case, a serious problem lurks in Nietzsche's attitude to the overman's art, for while it is clear what he prizes and what he despises, we may wonder why artistic creativity should be a better – truer – adaptation of the Will to Power than any other activity? Why indeed should not the use of tyrannical force be the supreme mark of the *Übermensch*? Above all, why does Nietzsche claim to know what is better than what, since he denies the existence of truth? All very well to proclaim, 'Will a self and thou shalt become a self': how are we to know what sort of self to will to become?

In short, Nietzsche's emphasis on the power of the creative will conflicts with his more metaphysical claim that there is no truth, only perspective: that each man thinks truth is what he perceives, and in the fashion in which he perceives it. We may wonder about his prioritising of the travails of artistic creativity over the activities and values of the herd. More pertinently, however, we must conclude that, while his attitude to truth points to nihilism, his claims about the overman and his superior creative nature point in a wholly other direction. As he himself admits, 'Truth is the kind of error without which a certain species of life could not live'. Yet and in the final analysis, if nihilism *were* Nietzsche's truth, would he not contradict himself in denying truth's possibility – even in the form of artistic creativity – by the very asserting of nihilism's ultimate status as a truth?

*

Much of Nietzsche's vision of the state of Europe was shared (as Nietzsche himself came to recognise) by Dostoevsky. The two agreed that its darkness was caused by the eclipse of Christianity, but whereas Nietzsche saw this, though threatening, as offering a glimmer of hope, Dostoevsky's conclusion, based not on theorising but on reflection of the events of his time and his own experience as a fellow prisoner with revolutionists in Siberia, is quite the reverse – and here one is mindful that Dostoevsky's experience of Christianity was of its Orthodax instantiation, whereas Nietzsche's was Lutheran. In the Russian anarchists of the 1860s, Dostoevsky recognises that the identification of the person as the will – indeed as the Will to Power – leads not to heroic creativity but to blind, even wilful, destructiveness. He offers a range of characters – from Raskolnikov to Stavrogin to the Grand Inquisitor to Peter Verkhovensky in *The Devils* –to illustrate the point.

Verkhovensky appears to be modelled on the terrorist Sergei Nechaev, leader of a group styling themselves *The People's Will* and author of *The Catechism of a Revolutionary*. Thus for Dostoevsky, elimination of God leads not to the elevation of (some) men to heroic stature but to violence and destructiveness for their own sakes, though dressed up in whatever revolutionary cause may come to hand. The death of God has led to the murder – often the mass-murder – of men once viewed as God's image but now *ex hypothesi* viewed as having no value.

Thus Dostoevsky identifies the outcome not only of Nietzsche's 'overman' but of Feuerbach's proclaimed destruction (or 'deconstruction') of the human self. Nietzsche saw the herd as 'despisers of life', as hypocritical enemies of the self-asserting Will which is the human spirit at its best. Dostoevsky, all too well aware of the would-be Nietzscheans around him, understood such people better. Nietzsche's however faulty analysis was to be more immediately influential; yet there seems no reason why in art, in and of itself, lies the remedy for despair. In our own age; artists (and self-styled 'artists') seem no less liable than the rest of us to even suicidal depressions, while experience has shown that art (or 'art') – in regimes where the cult of the Will is proclaimed, as in totalitarianisms more generally – soon collapses into the banalities of the manipulated herd. This can be observed both on the 'right' and on the 'left': in Hitler's Germany as in Stalin's Russia. Where art may contrive still to flourish and speak to such oppressed peoples, it will be in defiance of them: such was the case of Shostakovich, whose Symphonies often mocked the Stalinist regime.

Both Dostoevsky and Nietzsche perceived and offered similar diagnoses of the source of the impending destruction of old Europe – namely, as Dostoevsky put it, that Europe has 'lost Christ; that is the only reason' – but their prognoses differed, appropriately to their outlooks, as anxious optimism differs from grim foreboding. Subsequent history, especially in its totalitarian pages, would show Dostoevsky's foreboding as the more appropriate depiction. Put otherwise, and with obvious echoes of theorisings by Saints Paul and Augustine, and as cited by Paul Fussell (a more recent atheist than Nietzsche), what confronted the liberators of Nazi concentration camps displayed the fruit of the cult of the Will as 'a savage, insensate affair, barely conceivable to the well-conducted imagination and hardly approachable without some currently unfashionable theory of human mass insanity and inbuilt, inherited corruption'. And it had all been planned by bureaucrats and brought to completion by armed thugs 'just obeying orders'. A magisterial advertisement for totalitarian 'freedom' – *ARBEIT MACHT FREI* – remains in place where, with brutal cynicism, it was placed to greet the condemned and enslaved on their planned one-way passage into the Auschwitz concentration camp.

We shall return in a later chapter to the continuing role of the faceless, necessary but toxic bureaucrat as well as to some 'metaphysical' objections to 'just obeying orders': the defence of the commandant of Auschwitz and others of his ilk.

6 Scientistic Humanism

These things shall be: a loftier race
Than e'er the world hath known shall rise
With flame of freedom in their souls
And light of science in their eyes.

J. Addington Symonds

Just as Columbus and his fellow explorers had expanded awareness of the size and configuration of our planet, so in the following sixteenth century astronomers began to expand our view of the vastness of our universe – with such pioneers as Copernicus and Galileo to make demands on God's creative powers even infinitely greater than previously envisaged in a relatively circumscribed cosmos. The New Science would continue its attack on the old Aristotelian certainties with Bacon, Descartes, Harvey, Boyle and other seventeenth-century inquirers.

Along with Modern Science came scientism: a phenomenon largely unknown in earlier times, spawned by the new passion for experimentation. Perhaps there is nothing we humans cannot do; we may eventually be able to create ourselves (anyway, other people) in the lab; eventually learn to destroy not merely some inadequately fortified town but, if not the whole planet, anyway its fitness for human habitation. Fortunately all scientists are not scientistics, though too many are, playing God and flaunting a knowledge the 'layman' may regard with awe as partaking of a quasi-priestly superiority.

The comparison is apt, for the revival of science in the sixteenth century gave new life to the debate between faith and reason. This in some form had begun in classical antiquity, when Sceptics had argued that there is no good enough evidence to justify commitment to religious belief, Epicureans that their version of atomism implies the impossibility of a providential deity.

The empiricism of the sixteenth and seventeenth centuries, in demonstrating what could be explained in material and mechanistic terms, seemed further to diminish the scope for divine activity, inclining many to jump to the conclusion of there being no room for it: this despite more cautious thinkers (even Hobbes leaves us puzzled as to whether he should be accounted an atheist). That in turn encouraged philosophers – eventually and most influentially Kant – to argue that there must be something in human experience beyond what can be 'scientifically' explained, even if God is only needed as cause of the (now mechanistic) universe and guarantor that in the end Kantian 'duty' will be rewarded.

Scientism finds an obvious partner in atheism and the two fed off each other throughout the seventeenth and eighteenth centuries, reaching scientism's apotheosis in the early nineteenth century with the (very different) writings of Auguste Comte in France and Jeremy Bentham in England; nor have the glaring – though disparate – weaknesses in the thought of these and their successors done much to lessen a scientistic appeal now magnified through those media which authentic science has provided for us. Neither Comte nor Bentham was in any strict sense a scientist, though Comte wanted his 'Sociology' – the study of societies that he founded and so named – to be regarded as a 'hard' science – even though its methodologies plainly differ in kind from these. Bentham made no such claim, resting content with being moral philosopher, philanthropist and social engineer.

Comte further prided himself on his theory about the cultural development of mankind; this, coming to be believed by many beyond those who had ever heard of Comte, helped to lend plausibility to his very particular brand of scientism. According to Comte, first there was religion, superseded by metaphysics, that in course of time by

Science. As to what counts as a science, in wanting to add his new subject to the category, Conte imposed on his 'Sociology' a seemingly scientific, 'quantitative' character made to appeal to the Utilitarian mind by the plentiful use of statistics.

Yet examining human behaviour 'quantitatively' can only predict what is more or less likely to happen among groups or be done by individuals over time: statistical patterns cannot – as those who so examine it are liable to suppose, reductively – identify facts about individuals or their practices and preferences on particular occasions. If a certain percentage of a population is bald, that does not tell anyone whether I am bald. Nor can such a statistic as that 20 per cent of the population will at some time have cancer tell me whether I should ask my doctor for a check-up. The dehumanising risks of such implications and assumptions are obvious, leaving aside their being taken to suggest a new kind of religion. Comte would even propose the role of the sociologist as analogous to that of the traditional theologian – to the extent of elaborating scientistic substitutions for roles in the Catholic Church!

*

Jeremy Bentham's 'Utilitarianism' did not arise in a vacuum; at the theoretical level it depends in part on the reformist legal writings of the Italian jurist Beccaria and the anti-metaphysical atheism of Hume. But Bentham's role in the development of scientistic philanthropy as religion- and metaphysics-substitutes is curiously his own, depending on his belief – in line with the Industrial Revolution taking place around him – that applying technology to social problems, such as health and sanitation, will make the world a not merely better but even eventually a perfect place. Thus in addition to being a philanthropist, he is a forerunner of a Victorian philistinism coloured by overweening scientism.

At least, however – hard-headed as he was – Bentham recognised (as had Hobbes, his somewhat scientistically inclined predecessor) that philanthropy has nothing to do with rights; these he notoriously dismissed as 'nonsense upon stilts': appropriately enough in an atheist universe, but leaving contemporary and later disciples to attempt a pairing of Utilitarianism with some purely secularist theory that could justify them.

Like Comte, Bentham was a quantifier, and in his understanding of how to measure human experience, the dangers of quantifying, and the fallacies it is liable to engender, are glaringly obvious. Notoriously, Bentham held the aim of the moral philosopher to be to persuade us that we should ever seek 'the greatest good of the greatest number': if we bear in mind that principled target we can (he supposed) avoid reducing ethics (with 'the sentimentalists') to what we feel, or to matters of 'taste'. That Bentham had not resolved the matter appeared when, asked why he was a philanthropist, he is said to have replied (and certainly could have replied): 'Because that sort of thing gave him pleasure'. One must allow that giving the philanthropist pleasure can count (prescinding, that is, from the results of the philanthropy) as contributing something to the maximisation of 'happiness'. Only we might ask why we should prioritise what gives Bentham pleasure over, say, what gives some follower of the Marquis de Sade pleasure? Even if pleasing to others apart from himself, the sadist's activities might seem not to contribute so simply to 'happiness' and the overall good.

Beyond such immediate difficulties, Bentham's position raises the question, What is happiness? As also, How to compare items we distinguish as goods? His answers were simplistic, and Nietzsche rightly will recognise them as appropriate to 'the morality of the herd' in substituting a trivial and material satisfaction for 'freedom'. Bentham reduces happiness to a pleasure he fails to scrutinise and even considers measurable in units (his 'felicific calculus'), such that in considering possible courses of action, we should add up the number of pleasure-units each act or type of act will generate. To which it might be objected that, in comparing people's preferences for, say, apples or oranges, we can scarcely engage in some sort of statistical testing to ascertain which fruit, overall, will provide the greatest pleasure!

Then there will arise the question as to whether what we denote happiness and pleasure are not two quite different states. Many thinkers offer reasons why they are not to be identified, perhaps defining pleasure as a natural feeling which may arise when we recognise that a good job has been done, while happiness is (in Aristotle's phrase) 'an activity of the soul in accordance with virtue'. If I take up running for the sake of my health, I would answer misleadingly the question 'Why are you running?' if I said, 'For pleasure' or 'To enjoy myself', though I would be justified in saying that though I am running for health reasons, I experience pleasure when I run. Pleasure then, as Aristotle thought, seems to be an accompaniment of activity successfully carried out – raising the question as to whether it is not self-defeating to seek it for its own sake, when it perhaps is liable to take a dusty turn.

Bentham's activities as a philanthropist shed light on the simplistic nature of his theorising. It is obvious enough that if we develop better sanitation systems and pay workers an at least 'living' wage, the sum of happiness is increased or at least of misery decreased. We may grant Bentham that such projects will indisputably increase public well-being; even so, they only satisfy basic material needs, as for hygiene, food or shelter, ignoring what we may regard as our 'spiritual' needs, say for art or music or philosophy – even theology. And here the problem of priorities arises: given that resources are limited, is it better to build a hospital or a school or even a concert-hall? In the end it comes to the choices or preferences of whatever group controls our politics and (theoretically in a democracy) can persuade the general public that their balance of priorities is the best available. Ultimately such choices will be quite largely emotional rather than rational. Nor should we forget that increases in material prosperity may, beyond a certain extension, diminish rather than increase contentment, 'spiritual' or other – as by inflaming the (traditionally held diabolical) vice of envy.

Bentham's theories will also often raise questions as to the appropriate means to an end. In totalitarian states, long-term projects which may eventually benefit the wider public may be carried forward at almost any cost: thus Stalin achieved the industrialisation of the Soviet Union at the cost of the starvation of millions of its citizens. The means-and-ends problem, though always acute for consequentialists (including Utilitarians), becomes particularly agonising in times of war: thus in the World War II Hitler was defeated above all by the superhuman efforts of the Soviet Union, where victory was made possible by the sacrifice of soldiers in such numbers as no Western politician would have dared to contemplate. In this battle between two totalitarian states, the Soviet Union and Nazi Germany, means were sacrificed to ends on both sides, and those who sacrificed the most troops (and had sufficient numbers of troops to sacrifice) emerged victorious.

Neither side would appear to have given a passing thought for the greatest good of the greatest number, nor indeed could anyone determine whether Hitler or Stalin might be the less harmful to humanity as a whole. Certainly it was better for Western Europe that in this titanic conflict Stalin should prevail; he at least, and with whatever damage to its neighbours, was claiming to bring his country out of what for most had been a wretchedly servile past, whereas Hitler and the Nazis aimed to plunge theirs – and the rest of Europe – into a jackbooted tyranny of the 'Aryan' race. To this had descended the acclaimed German philosophical and cultural superiority!

The question of the greatest good of humanity as a whole is further illuminated by the Hitler-Stalin collision in that if we are prepared to sacrifice numbers on the scale demanded by the World War II, then our respect for each individual must be diminished; his or her role may become simple 'cannon-fodder'. 'Humanitarian' projects far less momentous than the defeat and removal of Hitler carry the same risk, as 'love of humanity' time and again stands in for the Hebraic-Christian 'love of *neighbour*'. Again, some sort of prioritising must be introduced if all commitment to individuals rather than to groups is not to be eroded.

One option (therefore normally ruled against by totalitarians) is to have, as the nucleus of our responsibilities, the family, from which a widening circle will include friends, neighbours – eventually one's nation and beyond. Even here is care needful not to lose sight of the individual, or we shall end up preferring to serve humanity rather than human beings. Edmund Burke, writing of the French Revolution, is careful to refer not to the rights of Man but of 'men'.

The contemporary distinction between agent-relative and agent-neutral actions helps us expand this point further, the paradigm case being that of Socrates who, confronted by the demand of a tyrannical system to take part in the arrest of a citizen scheduled to be judicially murdered for his money, simply went home rather than collude in the crime. That his action was 'agent-relative' appears in that he well knew that if he would not be an accessory, others would: thus in terms of getting the 'right' result, his action served no purpose. So how are we to measure that greater good for humanity Socrates achieved by his – in this case – inaction? That its effect (as in being exemplary) cannot be measured illustrates how quantifying goodness is liable to be a fool's game.

As early British Utilitarianism morphed into later versions, attempts were made, most notably by John Stuart Mill (initially an admirer of Comte, until faced with the 'ecclesiastical' roles that even to the serious Mill appeared as ludicrous), to measure pleasure *qualitatively* – that is, morally or aesthetically – as well as quantitively in terms of intensity and duration. This approach, involving the introduction of a metaphysical (originally Platonic) evaluation of pleasures according to their kind and 'target', conflicts with Bentham's attempt at quantifying pleasure according to a (hypothetical) 'felicific calculus'. Thus while seeking to be an improvement on Bentham's original proposals, it in fact – as was soon pointed out – negates him in setting a standard inadmissible on Utilitarianism's own principles.

Indeed Mill's proposal may make matters even worse; it is easier to envisage the quantifying of pleasures (say by some neurological testing) than to measure the qualitative pleasure, let us say, of listening to Bach rather than to Mozart: so much will depend upon an individual's perceptions, knowledge, or his or her 'tastes'. In responding to this, the Utilitarian is driven back on some such principle as, 'Maximise the good *whatever you suppose it to be'* – where the good becomes what each of us, despite our arguably mistaken judgments, inclines to prefer. Not that that makes measurement and prioritising any easier or safer – even should one accept that what is to be preferred is whatever 'good' is preferred by our political bosses (or in a democracy their followers – or dupes).

*

So far we have identified two factors promoting scientism in the early nineteenth century: the indubitable progress of the hard sciences, especially in physics with its mathematical foundations, and the Utilitarian belief that the technological harnessing of scientific knowledge to social improvement will render the world a happier, perhaps even a perfectible place. Science indeed might seem to provide the effective means of achieving the Utilitarian dream, viewed as it is in purely material terms. And in dreaming that dream society can easily shift from respect for science to its apotheosis and an unwarranted confidence in its high-priests: from 'Perhaps there is nothing they cannot achieve for us' to 'Perhaps we should give them a free hand'.

In the early days of modern science, few were as yet asking themselves whether or where the application of scientific knowledge should be restrained and – even though emphatically not to bring it into line with theological or metaphysical 'dogma' – whether there might be any considerations of ethical obligation: in effect, whether there are things we should not want to know, or at least should not want to practise 'scientifically'. In terms of the history of thought, such questions revive concerns in antiquity and in the Middle Ages about *curiositas*: a vice already identified by Apuleius in his novel *The Golden Ass* as the willingness to learn by resorting to magic, later applied more generally to forms of inappropriate and even – as in the legend of Faust – diabolical enquiry. Whatever the origins of *curiositas*, it is easy to see that it is no mere obscurantism but has application. There are no moral – though there may be scientistic or even scientific – reasons to want to know, let us say, how human beings react to novel forms of torture or the injection of known poisons: such experiments were not so long ago carried out on captives of the Nazis.

And since science after the seventeenth century has continued its exponential growth and is unlikely to decline – short of the denuding or destruction of the planet – we would expect that, wherever new grounds for enquiry were opened up, the ambitions of scientists (as of 'scientistics', and indeed of the worshipping public) would enter in. In the latter part of the nineteenth century two eminent investigators would provide that predictable impulse: Darwin and Freud. Both (it must be admitted) at times tottered on the edge of scientism, while many of their followers jumped over the cliff. It is a recurrent feature of human enquiry that professionals in one area of expertise too easily assume – or have attributed to them – competence in others.

As we have seen, in the eighteenth century, and most influentially in the writings of John Locke, older discussions of the nature of persons were transformed into questions of how to recognise them: that is, what we mean by personal identity. The normal solution offered was that it resided in consciousness and memory – bringing with it the anti-personalist implication that those who lose consciousness or memory by, say, illness or accident, are no longer persons, albeit still in some sense human. The findings of both Darwin and Freud enable us further to probe how we become conscious or how we acquire memory: in Darwin's case, how we have evolved 'beyond' other animals via other primates.

Darwin's research and writing carried much further, and in directions with peculiar relevance for our human condition, the expansion of our universe we recognise as opening up with Copernicus and Galileo. Physics and astronomy, in establishing 'The Big Bang' as our earliest starting-point, set us on the way to understanding the origin of our present cosmos, yet are of no help in establishing why there is a cosmos at all. Similarly Darwin's account of the origins of more 'advanced' (and why do we so regard them?) living forms vastly expands our knowledge (or apparent knowledge, for scientistic claims regularly blur the distinction between probable fact and tendentious, if learned, guess-work) of our own specifically human characteristics, or at least some of them.

While modern genetics did not exist as a science in Darwin's time – meaning the opportunity to discover the actual mechanisms implied by his theories was not available to him – what he could do (and as Mendel and others had done before him) was to observe and infer. Genetics, palaeontology and anthropology would subsequently be invoked to provide something like experimental verification or refutation of his excogitations – to be summed up in the theory of Natural Selection, according to which species able to adapt to the changing conditions around them survive, while the less adaptable die out. This theory as to 'The Origin of Species' (as Darwin entitled his bombshell book of 1859) has rather few immediate social implications – though if it could be shown that every human capacity is entirely caused by the chance events summarised as 'Natural Selection', the arguments against religious faith, indeed against the existence of God, would be substantially strengthened. To be useful for more than atheist propaganda, however, such arguments would need to be watertight, and this they certainly are not. Rather they suggest that the truth is more complicated.

But Natural Selection, reformulated by Herbert Spencer as the 'survival of the fittest', might also be applied within species, to include the human species, and thus to predict which groups of humans are likely to die out – namely those whose continuing existence might seem rather pointless: implying a Nietzschean distinction between herd and heroes – if not for such broader distinctions among human beings as those advocated by racists, a 'species' plentiful enough in the latter decades of the nineteenth century. Not only in Britain, where the birth of Darwinian eugenics coincided with the transformation of an Imperial 'mission' into a more racist project at the hands of Chamberlain, Milner and many another; similar and contemporaneous was the intensification of German colonial aims in the direction of a more extreme version of racist imperialism.

Darwin himself is not immune to such popular evaluation when he writes that 'looking at the world at no very distant date … an endless number of the lower races will have been eliminated by the higher civilised races throughout the world'. This looks to be more than mere prediction; the language of 'lower' and 'higher' implying a value judgment about the human quality of the individuals concerned and that a policy of eugenics would be in line with the inevitability of history. Implicit at least is that, by becoming aware not only of the theory of Natural Selection but also of 'primitive' natural deficiencies, we are in a position to co-operate with that inevitable progressive advance – or might we say a biological 'hidden hand'? – which Natural Selection would seem to indicate.

Nor was it only Adolf Hitler and ignorant 'social Darwinists' of his ilk who were to interpret Natural Selection along these lines. Social Darwinism popped up 'officially' almost as soon as Darwinism itself, and not only with imperialist politicians like Darwin's cousin Francis Galton, in whose honour a Chair of Eugenics was founded in Bentham's own foundation, University College, London, in 1911. Its first holder, the mathematician Karl Pearson, was only too willing not to limit his 'Darwinian' eugenics to inferior races abroad, but to look also to the Home Front, fearing that the imperial people faced corruption from weaklings as well as from miscegenation. In *Darwinism, Medical Progress and Parentage* (1912) he observed that 'As we lessen the stringency of natural selection, and more and more of the weaklings and the unfit survive, we must increase the standard, mental and physical, of parentage': an appeal not merely to the red-neck imperialists of late Victorian Britain and its colonies to rein in those denoted (in Kipling's words) 'lower races outside the law' but to similar action against inferior specimens at home. For both, the motive is Utilitarian in character – and ironically opposes that very miscegenation that is in practice seen to strengthen the species!

Marie Stopes – still regarded as a 'national' treasure in lands beyond her own – devoted much persuasion to the desirable elimination of 'lower' racial groups, more especially 'negroes' (though admittedly showing racial impartiality to the extent of disowning her daughter's marriage to a husband requiring spectacles for short sight). Bernard Shaw (who seems to have shared the view of Bentham that animals, or some animals, have moral claims similar to those attaching to human beings – or some human beings) reflected on the possible opportuneness of death chambers for the mentally and physically challenged. In such people (as in their similar, if more circumspect, followers into later times) we recognise that 'democratic' presentation of equality as uniformity signalling the totalitarian in 'liberal' and 'scientific' guise. Their Utilitarian background provides such 'philosophical' support for eugenicists, male or female, as may be helpfully invoked.

Bentham (and Shaw) may be right that in a godless world it is not easy to see why 'failing' human beings should be protected while animals are expendable. The present authors have noted that a Professor of Medicine in Aberdeen about a century ago had inscribed on his tombstone the boast that he had 'changed the genetic patterns of the North-East of Scotland': *scil.* by aborting (at the time illegally) offspring of indigent provenance. In such interventions we see how scientism of a Darwinian stamp can generate ethical 'problems', in the eyes of 'progressives' to be finessed by Utilitarian (so agent-neutral) appeal. We shall resume our investigation of the connection between scientism and more than one breed of totalitarians when we eventually reach the confusion besetting the largely rootless individuals who serve as our representatives and opinion-formers in the contemporary West.

*

In specifying individuals who have influenced the modern Western mindset, one cannot pass over Sigmund Freud – and not only because of his actual medical and wider, as he claimed, scientific work, but also because of scientistic conclusions which have been drawn from it. Despite his being now unfashionable – it would seem not least for his view of male homosexuality as a state of arrested development – much of his basic theorising has become mainstream, to the extent that no other psychologist has left a more significant impression on the popular mind.

In striking contrast to the view of Rousseau about the early period of our lives that we cannot remember, Freud considered that period of critical importance since the experiences which have slipped from our active memory have been retained in a normally unconscious stratum or 'subconscious'. The concept of a subconscious self in some form or other is not new with Freud; many philosophers have proposed its existence. Thus in the third century AD Plotinus believed that rising above our normal 'empirical' level we achieve a higher state in which we can identify ourselves with transcendent 'forms' such as Goodness and Beauty (to be understood analogously as attributes of God). We can also sink below our normal 'moral' level to identify with what we have suppressed, and which Plotinus' master, Plato, already noted could reappear in our dreams. As Plato explained it, what the good man dreams, the bad man does; he appears to have been thinking especially of 'Oedipal' dreams: very common in antiquity according to surviving 'dream-books' – and of particular interest to Freud.

However, whereas Plotinus and Plato thought that we should not want to access the 'lower' selves that may float into our dreams and fantasies, Freud (himself classically educated and son-in-law to a distinguished classical scholar) took a different view. For him, irrational 'neuroses' are a response to tensions arising from early experiences – especially our relationship with our parents – which need to be brought into the open to be resolved. Since we are debarred from doing that of ourselves, we need the services of a trained – that is, already 'analysed' – therapist or 'psycho-analyst' to prompt us to recall what we have forgotten and need to recover.

While Plato accepts that our subconscious self may obtrude itself upon our conscious mind, what really matters in his eyes is rather to recall the contents of a higher world we have lost, and not, as with Freud, a suppressed 'lower' stratum: to 'recollect', that is, not personal experiences but a higher and more inspiring reality which lies beyond our normal awareness but can be recovered by a disciplined programme of asceticism and reflective study. This we may be able to do on our own, but it helps to have a teacher – almost a psychoanalyst in reverse – who will ask the relevant leading questions, challenging us to recognise the fallibility of our normal judgments and see the need for the fixed principles concealed 'above' our normal life.

The problem with this is, how we are to understand what we may recover. And there is an analogous problem for Freudians which Freud himself recognised: how do we know that the analyst does not 'plant' in us our 'recovered' memories? Presumably the test of that will be if, when we uncover and face the relevant facts, our mental health improves: we become 'better balanced', happier individuals. Yet Freud himself noted a discouraging failure of his patients to progress to active ownership of the early experiences his therapeutic method claimed to uncover by 'associating'.

Not that such theories – well known to those who have studied Freud's writings about early childhood experience and 'transference', whereby the analyst replaces a parent-figure – are what the public understands to be the particular contribution of Freud to our social mentality. What signifies in the public eye is Freud's understanding that what we can uncover about ourselves will tend (at least in a 'repressive' modern society) to be of a sexual nature – implying that sexual 'errors' or confusions affecting our minds in early childhood and then forgotten – or rather 'repressed' – are key to the human condition: they in effect constitute the 'real' Original Sin. Again this should be compared with Plato, for the sexual drive – what the Greeks called *eros* – is fundamental also to his thinking and, as with Freud, it can and should be harnessed to a wider cultural and aesthetic project.

As himself a Classical scholar, Freud will have been aware of this, but he applies it to a very different world picture. Plato's project is to enable us to rise 'above' our empirical bodily life; Freud's is to understand and so dispel the distortions we have unconsciously imbibed from our early years, so as to live more 'healthily', which is to say more happily. Plato too uses the metaphor of a healthy bodily life and many philosophers have thought of themselves as 'higher' medical practitioners, but while Plato's project is born in a world full of gods and ultimately controlled by immaterial realities, Freud lives in an increasingly atheist universe – ex-Christian as he is in belief ex-Jewish – and for him the aim is to harmonise the self so that it may live in some sense productively, the causes of malfunction having been removed by 'analysis'. Understanding one's sexuality is key to that desired and desirable harmony – and one has to bear in mind that Freud's Vienna was more-than-average notable for sexual repression allied with deviancy and social hypocrisy.

Plato was happy to be compared to a doctor in the sense of a physician of the soul, and no one could mistake his position for scientistic. Doctor Freud does not and could not enjoy such immunity. Whereas Plato thinks we can be raised 'above' our normal 'empirical' level, because our higher self (as Plotinus will put it) remains 'above', Freud's claim is that the psychological theories he has developed (and that he always claimed would be found to have neurological analogues) will fit us to live well without recourse to 'external' metaphysical or religious aids. If Psychoanalysis can look like a religion without God, it is not difficult to see why – indication that in an atheistic world we appear still to need some such 'priestly' role as the analyst may fulfil.

Freud may not have recognised this possible aspect of his ideas. Certain it is that the effect they have produced in modern society is promoted by their central theme being sexual repression – 'sex' being, besides an indispensable, also an alluring function, making it liable to much scientistic attention. Hence is much indulgence in sexual experimentation, defended as therapeutic, an inheritance of our age from 'Freudianism' – however contrary to the intentions of its founder, that correct physician and *paterfamilias*, Dr Sigmund Freud!

Up to a point, then, Comte was right. Religion in the West has been replaced, as we have briefly chronicled, by metaphysics of various stripes, metaphysics by scientific enquiry. But to the 'scientistic' appropriation of science arguably Comte himself contributed with the new but highly inexact 'science' he named Sociology. And as sociology may be uncritically assimilated to the 'hard' sciences, so in the contemporary public mind science itself easily morphs into a scientism of which Darwin and Freud are viewed as original high-priests: Freud being, as we have noted, an atheist, Darwin preferring to style himself – in the term invented by his disciple Thomas Huxley – an agnostic: the distinction is scarcely relevant since, to the scientistic mind, God (whether or not He exists) is irrelevant. Hence the new cult, with its new priesthood, becomes less Comte's Religion of Humanity than a bowing down before 'Science' as humanity's arbiter. (We write even as 'Covid-19' has provided our government with a new cult-phrase and claims and exhorts simply to 'Follow the science'.)

*

Science being transformed into a new and, in the design of its faithful, a universal cult, what do its high priests have to say about the world-historical role of humanity? Recall that the title of this chapter is 'Scientistic' – not 'Scientific' – 'Humanism'. For there is a scientific (properly so-called) humanism, but listening to our contemporary 'priests' and their acolytes, we may be tempted to wonder whether this is not a contradiction in terms. Let us reflect on some of their gnomic sayings – very different as they are from those of Nietzsche, let alone of Nietzsche's model, Heraclitus.

Here are some recent specimens. According to physicist Steven Weinberg, 'living creatures just are very complicated physico-chemical machines'. Unsurprisingly, one of his echo-chambers, the philosopher Daniel Dennett, urges us 'to give up our awe of living things'. Notoriously Stephen Hawking identified the human race as 'just a chemical scum on a moderate-sized planet', and – waxing more cosmic – averred that 'because there is a law of gravity, the Universe can and will create itself from nothing'. One notes the deliberately dismissive phrases, 'just are' and 'just a'. In citing these examples we in no way wish to impugn any individual's proficiency in the hard sciences, only that their particular skills are no substitute for responsible thinking. Priests and gurus are traditionally and rightly castigated if they utter irresponsibly.

Such dismissive attempts to offer a reductionist, and above all anti-personalist account of human beings imply a rejection not only of fuddy-duddy Christianity but of any idea of human worth, to include that normally offered by 'humanists'. We should at least wish to be favoured with arguments for their utterance – better ones than that 'gravity' caused the Universe to 'create itself'! Admittedly it has been a bad habit of many a cleric – in the time-honoured sense – to pontificate rather than engage in serious debate; that is no reason to admit these latter-day gurus as their rightful heirs. Indeed their attitudes, whether or not intentionally, can only condone atrocities: if we are worthless, indeed 'scum' – why not treat each other as worthless? We have already observed how condoning atrocities is a recurring mark of the 'progressivist' mindset.

If according to our new 'humanists' – though better distinguished as post-humanists of scientistic bent – we are all (apart presumably from themselves) of little worth, what is to be done to keep us in order while unhindered they develop their 'improving' projects – designed as they 'obviously' are for our utilitarian good? Again and again the answer has been to lie and deceive: dark arts deployed by politicos from time immemorial, but traditionally held unacceptable (even immoral) if adopted by philosophers and political analysts. How then have they been made more acceptable as used not only by extremists of 'left' and 'right' but by the ordinary public figure, not least the public 'intellectual'?

To the question, 'How can you tell whether a politician is lying?', the facetious answer, as proposed in the case of President George Bush, is, 'See if he moves his lips'. But matters are not that simple, since politicians and others who hope to evade investigation – hence comprehension – of their proposals know that while direct lying is easily countered (unless one lives in a totalitarian state), the desired results can be secured in other ways. The two most commonly deployed can be heard on our airwaves almost any time a politician is asked a searching question, when he or she may decide to answer a question other than the one asked; this at least occupies the allotted time and by a barrage of words the listener – even perhaps the questioner – will fail to remember the original question precisely as posed.

The second of the more obvious modes of deception is the giving of a factually correct but incomplete response: thus, notoriously, Adolf Eichmann, asked about his role in Nazi Germany during the Holocaust, replied that he ran the trains – truly but not truthfully, since he omitted to mention that the destination of said trains was the Auschwitz death camp. In this case the omission was crude and obvious but that sort of reply, falling under the rubric of the Incomplete Predicate, can be effective and the listener needs to think quickly whether he or she is not being misled – and by an interlocutor groomed to deceive him.

At least from the Greeks on humanity has had to reckon with this kind of thing from politicians; indeed some might argue that politics is impossible without deception; this, if accepted, would to a degree diminish the distinction between blatantly totalitarian regimes and those exhibiting totalitarian symptoms. In our era of scientistic humanism, however, and with the present state of humanity denigrated by those who may hope by eugenics to produce a superior or superhuman population, the tactic is not limited to politicians but is often employed by opinion formers, including philosophers who have concluded (as from Hegel), that the 'truth' they traditionally sought is relative to time and place; or from Nietzsche that there is no such thing: that all we can offer are sets of perspectives, preferred or merely assumed; or from the Utilitarian tradition that when science bids, means may have to be subordinated to ends 'for our own good' – and it will be convenient if the public can be deluded into not noticing.

We can identify various contemporary motives for our opinion formers and self-proclaimed philosophers (better, sophists) settling to deceive. Clearly the media, especially the 'social media', form a handy conduit for them to do so. Further, they consider deception necessary to develop schemes (as perhaps eugenic) which *require* the public to be deceived. Finally, deception becomes for them an essential 'social glue' without which anarchy, or at least uncontrollable social unrest, will not be contained. Hence will Utilitarians or other consequentialists – those concerned with the good of Humanity rather than of human beings – be among the first to resort to it. Even the decidedly anti-utilitarian Plato is prepared to admit in the *Laws* that if the world is as the atheist politician would have it, deception of some sort is necessary if anarchy is to be fended off.

Not that Utilitarians deny all truth. They will hold it a truth that we should maximise the good of the greatest number, but make a distinction between 'long-term' and 'short-term' truths, the latter of which may where needful be discarded. They view themselves, that is, as engaged in a perpetual warfare on behalf of society, in which, as in real wars, some degree of deception – assimilated to the use of espionage in war – is essential for success. And of course if they are scientistics – many of them are – the deceiving of the *profanum vulgus*, the uninitiated herd, will in their eyes be the more desirable.

This we can recognise in the history of Utilitarianism itself. Where the problem first appears in clear light is with John Stuart Mill who, though purportedly a Utilitarian, was no egalitarian, his view being that the elite should call the shots, especially educationally, until the ordinary members of society can be educated out of their unenlightened state. Though claiming to be one of the few who had never been tempted by religious faith, he thought it 'perfectly conceivable that religion may be morally useful without being intellectually sustainable'; hence it should be tolerated if not actually encouraged. Or, as Marx was to put it, religion could be (and has been) a useful opiate to dull the restlessness and 'alienation' of the working class.

Thus far Mill's approval of such public deception may seem tempered. A more strictly Utilitarian – and sinister – approach comes into view with Henry Sidgwick. At the end of his extended *Methods of Ethics*, Sidgwick feels obliged to admit that he has failed in a major part of his project to resolve a problem going back at least (as we have seen) to Kant: namely how to reconcile duty with happiness. Some more recent Utilitarians assert that Sidgwick gave up prematurely, that the time had not come to despair, but Sidgwick himself saw no way out of his difficulties and wondered where next to turn. The problem as it appeared to him was not how could he improve his philosophising – or put traditionally, how to advance in the pursuit of truth – but whether his failure, if publicised, would lead to an intellectual confusion generating undesirable social effects. Why, even the elites might become disillusioned!

To Sidgwick it seemed the only solution was to keep the regrettable truth of the matter hidden; he thereby revealed a contempt for philosophical enquiry itself as well as for those he willed to mislead. We should remember that Sidgwick, like his master Bentham, was a humanitarian rightly credited with doing much for the education of women, not least in his role in the establishment of Newnham College in Cambridge. Thus what we already recognise in Sidgwick is an early and comparatively straightforward harbinger of too many of our contemporary gurus: an inability to accept that they hold conflicting positions, or positions dependent on conflicting first principles: as logicians put it, 'p and not-p at the same time'. We may presume Sidgwick hoped that the women he wanted educated would learn to be lovers of truth, not connivers in deception: it was another case of the signpost not going the way it pointed – for, of course, 'humanitarian' reasons.

Even the atheist philosopher Bernard Williams dubbed Sidgwick's attitude in this, 'Government House Consequentialism'. From our point of view it reveals the contempt of a self-identified elite, confident in their facile scientism, for the ordinary bloke: a contempt to be at all costs concealed from the bloke him- or her-self. This contempt, parallel to Leninist patronising of the ordinary worker, has extended its tendrils further among our contemporaries, for whom Utilitarianism, combined with scientism, is the basis of the mix forming their post-Christian 'humanism'. For a philosopher (as distinct from a sophist), that has to be unacceptable. Near the beginning of Western thought we find Socrates proclaiming the 'unexamined life' – and that will include the deluded life – to be subhuman. Yet and as we have seen, subhuman is – from a scientistic point of view – the state in which most are unavoidably trapped. Are we then (again) to put our trust in a eugenics, blatant or concealed, to rid us of such encumbrances and 'maximise the greatest good of the greatest number' – of at least the 'real' people: the people who 'count'?

7 World War, Bureaucracy, Consumerism

They will reap the whirlwind.

Hosea, applied by Air Marshal ('Bomber') Harris to Hitler's bombardment of London

In this chapter and the next we approach the contemporary scene. However, before introducing new intellectual projects bearing on our current cultural confusion, we must take a further look at the wider Western landscape after 1918. For, after the 'war to end all wars', political changes – particularly in America, the United Kingdom, Germany, Russia and China – have shaped the world in which Western thinkers now live, providing the backdrop for their social and philosophical theorising.

If the break with Rome by Henry VIII signals the beginning of a new and more 'statist' version of Constantinian Europe, and the French Revolution the partial eclipse of Enlightenment Man, the outbreak of war in 1914 similarly marks a radical change in the 'European' scene, not least because, by the close of hostilities in 1918, the United States had become a predominant 'Western' power. Other powers too had changed: gone was the Prussian monarchy that Bismarck had transformed into the German Empire, gone the empires of Germany's allies in the Great War, Ottoman Turkey and Austria – as well as the Romanov dynasty, for centuries Tsars of Russia. Britain was left standing apparently as she had been, but appearance did not match reality. Overstretched as she was by her own ultimately unmanageable Empire and deeply in debt, her disappearance as an imperial power was merely postponed, albeit this was hardly recognised in 1918.

It was not meant to be that way. A few years before the 'Great War' began, pundits had been saying that with the advent of new tools of destruction, the frontiers of Europe were more or less settled, wars between rival powers unthinkable, a thing of the past. In the event, even when the old authoritarian dynasties disappeared, two of them, Imperial Germany and tsarist Russia, were replaced by more ruthless totalitarian successors – now equipped with more highly mechanised military hardware. Yet only with hindsight can we see the old Empires sleepwalking to their doom in 1914. At first the assassination of the Austrian Archduke Franz Ferdinand at Sarajevo hardly ruffled the financial markets. Even when war broke out, in both London and Berlin cheering crowds were telling themselves it would all be over by Christmas. Overlooking the massive carnage caused by advanced weaponry as early as the American Civil War, each side assumed their military would quickly prevail. After all, the British had managed to mow down Zulus, Matabele and eventually even Boers, thanks to their Maxim guns. The Germans had done even 'better' in their new colony – what is now Namibia – their commander receiving the award *Pour le Mérite* for systematically exterminating the misguided natives.

After four years of huge losses on both sides, in 1918 Europe proceeded to 'lose the peace' when, at the signing of the Armistice at Versailles, France in particular (and much encouraged by Australia), insisted that Germany pay such huge reparations as guaranteed that the German economy would collapse and thousands of ex-servicemen prefer a para-military lifestyle, in the so-called Freikorps and other formations, to settling down to a jobless existence on 'civvy street'. In this they were encouraged by militarists who told them they had not been defeated but stabbed in the back by 'socialists'. The War, these 'patriots' insisted, had not been formally concluded. Reiterating sentiments uttered by generals as early as 1916, they declared, 'Next time we shall do better'. And with backs put to the proverbial wall, some fifteen years after the Armistice German factories were again turning out the most advanced armaments.

At the other end of the political spectrum, the Communists, led by Karl Liebknecht and Rosa Luxemburg, though not unsuspicious of Lenin's intentions, were happy to suppose that what their friends in Russia had achieved would be within their grasp – misjudging the resilience of their nationalist enemies, and in the first instance the genius of General Gröner, former wartime logistical wizard at the side of Marshal Hindenburg, then in 1918 delegated to tell the Kaiser that he no longer enjoyed the confidence of the Army and abdication was his only option.

Gröner too struck a deal with Socialist Chancellor Ebert to rid the country of Bolshevism, thereby securing for now that fragile Republic which had (perforce) accepted the savage terms imposed by the enemy. The enduring need for the political support of the Army exonerated it from blame; for the military failure – that fearful shock to national pride – the Left, the 'November criminals' (and not only the communists) who had 'stabbed the Army in the back', could be held responsible. The *Reichswehr*, the military machine sedulously built up by generals and politicians since the earlier humiliation by Napoleon, would survive: though greatly reduced in numbers, yet with prestige untarnished.

Many Germans – not merely the still tiny group of Nazis – took heart; in the longer run Germany would return to policies of military expansionism. In due course, Hitler, possessed of massive popular support, would only need to win over a sufficient number of generals and capitalists to subvert both government and society. In the meantime, as the new-fledged German democracy staggered from crisis to crisis, with Bolshevik and Nazi fighting for succession on the streets, the former would discover that the Russian model was less seductive than the cult of violence offered by their Nazi rivals to ex-soldiers and their supporters preparing to fight another day.

And insofar as the Communists were the less fanatical, so their chances faded when challenged by the adherents of a vengeful Will to Power. As early as 1859 Julius Froebel had written that 'the German nation is sick of principles and doctrines, literary existence and theoretical greatness. What it wants is Power … And whoever gives it power, to him it will give honour, more honour than he can ever imagine'.

By 1933 Heidegger was telling his exulting students not to 'let theoretical principles and "ideas" be the rules of your Being. The Führer himself and he alone is the German reality and law today and in the future'.

German philosophers since Fichte had maintained that the future of Europe lay in German hands – provided only German hands had the will to grasp it. Feuerbach – it might seem prophetically – had told them that in the right circumstances Man – or some man or men – will become god. Now the time of the god of destruction was at hand. Hermann Goering – he who claimed to flick the safety catch on his revolver whenever he heard the word *Geist* (Spirit) and for years Hitler's right-hand man – would claim at his trial at Nuremburg that, 'I joined the Nazi party not because of all the racialist nonsense, but because I was a revolutionary'. That is, he aimed to destroy the society around him without bothering too much about what – given the elimination of 'undesirables' – was to replace it. Germany in its philosophers had bequeathed to the world the thesis that it was the Will, not the Cartesian mind, that must forge the destiny of humanity. Now, in resuming its people's national destiny, it would demonstrate just what such 'Will' could achieve.

Sentiments arguably more international but parallel to Goering's were to be found on the Left. We have already noted how, in *The Devils*, Dostoevsky had based his character Peter Verkhovensky on the 'People's Will' leader: that Sergei Nechaev who had claimed that 'the revolutionist … knows only the science of destruction. His object is always the same: the surest and quickest way of destroying the whole filthy order'. In 1887 Lenin's brother, Alexander Ulyanov, had been hanged for active membership in the same 'People's Will': a will officially directed to the 'good of humanity', or some subset thereof – but significantly to 'humanity', not human beings. Or as Vladimir Nabokov, a minister in the Russian Provisional Government, later exiled, put it: 'The Lenins and Trotskys are completely indifferent to the fate of individuals'.

*

So much for the political backdrop. Our immediate concern is less with the atrocities of the Bolsheviks (or the Nazis) than with the mindset they helped to induce more widely among Westerners. In view of our earlier account of totalitarianism – and leaving aside the testosterone-fuelled excitement which may impel idealistic and headstrong young males (in particular) to violence – we should not be surprised that in the 1920s and 1930s many in Western Europe were happy to ignore Communist (or Nazi) atrocities or to pretend they had never happened. A habit of self-delusion about dictatorships – not only of the Left – had become well established. Among Britons ignoring or even denying the atrocities not only of Lenin and Trotsky but of their yet more savage successor Stalin, were numbered the Webbs (Sidney and Beatrice), Bernard Shaw and many other 'Fabians' who knew the facts but chose to ignore them: a mindset still much in evidence on the political 'Left'. If Communists were killing, torturing and raping in the Spanish Civil War, the retort of such would be that 'The fascist side is worse than ours' – a by no means demonstrable claim: both sides excelled in brutality and each, with their supporters, regarded their side as being in the right.

While the majority of such self-blinded individuals was happy to distribute blame among Hitler, Mussolini and Franco, these remained unwilling to heed Churchill's warnings that Hitler in particular was a danger not only to other Europeans but to themselves, hence that military preparation was necessary. Pacifism (an odd bedfellow for Communism, but with at least tacit support for and from the Left) had become a further fashionable self-indulgence, the 'peaceful' intent of obvious killers ever to be accepted, as truth gave way to ideology and wishful thinking – and not only in the heads of Communists and Nazis. While such attitudes might be more intelligible among an ill-educated general public, they had become increasingly common among 'fellow-travellers' of all stripes with claims to be regarded as intellectuals. Of these too many, refusing to accept that in politics the means must be in harmony with the end – more especially if that end is idealistic – accepted that intellectual and moral incoherence that both Plato and Aristophanes castigate, and is later summarised by Ovid as 'knowing the better and choosing the worse'.

We see an interesting example of this corrupt mentality being eventually rejected in one of its partisans when he witnessed the horror of what he was so cheerfully condoning and promoting. The well-known journalist of the period (and later editor of *Punch*), Malcolm Muggeridge, was a member of the Communist Party who decided to tear up his British passport and join the coming Socialist paradise. Living in a Soviet-provided flat in Moscow, he one day ventured (Did he already have misgivings?) to take a train for some fifty miles into the hinterland for a sight of the Soviet rural Idyll. What he saw was widespread starvation, even bodies on the streets.

In Muggeridge a certain integrity had survived the propaganda. From Moscow he wrote an account of what he had seen and sent it to his editor at the (then *Manchester*) *Guardian* – who refused to print the piece as being obviously false. Muggeridge returned to the United Kingdom and presumably reapplied for his passport; one deluded opinion-former had learned a lesson. Others would linger until the brutal suppression of the people's uprising in Hungary in 1956 compelled them to face up to the savagery of the totalitarian beast they had so long nourished in their role as 'useful idiots'; even then they might incline to put the blame for the catastrophe in Eastern Europe on Stalin, or possibly Trotsky: rarely on the original prime mover, Vladimir Lenin (he who – just for starters – had arranged the butchery of the entire Russian imperial family). Surely – so the 'idiots' seem to have assumed – some of these people must have had the good of mankind at heart; surely someone as intelligent and philanthropic as myself could not have been so wholly mistaken!

Mistaken they were – at best – and we need to understand how that came about, in the hope, however slender, that we may learn from such past 'mistakes'. Our specific problem is that it was the intellectual class (and not only in Great Britain) who allowed themselves to be misled. And why? Part of the answer is already clear: a misguided acceptance among the more educated (who often know more about ideas than about persons, being shielded from the problems of ordinary life in hard times) that the death of a few could be conveniently ignored for the sake of the coming paradise on earth. Or of a few million? As 'Iron' Felix Dzerzhinsky, founder of the Cheka, (first version of the Soviet secret police) had already explained, 'We stand for organised terror; this should be frankly admitted. Terror is an absolute necessity in times of revolution'.

Nor, as we have seen, was it only the would-be Lenins and Trotskys who took that view, albeit these may have been more willing to take personal responsibility for the 'necessary' brutality than would the privileged and ideologically excited onlookers. There were substantial numbers of ordinarily 'clever' people who should have known better and whose failure to know cannot be put down to ideology alone; we need to know why that ideology was so clung to. Part of the answer is probably common-or-garden cowardice; confronted by bullies, academics and intellectuals in general are notoriously prone to that vice, having learned to rationalise their implausible and self-serving pacifism as concern for humanity: indeed, the better you can reason, the better you can rationalise. Hence an unwillingness to fight or even encourage their more patriotic compatriots to do so: in effect, a willingness to appease the bad guys and let them get on with the killing. Only shut your eyes; in the end things will work out.

Yet ideology plus cowardice are arguably still not enough to explain the phenomenon, even though to go beyond those must be speculation, however plausible. That said, one can observe that the more 'educated' a person becomes – perhaps especially in the 'humanities' – the more he or she learns not only to rationalise but to see so many sides to a question as to be rendered unable to prioritise reasons for or against action – this leading to paralysis. And here we return from historical illustration to the need for the right-thinking mind and so to Aristotle, in this representative of the Original Tradition. For if he is right that the conclusion of the 'practical syllogism' is not a *thought* but an *action*, then this last stage of moral reasoning is what our intelligentsias have learned to avoid, while they dither, wait for others, or in last resort wring their hands and so (yet again) play the hypocrite. If Choice is now the leading Goddess in the new pantheon, then, as Mandeville prophesied and Hogarth painted, Lady Humbug is close behind her.

*

By the thirties German philosophers had for a century been telling whoever was listening that it is the Will that matters; hence were intellectuals entranced by Lena Riefenstahl's Nazi film, 'The Triumph of the Will': here was real 'Prometheanism'! Since at least the French Revolution, many intellectuals had been so attracted by the Will to Power as not only to ignore the atrocities such power-driven politics necessitates, but to become 'imitators of the men of violence', finding violence (and if concealed – even deprecated – no less malevolent) deliciously exciting. In Germany there must have been many such among the thirteen million who voted for Hitler in 1933 – and as yet they did not even need to join the Nazi party, for 'Adolphe Légalité' – so described by a French cartoonist – had secured totalitarian power by more or less democratic means, thus giving them the chance not 'really' to dirty their hands: illustrating too the uncomfortable fact that the mere holding of elections is no guarantee of democracy.

As we have observed, a very different evasion of reality was more appealing to British intellectuals in Bloomsbury and beyond. Don't follow the German model; reject patriotism (including the desire to protect your own country) as nationalism (the aim merely to make your country more powerful: the distinction had been made long ago by Plato in the *Gorgias*); hence decline to take national security seriously. Repeat the mantra of E.M. Forster that 'If I had to choose between betraying my country and betraying my friend, I hope I would betray my country'. Concentrate on being nice to your friends – with little more than the Utilitarianism of G.E. Moore to tell you what 'being nice' should mean: no place for metaphysics, just follow your own good – especially linguistic – habits – without noticing that the 'habits' of languages other than English may be very different. (This following of conventional social wisdom we as yet did not call 'virtue-signalling', but the term can apply.) When the expectable onslaught of German totalitarians finally precluded any native totalitarian growth in Britain, the refuge of nice Mrs. Leonard Woolf of Bloomsbury was suicide and we discovered – almost too late – that civic patriotism was requisite after all.

Moore apart, what had other thinkers been advising war-shocked Europeans after 1918? Existentialism and Phenomenology were developing in France and Germany but for reasons of clearer exposition we shall defer discussion of their perhaps unexpected arrival. After an attempt at the ideal (and unreal) language of Logical Atomism, Wittgenstein was not alone in falling back on clarification of ordinary language, explaining morals and aesthetics in terms of the 'family resemblances' of various sets of words and concepts within different linguistic structures. On offer here was a sophisticated view of conventional linguistic practices, seen as inevitable and determinative of value. The 'reformist' thinker Bertrand Russell would be reasonably unimpressed by this latter development of Wittgenstein's thought.

Nor were Communism, pacificism and appeasement – tempered by close, if temporary, friendships among themselves – the only evasive options available to the *ben pensanti*. After the carnage of a war caused by imperialism on both sides (disputed whose imperialism was the more problematic), clever people in many countries began to think that, if not nationalism and imperialism, then internationalism was the answer: perhaps the newly formed (American-urged though not American-supported) League of Nations could prove talking rather than shooting to be the way forward. Talking, however, came to an abrupt end when Mussolini embarked on Italy's belated attempt to get itself a glorious New Roman Empire.

*

One German economist, sociologist and historian had something more relevant to propose but died of the Spanish flu soon after the Great War: nor was what he offered calculated to please the conventional or wishful thinking. Max Weber is most widely known for arguing that modern capitalism was much stimulated by Protestantism's (in its more Calvinist forms) teaming up with the New Science to usher in an 'age of disenchantment'. He overstated his case, for features at least of the proto-capitalist world had appeared well before the advent of Luther and Calvin. Nonetheless, his *The Protestant Ethic and the rise of Capitalism* (1905) was important, not least in opening up a thesis that was less about disenchantment than about the materialist – and often totalitarian – hypnotisation of scientistic mass society.

This emerges from his extensive discussion of bureaucracy: outstanding feature of an age of ever-growing power blocs as having both civilian and military implications, and deemed an essential tool by philanthropic Utilitarians. Yet the bureaucratic structure of Imperial Germany – a powerful weapon in the hands of the Prussian imperialists – was in Nazi times to reveal its weaknesses when rival bureaucracies, established by Hitler as a means of dividing and ruling, would prove narrowly self-serving, so tending to lose sight of their overriding purpose.

Nietzsche had displayed a marked ambivalence in his attitude to the decline of European Christianity and its associated morality – by then often conventionalised whether in Kantian or Utilitarian form. Not dissimilarly, Weber demonstrated both the necessity of modern bureaucracy for an ever-expanding state (one of the more effective earlier bureaucracies had been developed in Caesaropapist Byzantium) *and* its dehumanising potential – welcome to totalitarians as destructive of individual responsibility and even humanity. In the modern state, noted Weber, bureaucracy is necessary for the organisation of huge and unwieldy groups of human beings, but will encourage specialists without spirit and sensualists without heart – until the last product of such a society can only imagine that he is human, living as he does in 'an iron cage'.

In a bureaucracy, Weber points out, individuals are sorted into specialist groups to perform the various functions of an administrative machine in which they are to become mere cogs. Such structures look rational, the individual being trained for his or her specific and it may be highly technical role – in effect carrying into social and political life the soulless Cartesian rationalism of the Enlightenment. This 'spreading of the load' ensures that no one is responsible for policy and its (possibly brutal) effects except those at the top of the pyramid, and these ensure that the 'specialists' are radically dehumanised. Yet responsibility is a prerequisite for anything resembling autonomy; we are not free unless free to make mistakes and pay the price for them; living in Weber's rule-driven 'cage', we can but imagine we are free. George Orwell's *Animal Farm* caricatured this situation in its sheep bleating, 'Four legs good, two legs ba-a-a-ad', while in mocking lyrics Tom Lehrer would gesture toward more specific implications of the bureaucratic mentality: '"If the rockets go up, who cares where they come down?/That's not my department," said Werner von Braun.'

Bringing us to statistics, the compilation of which is one major role of a bureaucracy, and notoriously easy to manipulate – most of those to whom they are fed being unable to evaluate them and relying on the facticity of what those who produce them wish to convey. Such manipulation, of obvious use to the totalitarian, is also helpful to those who use statistics to forward the Utilitarian objective of the good of the greatest number: a project always bringing strong likelihood of injustice toward smaller or less powerful groups of people whose actual neglect or mistreatment may be tolerated as enhancing the 'happiness' of the majority. Statisticians, by profession, are meant – at least officially – to be agent-neutral: concerned, that is, not with their own or their masters' desires and motives, but only with the proposed good to be achieved through information assumed to be accurate. Except that at times their activity might seem summed up as imagined philanthropy toward those they reduce to sub-human units.

It has been observed that 'the average human-being has one breast and one testicle'. In more cogent illustration of the delusory scenarios that may be opened up by statistics we might point to the way the public has during the (current) 'Covid crisis' been deluged with conclusions drawn from mathematical models. Being ourselves in the category, we take as example the model which has identified those aged over sixty-five as at greatest risk. It would seem reasonable to take such warnings seriously – always provided the model is well formed – and perhaps it takes us 'oldies' to remember how, in the 'mad-cow' crisis around the turn of the century, it was predicted that many thousands of beef-eating Brits would die inexorably of Creuzfeldt-Jakob-Disease ('CJD') – a prognosis much touted by righteous vegetarians and vegans but disappearing from view as the casualties failed to exceed a few hundred unfortunate susceptible persons. In such panics and pandemics, statistics reveal little about the particular risk for individuals in particular situations; rather they are of use (as Foucault might have pointed out) to scare their subject categories and so control behaviour with scientistic versions of what in a political context (that of 'Brexit') would be dubbed 'Project Fear'.

The contradictions built into bureaucratic governance may also negate any 'pastoral', Rousseau-style primitivism or such totalitarian dreamworld as Heidegger might envisage being established after the requisite mechanics of armed force shall have 'faded away', allowing paradise-on-earth to ensue. That bureaucratic structures, military or civilian, have a strong tendency to remain in place long after their original utility as organisational tools, might be seen exemplified in the kinder scenario offered by the recent history of Western ecclesiastical structures: fragments of an older world following the same pattern as their secular counterparts. One can note that as the Anglican Church in Britain has declined, the number of its bishops has increased, with those bishops performing rather as cogs in a bureaucratic machine, scarcely feeling the call to challenge family or other breakdown in a diminishingly Christian society. Enough for them to sound vaguely 'spiritual' – above all 'loving'.

We may conclude with Weber that the disenchantment he noted in the early Enlightened world, and which he shows contributing to the development of capitalism, is now inclined to morph into devotion to a set of self-perpetuating social institutions – to include many a committee or quango – operating both in the public and the private sectors. These bodies (seemingly designed more for talk than to encourage action) are staffed by scientistically-inclined bureaucrats and directed by technocrats who see their role as supplying the ingredients of a materialist paradise to a homogenised public. Similar quango-ism is by now patent in all modern societies, whether democratic, authoritarian or totalitarian. In the case of democracies it bears out the appositeness of De Tocqueville's recognition, based on the earlier United States, that homogenisation is not only a feature of blatantly totalitarian structures but can take an apparently more democratic and egalitarian form while yet tending toward totalitarianism.

As we have recalled earlier, to run a totalitarian state the Leader must normally control at least two of its three essential – and essentially bureaucratic – power-structures: army, Party and police. The army must be homogenised as a single-minded 'killing-machine' with independent thought severely discouraged, such that – as an old joke goes – 'Military Intelligence is a contradiction in terms'. As Weber noted, the disadvantages in terms of initiative – and therefore efficiency – are obvious and need correction.

If possible! For it is the role of a totalitarian police-force precisely to prevent such challenges to Party instruments. And of course, as the army and police, so the Party itself must be bureaucratic, the apparatchik always defining him- or her-self as 'just obeying orders' and enforcing them. Insofar as in democratic states a Party tends toward such thought-control, it is becoming not only more 'homogenised' (as required for its success) but also more bureaucratic: a tunnel-visioned aggregate where rules identify exactly in what job each individual is to be employed, looking not to the ultimate goal of government but to the immediate (however trivial) task in hand. Whereas in genuinely 'pastoral' societies lack of resources will render individuals resourceful at undertaking any job required in the community, in a bureaucracy the opposite is the case. For the bosses – especially if totalitarian – it could be dangerous were it otherwise.

Before leaving Max Weber's prescient account of bureaucracy, we pause to note that some among our totalitarians, having understood the unavoidable drawbacks in bureaucratic structures to which he drew attention, have acted with the requisite brutality. For their apparatchiks (and not only those at lower levels in the hierarchy) may fall back into such older 'bourgeois' practices and human failings – corruption, nepotism, obstructionism or mere careerism – as (even apart from the ensuring of the authority of the Leader) may call for a new type of 'purge'. The purges of Stalin in the thirties may be put down rather to paranoia than as necessary reaction to real threats to the central power. Chairman Mao would understand the human herd more rationally.

Mao seems to have grasped that a 'surd' factor in human nature – once called Original Sin by Christians of the Original Tradition – will operate even in the communist near-paradise, Marx and Lenin having erred if they thought that the achievement of this paradise could be a once and for all event. Academics, middle-rank officials, even generals and high party chieftains, may fall into older and 'capitalist' habits: hence the necessity for continual renewal, involving continual 'purges'. Nor will only a few dissidents need to be eliminated from time to time (in the Soviet Union under Stalin these 'few' included almost all the surviving 'old Bolsheviks'), but the whole apparatus must be regularly – as it were cyclically – purified. In seeing this, Mao may have been right: small comfort for apparatchiks at all levels who might have supposed servility combined with bureaucratic competence – 'just obeying orders' – to be all that was required of them.

*

After Churchill had persuaded Britain to continue the struggle against the Nazis alone in 1940 – while calling for and soon securing American support, plus alliance with Stalin after Hitler had turned on his opposite-number dictator – World War II in Europe developed essentially into a battle between the two totalitarian giants, Nazi Germany and Soviet Russia, with Britain and the United States giving very substantial assistance to the more remote and less immediately threatening Soviets. In world-historical terms, however, the most significant result of the more substantial and effective Western military activity after D-Day was to prevent Stalin from ruling Western as well as Eastern Europe. In the Far East the situation was different: the American military-industrial machine, once fully revved up, finally subdued the militarists in Tokyo, whose chances of eventual victory – as their more perceptive generals realised – were always a virtual zero: Yamamoto, the Japanese commander organising the attack on Pearl Harbour, had observed that by attacking the American Fleet he could delay defeat by one year.

No one would denote World War II 'the war to end all wars', as they had World War I, yet German and Japanese atrocities – and the eventual use of atomic weapons – convinced many in the West that the failed internationalism of the League of Nations should be given another chance: that since national governments, especially if totalitarian, could not be called to account by their own citizens, some international body could and should arbitrate. Again were obvious facts to be conveniently ignored, the first being that if a smaller body is corrupt (even brutal), there is no guarantee that a larger one will not be similarly disposed, though on a bigger scale. Augustine tells us that God permitted the Tower of Babel because plurality of languages and the diversity they encourage lessens the chance of single-ruler tyranny over too extensive a proportion of humanity.

More basically perhaps, Western idealists, such as Jacques Maritain, who advocated internationalism, neglected that, while it might be possible for the United Nations (normally via the United States) to rein in smaller powers with atrocities in mind, it would entail too great loss of life to restrain such grandiose criminal states as the Soviet Union and soon Maoist China. Not only would such be given a free hand, but they would gain a strong say in prescribing to the international organisations their duties and when and how they should – or should not – perform them. Not to speak of the fact that 'international (i.e. "United Nations") law' was to be developed and misused to castigate those conveniently adjudged by majority vote international pariahs and enemies of 'peace': in particular a state the United Nations itself, and for good reason, had guaranteed.

The United Nations General Assembly has (vainly) condemned the state of Israel dozens of times for alleged human rights abuses, while remaining largely silent on self-evident abuses committed by such professed Israel-haters as are to be found in the Islamic world (who may 'legitimise' this in various ways, but underlying them is their claim to rule in perpetuity over their *Dar al Islam*: that is all territory ever 'converted' to their religion: in theory to include a good part of Spain, Greece and most of the Balkans). Such as these plot the destruction of the territorially diminutive Jewish state, at times even avowing to murder its entire population. Meanwhile, by invoking the principle of 'geographical distribution', the ill-judging United Nations – many of whose members are themselves large-scale human-rights abusers – can find it appropriate to appoint representatives of oppressive dictatorships (such as Ghaddafi's Libya and the Iran of the ayatollahs) to oversee possible abuses of human rights: apart, of course, from any at home. The circus goes on its rounds – ludicrous were it not deadly threatening to justice and peace.

The aim of those Western idealists who promoted political internationalism – commercial globalisation is a different, though related question – was to control abuses by totalitarians of both 'right' and 'left', and not least to prevent refugees being rendered stateless and thus without protection: too little of which came about. What did come about was a huge international bureaucracy, often staffed by corrupt, even murderous, officials from petty dictatorships, strangely believed able and willing to develop and enforce international laws binding on all member states – though in reality only ever on those who accepted to treat them as binding.

Furthermore, although the United Nations was largely dependent on the United States for its more humanitarian rulings to be carried out, it was left free to elaborate 'human rights' well beyond its original mandate: to become, in effect, the 'guardian' of any rights which (primarily Western) lobby groups were able to procure. The result has been that (as latterly over the Coronavirus pandemic) the tendency in the United Nations and its agencies is to the favouring of commercial and political interests of the most insistent: in this instance China, actual source of the pandemic.

Be that as it may, largely as a result of the establishment of the United Nations and other supposedly humanitarian bodies such as the European Union, the character of rights-claims themselves has changed radically. We started after World War II with traditional demands: for the right to vote, for women's suffrage, for the protection of stateless persons, for the stamping out of torture (legal or other), for the prevention of any repetition of Nazi-style genocide. Even this last was rarely secured if the United States failed to make itself felt – as we saw at Srebreniça and most strikingly in Rwanda.

For instead of upholding traditional and more easily justifiable rights-claims, the United Nations is inclined to move with alacrity to where it may act with greater impunity. The rot began with the Declaration of Human Rights itself – of which Maritain was one of the advocates, apparently deluded into believing that secular 'rights' were the equivalent of traditional Catholic teaching about human dignity: for which, however, 'dignity' does not equate to just (some) 'value'.

Human dignity as a concept derives from Judaeo-Christian teaching about Man's creation 'in the image and likeness of God'. With God absent from the United Nations Declaration (as later from the Preface to the Charter of the European Union), the light was set green for any 'right' some powerful pressure-group could by fair means or foul claim. Normally top of the list were 'rights' to sexual 'freedoms' formerly thought of under the heading of libertinism if not crime: first of the latter being the (mother's) right to abortion. This has been followed by other so-called reproductive (though more accurately non-reproductive) rights, notably for 'gay' (oddly inappropriate shorthand for homosexual) and 'transgender' rights. Bestiality rights have not so far followed: perhaps there is sensed to be a limit; perhaps animals are held to have some sort of moral standing. In the case of children claiming to change sex, *parental* rights have actually been denied.

The case of abortion is – as often – particularly informative, not 'merely' because the right awarded by international lawmakers to mothers and doctors entails inexorably death for millions of unborn humans (predominantly female), but because it enables scientistic eugenicists in both East and West to expand their policies into something resembling a new world-wide religion. The goals of such as Chairman Mao, who hoped to reduce the population of China by about a quarter (by 'judicial' murder if forced abortion would not do it), thus are reflected in the Western 'humanitarianism' of the great financiers of abortion and other causes dear to them: such are George Soros, Bill Gates and their ilk, poised to become our actual though unelected rulers. And all but inevitably, the 'rights'-based road descended by the United Nations would be followed by those like-minded 'reformists' able to take over originally charitable organisations now dubbed NGOs; such is Amnesty International, once famed for its campaigns against torture, but hijacked to become promoter of the lobby-driven killing of the unborn.

*

One of the effects of the recent internationalist outlook is the further expansion not only of the international political bodies themselves but of globalising companies (with their high-profile and largely unaccountable CEOs), some of which have a GDP far in excess of even quite wealthy nation states. If we ask why this has been so easily tolerated, part of the answer is that such companies – often by virtue of employing 'out-sourced' sweated labour – can provide a massive array of cheap consumer goods while still maximising their profits. For the consumerist mentality now dominant in the West demands ever increasing economic growth – somewhere – and not least in the supply of largely superfluous items promoted as fashionable 'must-haves'. A side-effect of such 'global' habits is that local businesses rarely profit. Smaller purely national organisations, if obliged to pay a more just wage, are driven out of business, their products replaced by 'cheap' (in every sense) international versions of inferior quality and even designed to need early replacement.

In a world dominated by Consumerism – with shopping the new Sunday worship, malls its new cathedrals – immediate gain trumps concern for the long term. Well-meaning individuals (especially bishops) may prate about 'the common good', but that shibboleth of a now passing society has largely lost its reference in a Western world of increasingly isolated, lonely, even 'virtual' individuals. Philosophers in their protected Chairs may persuade their students and readers that the new 'individualism' marks a recognition of our unique autonomy; in practice it may turn out to promote 'bread and circuses' for the masses.

The paradigm case is of course China, where economic prosperity is held out for a proportion of a homogenised population, the price being the toeing of a totalitarian government's line, increasingly enforceable by digital surveillance. The rulers of Communist China and the bosses of the big international companies are basically playing the same game, bribing their donkey-like populaces with rather similar 'carrots' – though the Chinese could at least make the case that if you are starving you don't need to worry too much about freedom. Unlike their Western corporate competitors, they can boast of keeping much of their population alive and fed – not least by pampering the wider world with cheap electronic gadgetry often produced by forced labour.

Meanwhile we in the West now nourish a novel breed of international companies, more or less unchecked and presenting great opportunities for 'progress' in a totalitarian direction. 'Big-Tech' giants such as Google, Facebook and Twitter may at times be justly lauded for enabling political and social abuses in various parts of the world to be brought to light, but are also in the business both of supplying 'fake news' and of promoting some insidious so-called liberal and speciously 'progressive' agendas. While these companies purport – in this like the Chinese regime – to be benefactors of humanity, they primarily are concerned with the making of money; so if the Chinese (or any similar) regime were able to buy or otherwise gain influence among them, further aspects of totalitarianism – in 'liberal', 'free-market' disguise to begin with (a recent example being the hi-tech company Huawei) – could be imposed by stealth on our blithely materialist populace.

As we noted, 'plains men' – in the language of Herodotus, but in this case our comfortable selves – can be induced by these Tech-Giants to sell our birthright of freedom in exchange for more gadgetry – touted as more 'commodious living' but more usually its clutter! As also by China: almost weekly we hear preached the need to do more business with China because that is where the profits can be made. We are even invited (once sufficiently confused) to think that by buying their goods we can influence them to become 'nicer'. In reality, we need to face up to a self-indulgent mentality apt to tolerate an increasingly totalitarian society for ourselves and others through its consumer-driven failure of critical judgment: to recognise how in a world of increasingly bureaucratic conformity our lust to consume will encourage mental confusion: replacing the needed clear thinking with (temporary) felt satisfactions.

8 Sexual Liberation and the Subversion of the Person

Despite Britain being finally bankrupted and its Empire soon to be dispersed, and while Eastern Europeans were sold down their various rivers to Moscow, in Western Europe and North America, the immediate moral and social scene after World War II appeared at first chastened but not radically changed from its state of inter-war complacency. Certainly there arose a feeling in many lands, and immediately in the United Kingdom, that the old social injustices must be remedied: this time the peace as well as the war be won. The reformist Attlee government swept away some long-standing social evils, most notably by the construction of a National Health Service.

Similar developments would occur in France, Germany and Italy, after substantial American support for the assimilation of thousands of refugees left stranded after the Nazi defeat and with the Marshall plan enabling some basic social reforms. Thus the United States, for a while the sole great power both surviving and equipped with atomic weapons, gave Western Europe not only military protection but the opportunity to plan a greatly improved social structure and make the opening moves, in the form of the internationally welcomed Coal and Steel Community, toward what would become the European Union.

That project, while successful in securing its first aim of a lasting peace between France and Germany, was always ambiguous as to the type of political construction intended. Some among the original architects were harking back to a long-lost Christendom, but would be overtaken by those who, with hindsight, can be recognised as taking first steps toward a United States of Europe – while aware that this would not be welcome to all their constituents, and at that time to virtually none in the victorious (if exhausted) United Kingdom.

Hence the understanding to proceed by stages and by stealth, planning first an Economic Union such (as they but not their public understood) as could work effectively only if economic union were followed by a common financial policy and so with common finance reaching an at least federal state. What these would-be 'Founding Fathers' failed to divulge was the degree of centralised bureaucracy and unelected leadership their project would rely on, its officialdom backed by a European Court whose judges would sort out rights-claims.

Thus did we trundle on through post-war Austerity and the fifties, happy to be rid of the Nazis while still threatened by Communism – seriously in Greece and Italy, less seriously in France – and by The Bomb, now also in the possession of the Soviets: hoping, though materially times were still hard, soon to achieve a plateau. Yet Marxism, in its Stalinist form and soon in neo-Marxist variations, was still attractive to many among both elite and 'rank-and-file'. Particularly in Italy was the 'national' totalitarianism pioneered by Antonio Gramsci widely admired – and boosted by magnification of the heroism of a small and ruthlessly Marxist-controlled Resistance. The Communist boss Palmiro Togliatti – almost every town even now has a street named for him – took his orders directly from Moscow as to when to murder opponents (including earlier non-Communist opponents of fascism) and when to refrain. So was injected into the political life of that defeated country a myth-fuelled poison which, though happily dispersing, persists still.

As for intellectuals more generally, many in continental Europe still had not learned from the thirties that flirting with Marxist-Leninist dictatorships was a risky game: seeming naively to assume it posed risk only for that bourgeoisie so hated by those new 'divinities', the Parisian Jean-Paul Sartre and Simone de Beauvoir: of which duo, and despite her secondary role while their *liaison* lasted, the impact of De Beauvoir would in the longer run be much greater.

As Sartre's value-free 'existentialism' and strong theory of freedom, combining (somehow) with more traditional Marxism, grew outdated and unfashionable, De Beauvoir, following Engels rather than Marx, was generating theories whereby Marxist identification of the industrial and peasant proletariat as victims of the Capitalist System was displaced in favour of any group which could – Rousseau-style – assert its victimhood. For De Beauvoir herself the 'new proletariat' was women, largely understood in social terms – so she argued – as the construction of men. With this claim she elaborated one of the earliest neo-Marxist theories of 'alienated' groups, with its call for remedying – even if violent – action.

By the sixties of the last century women were not the only sector to be recognised as victims. Of at least equal political urgency in the United States were demands for the civil rights of the black population: Afro-Americans as they now demanded to be distinguished. Yet, and while even De Beauvoir did not regard women as the only group requiring deliverance from 'alienation', it was women whose 'liberation' (however understood) was destined to have the widest repercussions on Western society and eventually on a wider world. From the standpoint of a study of changing Western mentalities, the question to answer is how in the sixties De Beauvoir's challenge – followed up in America by Betty Friedan and others – would usher in what is now seen as a second, more radical feminist wave.

For as we have noticed, De Beauvoir was far from the first to advocate some form of feminism – and nor was Engels, her primary Marxist source. Some of the demands of 'second generation' feminists had been made not only by Olympe de Gouge, Mary Wollstonecraft and Tom Paine at the end of the eighteenth century, but by thinkers as far back as Plato, with his claim that women could and should take part in intellectual and political life. Nevertheless, the theories of Plato (to some extent repeated by John Stuart Mill) and even of Engels, were significantly different from those now advanced by De Beauvoir.

To begin with, Plato had believed that sexual differentiation was simply physical, while all human minds are 'male'. That encouraged him to claim that for elite women the burdens of reproduction, as enshrined in traditional marriage, should be removed in the interest of putting their gifts at the disposal of society. To that he added that families as traditionally conceived by the ruling class constituted a social threat – as indeed they often did, since loyalty to family and clan could override loyalty to the wider community, generating violence and even civil war.

Engels' view of the family was similar but cruder. A political homogeniser, he recognised that family loyalties would compete with loyalty to The Party and thus ultimately to the state as The Party conceived it. Therefore the family, a 'bourgeois' phenomenon, must go: a position appropriate to one who has no concern for the uniqueness and beauty of human individuality (as distinct from mere individualism). Nevertheless, while Engels' dismissal of the family arises out of his account of the historical inevitability of a socialist succeeded by a communist state, De Beauvoir's theory is universalising. In her view, woman as 'the other', the alienated 'neo-proletarian', will be found in all societies unless not merely political but social mentalities are radically changed. The whole relationship between men and women must be rethought: a challenging, though of itself not unreasonable proposition.

A major difficulty with De Beauvoir's thesis, as with that of other revolutionary theorists (including Marx), is that she found it easier to define what was at fault than what should replace it and how the replacement should be carried out. From the outset her account of the proper relationship between men and women is problematic. Relying on Sartre's notably narcissistic and ultra-individualist account of 'authentic' human nature, she argued that in relations between the sexes each party should want to possess the other without trading away (her or his) autonomy: hence there can be no true 'giving' in the relationship, only mutual 'profit-taking'. (Aristippus, a Greek thinker who managed to combine hedonism with admiration of

Socrates, had expressed something of the same idea more succinctly, defining his relationship with a notorious courtesan as: 'I have her, but she does not have me'.)

Accompanying De Beauvoir's views on autonomy and alienation was her Rousseauistic belief that sexual relations were properly entirely spontaneous: thus marriage is an 'obscenity' because it imposes duties, rights, rules and responsibilities on what should be a purely instinctual (and polymorphous) activity. One implication of this is that since the woman (equally with the man) is to be protected from 'enslavement' to her sexuality, any expectation of offspring (prime among aims of traditional marriage) must be abolished, with the corollary that since a pregnant woman's autonomy is threatened by her unborn child, she should have the sole right to decide to kill it. Where this rule and 'right' come from is hardly explained; implied is that its validity depends less on rational argument than on giving women the power to enforce it.

Perhaps because this conclusion conveys too totalitarian a contempt for human life, those who followed De Beauvoir would pronounce the unborn child not (yet) a human being – leaving the question open as to when he or she becomes one. At birth? On attainment of the age traditionally taken (by the Church!) as that of reason – which could imply the execution of children of under six or seven years of age? Whatever the answer, De Beauvoir and her followers would have women choose between their own short-term 'interests' and those of the future of the human race. While it was fun playing the Sartre-De Beauvoir-style sexual game, getting pregnant from it is a misfortune to be 'corrected' by the woman becoming unpregnant. Certainly the newly developed (contraceptive) 'pill' would help; its effects were soon being seen in the ageing societies of Europe and Japan and most spectacularly in China where the 'one child policy', with its fallback forced abortions, would result in an onslaught predominantly on the female foetus, with resulting lack of partners for the generally preferred males. Female-on-female killings might seem an odd result for a project claimed to benefit women. It becomes intelligible within a totalitarian mindset.

*

De Beauvoir, though by far the most influential sexual revolutionary of her period (her book, *Le Deuxième Sexe*, appeared as early as 1949 but gained its wide popularity at a rather later date), was far from a lone voice, even apart from more orthodox followers of Engels. In the United States, where 'second wave' feminism was to be followed by a more anarchic third wave, two thinkers would be especially influential. The first was Herbert Marcuse, though his immediate vogue was partly eclipsed by his own admission of error. A theoretical forerunner of the libertine sixties, he had published *Eros and Civilization: A Philosophical Enquiry into Freud* in 1955 but retracted its basic claims in 1964 – by when the genie was well out of the bottle and few would be impressed by what could be dismissed as a 'failure of nerve'.

Marcuse's approach had been to blend Marxism with a bastardised version of Freud's analysis of sexuality: retaining, that is, Freud's 'pleasure principle' but ignoring that 'reality principle' to which, as Freud argued, the pleasure principle will need to be subordinated in the well-integrated and productive individual. By treating of a sexual 'sublimation' lacking recourse to such realism and claiming to liberate sex from 'alienation' (with its 'capitalist' implications), Marcuse was in effect writing a libertine's charter, and as was hardly surprising, the sublimation failed to occur, the fornication continuing on its merry path. The appearance of 'the (contraceptive) pill' was welcomed by Western women seizing the chance to imitate male libertinism – as well as the many men happy to encourage them to do so.

Marcuse's arguments might – from a distance – seem largely frivolous. The same cannot be said of the next prophet to follow in De Beauvoir's train. In 1963 Betty Friedan's *The Feminine Mystique*, while generally avoiding ideological premises, certainly probed a raw human wound. After World War II, with the returning home of the GIs, there had been a revived version of the domestic idyll, with consequent birth of a multitude of 'baby boomers'. But under the apparently smooth surface, Friedan discovered a deep unhappiness in many American 'dolly-birds', especially among the more educated, now stuck at home looking after the children and expected not to get bored and frustrated doing nothing besides. Friedan's call was for an end to the 'mythology' and a much greater participation of women in the public sphere: not on grounds of ambition nor even for the general economic good, but for their psychological health. Her book was a runaway success, understandably treated by many, especially in the United States, as a Gospel of liberation.

Despite such writings – and many less well known – the Sexual Revolution, in all its aspects, took the world largely by surprise, leaving the leaders of conventional society baffled about how to meet it and many deciding to cave in to the new and 'modern' ways – presumably on the principle of. 'If you can't beat 'em, join 'em'! The sight of fifty-five-year-old men undergoing the 'male menopause' while attempting to be 'lads' in the new-found freedoms, was at least a source of entertainment. In universities, professors seducing their (more usually graduate) students – or being seduced by them – became part of a scene, in Britain assisted by the abolition of the legal concept of students being 'in statu pupillari' which had made their mentors officially responsible for them. More widely, T-shirts were seen proclaiming, 'Help stamp out virginity', or 'A nymphomaniac is a woman with the sexual desires of the average man', while 'fuckin'' replaced 'bloody' (originally 'By'r Lady') as the expletive of choice, sexual imagery being more appropriate than religious to the phallocratic age.

It all happened so fast. It would be of the still recent fifties that the society novelist Margaret Drabble would pronounce, 'We thought we were the first of the free. We found we were the last of the frumps'. The ambiguity of her observation transpires in no doubt many examples from those happy days, but here are a couple of memories from the authors of this book, undergraduate students at the

University of Cambridge in the mid-to-late 'fifties. One is comparatively trivial and local; the other indicates the delusions at the heart of what remained of the older European Christian establishment.

At this time its statutes, apparently propped up by Parliamentary legislation, decreed that our University might admit women in a proportion of one to ten men. (One regrets to record that this select quota of women was known – even among themselves – as 'undergraduettes'!) The more 'progressive' among us ritually complained about the statute, yet never would have thought it would be swept away within the next ten years – as would segregation by college – with very little protest: providing an example of a piece of institutional inertia easily abolished in the early stage of a social revolution.

At about the same time a much more significant change impended for what remained of the authority of the Christian Churches over sexual morality and the appropriate relationships between men and women. During the Second Vatican Council (1962–1965), Pope Paul VI removed the subject of artificial contraception from the agenda, reserving to himself a decision that was obviously required. He may have feared the Council Fathers succumbing to the urge to show themselves 'contemporary': after all, his predecessor, Pope John XXIII, had called the Council in the name of *aggiornamento* or a bringing-up-to-date.

Be that as it may, when eventually Paul took his lonely and fateful decision, neglecting the advice of his appointed counsellors in order to reaffirm the ban on artificial contraception, he was astonished not (one hopes) that he was pilloried by the secular press, but at so many Catholics rejecting what he taught – as their formula for Confession has it – as to be followed in 'word, deed and omission'. That he was apparently unaware this was likely to happen may suggest he was no longer in touch with the world in which it was his calling to teach.

There ensued a not-unrelated 'awakening' of his clergy, many of whom, instead of following their leader's decision, bolted from the stable in the happy belief that, as on other matters relating to 'empowerment' of the female, times they were a-changing whatever the Pope said. These left the clerical state in droves, throwing over their solemn vows in favour of the new freedoms all about them – formerly met chiefly as sins confided in the confessional. Some of us referred to them as 'late bloomers' and wondered what could have been their state of mind only weeks earlier. But it seemed more pathetic than amusing.

All this in the 'sixties was indeed a revolution, and in revolutions, whether political, social or religious, the tendency is for more extreme prophets to seize the advantage from more moderates: thus Mirabeau is succeeded by Robespierre, Kerensky by Lenin, Hindenburg by Hitler. The Catholic Church is not supposed to provide, like the nation-state, an arena for power-grabbing; however, its very hypothesis implies that there too – or especially – the devil has his designs! And there too one can observe the secularising challenge of Loisy, Tyrrell and other early twentieth-century 'Modernists' (even after being apparently absorbed by a constructive reformism of such as Congar, De Lubac and Daniélou) returning in strength with an overtly anti-traditional programme associated with actual religious indifferentism and inevitably issuing in moral license.

This trend – claiming to invoke the 'spirit' of the Second Vatican Council rather than that Council's decrees – could best be seen in the post-conciliar avatar of the Society of Jesus, culminating in the election of the first Jesuit Pope, the Argentinian Jorge Bergoglio. Deliberately ever ambiguous lest intended changes appear too revolutionary for even episco-bureaucrats and clerical time-servers to swallow, the Pope of the disarming name Francis I might be well denoted – in the words of Tacitus of the Roman Emperor Tiberius – *occultior non melior*.

*

The pursuit of sexual liberation did not end with De Beauvoir, Marcuse and Betty Friedan, none of whom yet attempted to induce

Westerners to disbelieve the evidence of their senses. That totalitarian advance into madness remained for such 'third-wave' feminists as Judith Butler, Susan Moller Okin, Adrienne Rich: those whose revised claims were not limited to the rectifying of perceived wrongs suffered by females, nor even the demand that 'male' libertinism should be enjoyed by women. The whole concept of sexual difference as understood by humanity since Adam and Eve – and of course as represented by Western Christianity and post-Christianity – had to be recast. Philosophical tools were to hand to misuse in the work in progress. With access to levers of power exercised in a world where, in universities and other one-time homes of free debate, such debate might be increasingly subverted – and even denied, with speakers being blackballed – the operation has been corrosive of truth and rationality.

Of the philosophers to be misused, first was Nietzsche, who denied the existence of truth (except, that is, those truths perceived by himself), his view being that all we have is varying perspectives. Not that that implies the perspectives are not true, but that often they are limited or incomplete; nor, although perspectives may be different, is there anything objectionable in asserting what we really *believe* to be true. Only some of our beliefs will be madness: the more mad will include those unintelligible to others as not corresponding to reality as enshrined in a common language.

If I think of a knife as a cutting instrument, I do not know its essence, only that what I call a knife can cut; others will use the word 'knife' in the same way, and thus is language formed by the agreement of groups of people that certain words are used to denote certain objects or purposes: we approach a knife from similar 'perspectives' and thus learn the sense of the (English) word 'knife'. Nietzsche's account of truth as perspective neither prevents us from knowing enough about a knife for most ordinary purposes nor from knowing to what the word 'knife' refers: nor – as is recently more apposite – to what the (English) word 'boy' or 'girl' refers. Hence if we agree on certain visible signs, we name a newborn (or now preborn) person a boy or a girl; thus confusion does not arise.

Ah, now comes the reply: we do not have to identify people by what we see. When the midwife sees a newborn baby's penis, she says she sees a boy, but we can deny that, claiming she has merely identified the child conventionally as a boy because it has 'male' genitals – and this is misleading because 'it' did not choose to have them and is not to be identified by 'its' bodily manifestations. Notice that this claim does not merely deny that a feature identifying male or female, is the genitals, but further that bodily form has nothing whatever to do with sexual identity. According to this supposition, we would be non-bodily – perhaps, 'angelic'? – beings. Or perhaps our identity resides only in our will (as in some sense Nietzsche believed), our bodies being accidental appendages. But then we must ask: to what are they appended, and how? 'Third wave' feminists debar themselves from being materialists or even soul-body dualists; indeed what account of the whole person can they give?

In this dilemma they may turn to Nietzsche again, at least as interpreted by Michel Foucault, or to so-called post-Modernists more generally. Yet in so doing they would seem to neglect that post-Modernism (as normally understood) seems to combine two apparently irreconcilable claims: first that autonomy is all (the tradition inherited from Kant and Rousseau) but at the same time that individuals are to such an extent the products of society and social conditioning that, as Derrida concluded, there is no such thing as 'an author': merely an echo of the society to which the (supposed) author belongs. (Whence an academic 'urban myth' to the effect that Derrida would have no claim upon someone who translated one of his books without permission, the translator defending himself on the grounds of Derrida's own claim that there is no such thing as an author.)

Leaving the contradictions inherent in post-Modern theory and returning to the influence of Foucault on third-wave feminism, we learn that not only are we basically our unattached will, but we must rebel against – and as necessary penalise – those (dismissed as mere 'patriarchal' power-players) who would insist that our hormones, chromosomes and more superficial bodily features have anything do with our authentic and sexually fluid selves. Our world is to be entirely created by our changing social beliefs – about facts or ideas and most assuredly about sexuality, where seeming facts are to be treated *as* (mere) ideas. Easy to see why 'third wave' feminists find strong allies not only in Foucault but more widely in the community of homosexual activists that also claims to rewrite nature according to will. For such 'revisionists' there is no necessary connection between genitalia and procreation; something or other has given us genitals as toys to play with in whatever way we prefer; there is no heterosexual norm.

It has been claimed that at times during the World War II American soldiers who referred to their rifle as a gun were marched around camp, rifle in one hand, penis in the other, proclaiming: 'This is my rifle and this is my gun; the one is for fighting, the other for fun'. For 'third wave' feminist disciples of Foucault, that would be based on a false premise if the military disciplinarian assumed the fun to be specifically male and heterosexual. Since for Foucault social, and especially sexual activity is largely reducible to power-plays, he presumably would approve the identification penis=gun – and the slang 'my tool' carries much the same idea: both figure the penis as an instrument of control – therein concurring with a Freudian view of 'third wave' feminists as governed by penis-envy: engaged in a battle against a sensed deprivation of 'phallic' power.

In pointing to this absurdity in such feminist exaggeration, it is important to note that the sociology of 'gender' – that is, of how a given society holds that men and women should behave – can be a significant discipline, with views judged good or wanting: which is to say humane or inhumane. Put otherwise, it makes perfectly good sense to study what a given society expects of males and females, without straying onto the ground of what males and females actually *are*. To study such material sociologically does not demand any denial of the evidence of the senses, nor commit one to a theory such as that we are 'really' just our own will to power. It is intellectually disreputable – before it is socially destructive – when Women's Studies in

Western Universities indoctrinate women (in particular) to accept as dogma what is merely a view – more especially if a perverse one.

It should not have so turned out. Yet universities, institutions supposed to encourage thoughtful criticism of any and all orthodoxies without fear or favour, without lying and the misrepresentation of opponents, have from the latter part of the twentieth century till now – and among them the more prestigious – signally failed in what they were established to do. Two devices in particular have been used to suppress challenges to orthodoxies given the seal of approval by Hollywood, much TV and social-media wisdom and the bosses of Silicon Valley.

The first device is the regular employment – in the 'liberal' West – of euphemisms common enough in Hitlerian or Stalinist regimes. The Nazis spoke not of the murder – nor normally even of the extermination – of Jews but of a 'Final Solution of the Jewish Problem'. Not dissimilar is naming the intervention to end the life of an unborn child a 'termination'.

The second device – also traditional among totalitarians – is censorship, which may be open or covert. Openly it takes the form of banning books, arresting those who write (or speak) what is too challenging to those in power – as latterly for their 'snowflake' adherents. There may be a threat to bring the authors to court on politically-motivated charges, and whether legally or in the court of public opinion, those so convicted may be dismissed from their academic posts: thus those who argue that children are damaged by being brought up by two homosexual 'parents' are branded 'homophobic'; meanwhile anyone arguing (from history) that Muhammed was a warlord is 'Islamophobic'. Such is the 'left-liberal' mindset and agenda, governed not by truth, let alone principle, but by an assortment of disparate and unexamined assumptions, if not of lies.

This persecution is now regularly extended to figures of the past: thus in a number of universities in the United States, the once revered George Washington is merely vilified as a slave-owner. Which he was, but not all that he was, and to write him off so is to preclude recognition and study of his other, often highly important and worthy activities. Indeed both in universities and more widely in public media, things have almost reached the stage where anyone accusing another of racism or of being a white-supremacist or an imperialist can be assumed to be engaged in some kind of ideologically-motivated deceit, whether by character assassination or by the reduction of debate to a moronic simplicity where anything goes so long as we can get some ignoramuses to accept it uncritically – thinking perhaps that they are being thus 'empowered'. That is the level to which Humanities departments in many of our universities have sunk.

For the ultimate aim of 'liberal-totalitarian' programmes, in universities and elsewhere, would seem – again – to be not understanding (or even 'enlightenment') but homogenisation. Thus that we are all to an extent sexually fluid is exaggerated into the claim that we can make ourselves what we will and further that no particular lifestyle can have any special value or dignity; we are human machines and may be manipulated at our (or – and more ominously – others') will. Indeed it can seem that the aim of 'third wave' feminists and their dupes is to indulge their interpretation of Nietzsche's Will to Power at the expense of the wider society. For Nietzsche's 'over-man', we are to have the dominance of the over-woman ('over-men' if they so choose to call themselves): another example of the reduction of democratic equality to a willed identity – with a claimed elimination (by mere denial) of human difference, sexual or other.

Nor are Nietzsche and Foucault the only philosophers enrolled as supporters of 'third-wave' feminism and its (frequently homosexual) backers. The writings of J.L. Austen may be misused to the same effect, where Austen draws to our attention that some verbs act as 'performatives' in bringing about – 'enacting' – that of which we speak. 'I take thee (X) to be my wedded husband/wife' commits me (in the appropriate social circumstances) to be 'married to' the person named. Somewhat similarly, taking the required oath in court commits me to be an honest witness. But not all verbs are performatives. If the midwife states of the newborn, 'It is a girl', she is not making it a girl; nothing performative is involved in the assertion; simply noted are bodily features of the newborn child. Whatever she or the doctor or anyone else says can in no way affect the hormonal and chromosomal make-up of this child, this person – let alone its 'essence'. To pretend it does is at best sophistry.

But things can get even more bizarre and socially threatening. Some third-wave feminists will claim that all heterosexual penetration – which they refer to as part of the culture of compulsory heterosexuality – is to be labelled as rape, whether the female partner welcomes it or not; they thus would deny her (and all our) ability to distinguish between violent and non-violent (or indeed undesired and desired) sexual behaviour. How on earth, we may wonder, could such sophistry be taught in universities?

The kinder Freudian explanation might be that such claimants are sufferers from hysteria. Otherwise we are here confronted by wilful distortion. It is of course the case that some women are forced into marriages they do not want. That might be thought of as a form of rape, but to claim that all marriages are rapes is nothing more than a particularly blatant attempt to prevent us doing what we have argued in the Introduction is a key task of philosophy: the making of proper distinctions. Happily, with a view to the empowerment of women remaining in touch with reality, a safer guide than such ideological sophists had already spoken. That, however, must be deferred for the following chapter.

*

After inspecting the radical, if bizarre, anti-human projects of the twentieth and twenty-first century sexual ideologues, we might perhaps hope to find relief in the more sophisticated and acclaimed philosophical performers active in the same decades; however, if we expect to find refreshment we shall be disappointed. Normally in recent decades, 'Anglo-Saxons' have had to choose between the philistine materialism of the Utilitarians – by now no longer agreeing on what 'goods' should be 'maximised' – and Kantianism without the necessary (but rather necessarily to be discarded) 'noumenal-phenomenal' distinction required to make it intelligible. 'Continentals' also might opt for Kant – otherwise Hegel, Marx or some post-Marxist ideologist: even Heidegger's star has hardly waned among his more die-hard admirers, in despite of his membership of the Nazi party, his not unconnected antisemitism and his value-free emphasis on the Will – if not to Power then to 'authenticity'.

Heidegger's understanding of the human person had taken a knock before his 'late period' began with his Bremen Lectures of 1949. It may be presumed that the events of the 'forties, culminating in the defeat and near-destruction of Germany, had persuaded him to substitute cultural superiority for his earlier racial – and distinctly racist – predilection: for Germans in particular, for whom he claimed an 'inner relationship' with the language and culture of the ancient (preferably pre-Platonic) Greeks. Perhaps it might not have surprised him that his stance has something important in common with that of a mere Anglo-Saxon luminary, Derek Parfit.

Heidegger had wanted to diminish the individual by assimilating him first to the state, then, apparently, to a higher Culture wherever to be found (by 1949 not necessarily in Germany). Parfit too, apparently without political ambition but in an attempt to make Utilitarianism more palatable, argues that we overestimate our individual importance – being in this influential in an intellectual trend toward a more scientistic impersonality. As revised (Lockean) 'serial selves' precariously tied together by a new understanding of memory-chains, we 'matter' much less than we suppose. If we would only recognise that, we should be less self-obsessed, *ergo* more altruistic. (This goes against the more normally accepted view among psychologists such as Erich Fromm, that unless we have respect for ourselves we are unlikely to have much for anyone else.) If only, continues Parfit, we could recognise that a clone would be 'as good or almost as good' as ourselves, we would also worry less about our coming death; thus would be diminished the curiously modern fear of extinction – relieving Heideggerian fears of 'perishing like savages who have no history', rather than dying 'authentically' like Nietzschean (or Nazi) heroes.

Parfit's claim as to the low worth of the individual is part of a wider thesis about moral philosophy. His explicitly godless ethical stance – if viewed from a theistic standpoint such as that of the Original Tradition – makes our comparative worthlessness more explicable. 'Disbelief in God', he tells us, 'openly admitted by a majority,' (he means, presumably, in the West) 'is a recent event, not yet completed. Non-religious ethics is at a very early stage and we cannot yet predict whether, as in mathematics, we will all reach agreement. Still, and since we cannot know how ethics will develop, it is not irrational to have high hopes.'

Parfit's claim is more honest than current alternatives that aim to justify Utilitarianism by reviving Mill's (or Sidgwick's or Moore's) more sophisticated recasting of Bentham's original project; at least we do not have to resort to deception, offering an alternative and 'virtual' morality as others in the past have offered a virtual religion. Parfit does not encourage the herd to carry on praising the older virtues and rejecting the older vices (especially lust) in the interests of 'social glue' – with the sophisticated elites well aware that there are no good arguments for any claim to moral objectivism, nor for that matter for any version of free will. As his thought develops, however, further oddities appear. In a second and massive book he professes himself surprised that his claims about our diminished importance have been taken to point to nihilism; he holds that they point to a helpful assimilation of Kant with the Utilitarians. Not only is he no nihilist himself; rather all moral theories *other* than his own point toward nihilism!

Parfit supposes that we should all want to eliminate pain and maximise happiness, neglecting that some pains may be morally (as well as physically) beneficial and that he has nothing not merely conventional to say about happiness. Moreover, where does that 'should' come from? Is it not – as so often – deduced from what some philosopher thinks we would rightly (ought to?) *prefer*? Parfit denies that too: he is, he claims, an objectivist, though holding that moral 'truths' have – like the truths of logic and mathematics – no 'ontological status'. They are, that is, useful devices, but what does that analogy imply? What relation might he assume logical and mathematical necessities have to *moral* truths?

Perhaps Parfit has fallen back on some version of Kant's implausible claim – discussed in an earlier chapter – that to be moral is no more than to manage to be rational. Or can it be that, in elaborating on his earlier account of our fragile serial selves and our comparative worthlessness, Parfit's introduction of logical necessity is merely a way of protecting himself against the charge that in his earlier writings he had failed to notice the nihilist implications of his arguments? For others had pointed them out, and it is worth noting that deconstructionists had pontificated on similar lines with more specifically nihilist intent: Derrida, in particular, introduces 'serial selves' to support his claim that all notions (of, say, friendship, empathy, etc.) can be unmasked as incoherent, therefore unintelligible.

For Derrida, of course, the positing of serial selves is merely ancillary to the more fundamental, if seriously flawed, claim that, though we think we have limited understanding of some moral or aesthetic concept (again say friendship or empathy), we have no knowledge of its 'essence': hence can only speak of it incoherently. In fact – as we noted earlier – in such cases we do not have to know the essence (whatever that is) in question, but only how the word, descriptive or evaluative – 'the rigid designator' in Saul Kripke's technical language – is used for specific purposes in intelligible speech. Following such conventions does not in itself make us incoherent. If Parfit disappoints in ethics, Derrida fails in epistemology.

Noting in passing that post-modernists, here as elsewhere, do nothing to reduce current confusion – noting too the parallels in recent evolutions of Anglo-American and 'Continental' philosophy – we conclude that Parfit's anti-personalism – in its own way reducing humanity to the evolving animal, the consumer, the bureaucrat, the phallocrat, the near-nonentity – is no argued objectivism but a construct of its times: Heidegger in softer, more trivialised guise.

9 Personalism, Virtue Ethics and the Original Tradition

Universally Man is the father of Man, but there is no Man, but Peleus is the father of Achilles and your father is the father of you.

Aristotle

In the last two chapters we have traversed much ground in order to set out the immediate backdrop to our contemporary social, and more specifically intellectual agonies. We have identified both political actualities and theories (whether or not these have always been correctly understood) of philosophers in the main German – plus wilful blindness, both political and intellectual, in European and Anglo-American thinkers and readers more generally. We have looked at Fascism, Communism, Internationalism, Feminism, postmodernism, consumerism, 'Big Tech' and the 'sexual revolution'. We now return to the present state of our Original Tradition, still available and a possible resource as we attempt to resolve our contemporary perplexities – yet increasingly drawn on only as a desperate (and often unadmitted) last resort.

As we have shown in Chapters 2 and 3 of this essay, the centuries between Plato in the fifth century BC and Aquinas in the thirteenth century AD witnessed the gradual formation in Europe of the concept of a universe created by a monotheistic, though Trinitarian, God, in which the laws of nature are of divine origin and human beings – composed of body and soul – are the supreme product of that creation and formed in God's 'image and likeness': hence reflecting in their personhood the divine 'dignity'. In brief, they – we – matter. And though we humans have become corrupted so as to live in a now 'fallen' world and subject to sin and death, we hold – unless we are

Calvinists – that we are not entirely corrupted, and that at least some of us, salvaged by God's 'grace', shall live with a 'spiritual' body and a purified soul in God's Presence that we denote heaven.

This enchanting, if in some respects terrifying, picture was a fragile construction and its portrait of both man and universe too easily (if often irrationally) picked apart. In subsequent chapters we have dwelt on features of an alternative world, constructed as that Judaeo-Christian picture was widely rejected: with wars of mass destruction and deadly weapons hitherto unimagined; with bureaucracy, totalitarianisms of differing stripes and an increasing belief that man, in his desperately claimed autonomy, can manipulate not only material nature (as Descartes and others had hoped) but also his own. Westerners had come to believe that, the human race having evolved from lower life-forms, that process of evolution is now in our own hands. As 'persons', as once we had learned to understand them, were subjected to political manipulation and explained away by the scientific (or scientistic) use or abuse of new knowledge, so in self-proclaimed 'liberal' societies it was coming to be held that humans and humanity no longer 'matter' much, if at all: it is the system – hence power – that comes to matter.

Indeed, with God dead, why should we humans matter? And not only was God dead, but any kind of 'transcendental' metaphysic implying that raw or transiently formed matter was not all there was increasingly disappeared from view – except in vague notices of 'spirituality', often in the context of the 'arts', whether 'graphic' or of literature, music or architecture: and it might be noticed that these had tended over the past century or so to collapse into less appealing, more utilitarian or crudely provocative forms. Such have come to seem like mere ghosts of a past account of the world, with much 'art' reflecting the now trivialised person and, even if often ingenious, abandoning any intention to 'inspire' its readers, viewers or listeners; rather it will invite us to indulge in vicarious sexual excitement or specious lamentation on how grim things have become – at least for others. None the less do those who, with whatever justification, still call themselves artists, hail themselves and are hailed as the nearest approximation to gods we can entertain. Assuredly they may be thought less dangerous (at least in the short run) than other claimants to a virtual divinity in more blatantly totalitarian regimes.

Yet some still cling to glimpses of a brighter future. Persons may still matter; 'personalists' have re-appeared as a minority group on the philosophical horizon. At first these may have looked more nostalgic than realistic, some apparently longing for a return to the older 'Christian times' (*tempora Christiana*). Naturally it was to later heroes of those times that they first appealed: the 'summations' of a Christian world-view as 'Summa''d in the thirteenth century could be reconstructed. In 1879 Pope Leo XIII's encyclical *Aeterni Patris* urged more serious attention to Thomism, hopefully in its original form, rather than via various deformations to which it had succumbed since the Reformation. Yet he and his advisers normally failed to recognise that the Thomism of the more 'modern' Suarez was not the Thomism of Aquinas himself: an error it has taken time to correct.

Leo's efforts to stem the tide of 'liberalism' and Marxism would give rise at first either to attempts to blend the old with the new and trendy by reading Thomas Aquinas as a Kantian, or alternatively to follow him slavishly in what was thought to be a 'Thomism of strict observance'. Still, on the horizon appeared the possibility of blending the best of the older metaphysics with a serious navigating of the anti-metaphysical minefield sown by the labours of Hume and Kant and still causing mortal injury to the unwary.

One possible centre for further advance seemed to be Paris, where Emmanuel Mounier founded the 'personalist' journal *Esprit* in 1932. Mounier's ideas were publicised by Jacques Maritain, whose influence was strong in North America as well as in Europe. Maritain held 'personalism' to be a legitimate extension of the thought of Aquinas, offering a metaphysic with psychological and ethical attachments which might have satisfied Leo's intentions. However, although his memory is still revered and there are philosophical organisations dedicated to keeping it green, Maritain debased his 'personalism' by overhasty acceptance of the transformation of older accounts of human dignity into more recent and problematic versions of rights-theory: so indeed had Leo. Maritain also – as we have noted – entertained fantasies as to the Christian potential of the post-Christian new world of international organisations to clean up the ghastly political landscape through which he and his converted Jewish wife Raissa had lived in the earlier twentieth century.

The real breakthrough would occur not in Paris but in German-speaking lands, with Franz Brentano (1838–1917) whose revised Aristotelianism opened up the road to a more viable form of personalism. Edmund Husserl (1859–1938), Brentano's pupil in Vienna, would dismantle the Hume-Kant barrier, leaving the way open for an improved psychology and consequent ethical theory able to blend with a comparatively traditional, though less exclusive, Thomism still in need of 'personalist' and other modifications. Husserl's emphasis on the intentionality of consciousness pointed to an account of human action less drearily determined or manipulated, less to be explained as based on merely subjective constructions; his students' slogan would become 'back to the things themselves', indicating their recognition that his challenge to Hume's account of what is given in perception (disastrously accepted by Kant) called for a first-person, less scientistic account of everyday life and experience without falling back on subjectivism.

Husserl, originally a mathematician who eschewed traditional metaphysics, developed Brentano's concern with intentionality into an investigation of experience from a first person point of view, thus allowing for a humanistic – as well as (not instead of) a more statistical, third person account of the human condition. Some of his students – notably Edith Stein in Germany and Roman Ingarden, who would introduce phenomenology into fruitful soil in Poland – thought that he eventually succumbed to the very 'idealism' (that is, subjectivism) to which he originally objected; still the spell of that idealism had been broken in the lands where it originated.

The phenomenological movement managed to penetrate the Anglo-Saxon world to a rather limited degree, forming a minority tradition in the United States.

Phenomenology is not a metaphysic but an approach to human experience and behaviour; therefore if it was to pass from the capacity to provide a better *description* of human beings to allow for a defence of the claim that human beings *matter*, it had to be allied with some metaphysical or theological construction, rather than rely solely on epistemological and psychological analysis. Husserl himself was inclined to fall back on a version of Cartesian-Kantian idealism, and among his followers the influence of Kant proved hard to eliminate. Thus Max Scheler, delivering what he took to be a metaphysical and psychological account of human nature based on the 'feeling' he considered to be love, still insisted that Kant's ethics superseded anything more Aristotelian, even though admittedly too 'formalist'. According to Scheler, Kant had shown that what the autonomous self wills to be right *is* right insofar as it is rational – but since Kant had failed to explain the 'content' of rightness, and hence of goodness, he had been far from able to account for human worth.

Scheler accepted Kant's attempt to explain persons in terms not of Aristotelian substances but of consciousness: 'The person must never be considered a *thing* or a *substance* with faculties or powers ... The person is the immediately co-experienced *unity of experiencing*; the person is not a merely thought thing behind and outside what is immediately experienced'. Here Scheler has followed Kant in identifying a single aspect of persons as what 'really' makes them persons: thus 'it belongs to the essence of the person to exist and to live solely in the execution of intentional acts'. True, the sense of 'intentional' is ambiguous, but it suggests that if I am rendered unconscious by accident or illness, and thus unable to perform intentional acts, I cease to be a person. That this is indeed what Scheler meant is made clear when he continues: '[The word] person is ascribed only to a certain level of development of man. A child manifests ego-ness, possession of soul, and consciousness of self but this does not make him a person in the moral sense'.

The question-begging phrase 'in the moral sense' implies that children (and others) are not persons and therefore lack the value which persons, according to Scheler, possess. Thus Scheler demonstrates once again that a merely improved description of human capacities is not enough to guarantee intrinsic value to human beings as such. He has in effect again defied the more Aristotelian position that the young are persons with potential for development, substituting the undefended (and indefensible) assumption that they are 'potential persons'.

A very different, more contemporary phenomenologist, Karol Wojtyla, recognised that Scheler's phenomenology (devoid as it is of any Aristotelian, or better Thomist, metaphysic) is unable to offer an objective account of persons which would allow for their possible dignity. In *The Acting Person*, *The Theology of the Body* and elsewhere, Wojtyla developed a description of the sexualised human agent that serves as useful correction to the Christian tendency to prudishness. Yet though managing to sound more contemporary – and doubtless preoccupied after his election as Pope John Paul II – he failed to advance his metaphysical supplement to phenomenology much beyond that of Aquinas' original.

Nonetheless, much necessary corrective to that original, with reference both to the radical nature of sexuality in the human psyche and to the inadequacy of Aquinas' account of individuals, had already been placed on the philosophical table, and appropriately by a woman. Edith Stein, a German Jewess, was Husserl's boldest and most original student – Heidegger perhaps apart, but while Heidegger would end by contributing to the catalogue of human perversion, Stein, lacking his fatal attraction to Nazism, would prove rational and level-headed – even, it appears, when arrested in Holland and transported to die in Auschwitz.

*

Stein's doctoral thesis under Husserl was on empathy – an eighteenth-century theme she examines in a new and more sophisticated phenomenological setting. This would prove especially helpful in her later controversy with Heidegger about the proper understanding of death. She was for several months a military nurse during World War I and that experience, combined with her Husserlian concern with what is given in perception, enabled her to reject Heidegger's account of the isolation of the person (*Dasein*) and thus by implication his view that the only – and temporary – 'redemption' lies in assimilation to the will of the state. According to Heidegger, our attitude to death will show whether we were capable of an 'authentic' – that is an honest – life; however, the state becoming irrelevant as the individual dies, the ordinary mortal will be overwhelmed by the prospect of extinction, hence 'perishes' alone rather than performing the authentic 'act' of dying fearlessly. (Even the later Heidegger, advocate, after 'the turn', of assimilation to Culture rather than the Nazi state, still spoke of 'perishing'.)

Before recounting Stein's commentary on this, it is important to recall that Heidegger's Wagnerian attitude to death can help us understand a radical difference between contemporary man and his medieval and Graeco-Roman predecessors – for whom what was feared about death was normally not extinction but survival: what might happen to us after we have died. Rejecting this fear, Socrates had argued that, the nature of the gods being as it is, the next life must either be better than this one or at worst a peaceful cessation of labours; that since on the latter scenario we have no sensation, death is 'nothing to us'. Epicurus, though rejecting the hope of a better existence after death, concurred that with loss of sensation we have nothing to fear. Thus the fear of extinction – for Heidegger characteristic of modern man – was no acknowledged problem in ancient (or medieval) times. To the contrary: for the Socrates of the *Phaedo*, philosophy itself is a 'practice for death' and our ensuing survival.

Stein's account of dying, and the possibility of empathy with the dying – perhaps the most perceptive yet proposed, as enriched by her experience as a nurse – is a rejection of Heidegger's and implies a very different view of humanity which would accompany her to her violently truncated earthly end. It is not nothingness we fear but the loss of what we have and have been *given*. What we desire to continue to receive is the 'ever-new gift of Being', for we are not, as Heidegger supposed, merely 'thrown into' being; we receive it as a gift, this marking, as Stein explains the phenomenon, the necessary dependence of each of us not only on one another (as empathy testifies) but on the giver and our source. Hence she can move, from a phenomenological vision of human life as given, to a religious and metaphysical account of that 'given' dependency. By recognition of the 'necessary' (that is, non-dependent) existence of our source we add an intelligible account of our perceived dignity to a better understanding of our dependent nature.

Eventually Stein would conclude that a revised and where necessary improved version of the 'perennial philosophy' of our Original Tradition as given by Aquinas could still provide the metaphysical groundwork for an account of the Catholic faith she had adopted and which in no way contradicted what she saw as necessary phenomenological understanding and objectivism. No 'Thomist of strict observance', she corrected a significant weakness in Thomistic theory, going on to develop some corollaries and implications of that correction.

This required correction was that in reflecting on human nature we must pass beyond universals: that is linguistic items which sum up the characteristics of various natural sets; such are humans, elephants, fleas, trees, etc. We must take more seriously the metaphysical uniqueness of each human being. According to Augustine – whose emphasis on that uniqueness had usually been forgotten – this implies that metaphysics as traditionally developed cannot account for human individuality but must be supplemented by biographical or autobiographical accounts of each individual life with its unique set of characterising causes, whether genetic (as we would now say) or arising from lived experience. But perhaps what has been traditionally developed in metaphysics can be developed further.

Stein came to understand that human beings cannot be summed up 'without remainder' as members of a numbered set; we need more serious *metaphysical* reflection on the first person aspects of each human individual. (She does not discuss unique differentiations in animals, though her theorising would allow for it.) In this she remained in line with her phenomenological training while acknowledging the influence of Duns Scotus, as also of Plato and the Platonic tradition, not to speak of her beloved Teresa of Avila. She did not know that her conclusions would be compatible with coming theories of genetics where the structure (i.e. form) unique to each individual is confirmed by the differentiated DNA. What she had shown – and enabled us to understand – is that where in the older tradition of Christian metaphysics we could differentiate Jim from Jack numerically, we could now do so qualitatively – as also, and for her importantly, Jack from Jill, as well as Jill from Jacqueline.

The problem Stein had to face is that Aquinas, supposing he was following Aristotle, held that individuality is determined with reference to matter alone: 'matter distinguished by quantity'. But for Aristotle raw or 'prime' matter is merely a convenient abstraction, since actual matter is always 'formed' in some way: thus wherever there is matter there is form – and wherever there is *living* form there is 'soul'. As for Aquinas, his reading of Aristotle was addressed not to *differences* between individuals but only to the *plurality* of individuals within a set. The incompleteness of such analysis, Stein knew, had been identified by Scotus – though earlier, as we have observed, the Stoics and Plotinus had been aware of it.

As we have noted, Scotus wanted an explanation of 'thisness' (*haecceitas*). His solution, which he thought of as in the Aristotelian tradition, was that we need to posit not only the Form of Man, but individual forms of individual men and women. There he had stopped, not asking whether the souls of men and women significantly differ not only as distinct human beings but also as differently sexed human beings. Nor did he conclude that a Form of Man (in general) must be a reified, formal concept, useful for referring to a common human nature that is only instantiated in interrelated individuals. As Aristotle himself had put it: 'Universally, Man is the father of Man, but there is no Man, but Peleus is the father of Achilles and your father is the father of you'.

From her Scotist principle Stein now drew the requisite conclusion with its significant consequences: namely that the most fundamental distinction among humans is between male and female, these yielding two subsets of humanity. To explain the nature of each human individual we must first recognise him or her *as* a human being, then distinguish to which sex this individual belongs, then his or her particular characteristics within members of the same sex. From that Stein further realised that Aristotle was right to argue that where there are physiological differences there are also psychological differences – even while wrong to infer that one subset of humans must be superior to the other: the two 'forms' of humanity are equally human, but women are differentiated from men not only by their female bodies but by female souls ('forms' in the stricter Aristotelian sense). Thus not only are there forms of individuals but roughly half of human individuals have male forms (or souls: as we saw, Aristotle uses both terms), half have female.

Stein's argument that we need to account not only for individual differences between members of the same set but also between the two sub-groups of the wider 'set', namely males and females, enables her to offer a much superior account of the relationship between the sexes than would De Beauvoir – let alone the 'third wave' feminist propounders of gender fluidity and polymorphism who were to follow at the end of the twentieth century.

In her account of the female of the human species, Stein claimed to be influenced less by orthodox Thomism than by Plato and Augustine as well as by Scotus. In line with Plato's original insight, therefore, she was able to agree that although there are significant differences between males and females, these have nothing to do with capacity or incapacity for intellectual or public life; what they do is enable the same problems, intellectual or social, to be tackled from different but complementary angles, without implication that one angle is necessarily superior to the other. Hence at a stroke Stein eliminates the Aristotelian-Thomist – indeed more general – view that women are inferior to men, or are defective males, while upholding their ineradicably distinct roles in the reproductive process.

Within this wider framework of equal capacities, Stein is still able to argue that women normally – and not merely by social convention or environment, but by what we since her day understand as genetic factors – incline more to the personal, men more to the abstract. Hence too their characteristic vices: men being liable to become one-sided, liable too (in the fallen condition) to attempt a brute domination; women, being more concerned with the personal or 'holistic', more prone to superficiality and to sensuality in securing their immediate goals.

The true feminist (female or male) will rejoice that Stein goes thus far – even though some will mislike her claim that men will exhibit 'male' characteristics (shared by the 'stronger' among females) and women 'female' characteristics (shared by the more sensitive male): these at least more consistently than vice versa. And that while the 'sensitive' man will display this 'feminine' side to his masculinity, so the 'strong woman' tempers her feminine propensities with 'male' virtues; thus indeed – and since in the end the personal is more closely associated with human dignity than is the abstract – among those who approach the goal of a full humanity there may be more women than men. Having become a convinced Catholic Christian (while still owning her Jewish identity), Stein was well aware of the two Jewesses named in the Gospels as Mary (Miriam), Mother of the Lord and the Magdalene, His disciple and the first witness to His Resurrection – praised too by Augustine as 'excelling in affect'.

Stein was able to show that even in the modern world – and in modern philosophical and social conditions – the radical homogenisation of individuals and its totalitarian parallel in societies is not the only option. It is thus singularly appropriate that not too long after, in 1933 when it still might have had some effect, she had addressed a letter (unanswered) to Pope Pius XI appealing for his repudiation of the daily atrocities against Jews being perpetrated in Germany, she was herself arrested, with her sister Rosa, in Holland, to be murdered by the Nazis in Auschwitz – where she was last recorded as tending to her fellow-prisoners, especially the children.

Stein's philosophical work has been largely ignored by the intellectual stars of modernity and post-modernity and their acolytes, female as well as male: this may result from her having – once excluded by the racial laws from teaching – fulfilled an old desire in taking the habit and so dying as a Carmelite nun: not a choice calculated to recommend a philosopher to an academic and mediatic fraternity which has settled on agnosticism (at best) as its default position! Yet it was during her years as a 'religious' that Stein would complete her most important philosophical book: written, indeed, under religious obedience, her superior having required it – and Stein is on record as exclaiming, 'Mercifully it is Sunday and I don't have to write!'.

In the language of a fellow phenomenologist, Robert Sokolowski, Edith Stein (Sister Teresa Benedicta of the Cross) was an 'agent of truth' in a world which prefers to deny all but what itself puts forward as truth.

*

Personalism in phenomenological form, combined, as in Edith Stein, with an enhanced Thomism, is not the only form of specifically contemporary thinking capable of further enhancing the Original Tradition. A second variant can be recognised in what is now called 'virtue ethics': essentially a revival of Aristotelian or Thomistic practical reasoning enriched by the linguistic precision characteristic of much analytic philosophy. Of this development there are two versions, one more Aristotelian, the other more Thomistic, the latter (as powerfully expounded by Elizabeth Anscombe and less narrowly by Alasdair MacIntyre) being framed within a theistic metaphysic. Such 'analytic Thomists' are well equipped to argue with their colleagues in secular departments of philosophy so long as they keep their transcendental metaphysics in the background; however, their version of Thomism is only rarely enriched by personalist, first person insights or, as with MacIntyre, by rich historical and sociological insight, so tends to appear as a more careful version of the older, more arid Thomism 'of strict observance'.

As for the secular version of 'virtue ethics', though it has the huge merit of compelling contemporary moral philosophers to recognise in Aristotle's writings an antidote to a by now moth-eaten Kantianism and Utilitarianism, it lacks any metaphysical foundation, holding Aristotle to advocate the 'autonomy' of ethics – as indeed he does in his non-Platonist moments. It thus tends to fall back not on what Aristotle himself thought of as the correct canon of Hellenic virtues, but on the 'bourgeois' virtues of the more 'respectable' elements of our own society: rather as Hume fell back on the ethical code of the eighteenth-century English gentleman!

10 Culture, What Culture? 2021

> Overheard at a funeral in Toronto:
>
> First Lady (with a sigh): 'Ah well, you have to be philosophical about these things.'
>
> Second Lady: 'What do you mean, "philosophical"?'
>
> First Lady: 'Oh, you know: don't think about it.'

Having completed our survey of the smorgasbord of moral, political, social and cultural traditions now temptingly spread before contemporary Western man, we may proceed to recall some (though far from all) of their variously contradictory features. In so doing we shall illustrate how we may imagine we deploy a coherent set of beliefs while following successively disparate traditions – and as a result may ask whether we do not find in our contemporaries a certain preference for ignoring or actually encouraging confusion?

We shall of course concentrate on those features of each tradition which live on and are hence of more than academic interest, separating them from whatever is no longer relevant: we no longer need to concern ourselves with whether the earth is round or flat!

In looking at implications of what we have laid out in the previous chapters, we start with the assertion of that intellectual and cultural tradition that began with Socrates, reached its high point in the High Middle Ages and, though thereafter often diluted or lost sight of, remains capable of further development. This dynamic process we named the 'Original Tradition', in that though it exhibits some variations, it remains sufficiently uniform to warrant recognition as a single and persisting mindset. In the later Middle Ages and with increasing rapidity in the Early Modern period, its hold was broken, to be largely replaced not by any coherent outlook to which the vast majority of Westerners, and especially 'Western' intellectuals, could subscribe, but by an ever growing number of alternative traditions which (like the post-Reformation Protestant Churches whose fissiparous tendency has connection to it) would hive themselves off in sometimes radical varieties. As the three major lines along which the new traditions developed, we identified Enlightened man, Totalitarian man and Scientistic man: the last deriving from perverse interpretations of Enlightenment Science.

For the sake of convenience and of defining these new variants with reference to their common rejection of the Original Tradition, we shall refer to them collectively as the 'Alternative Tradition'. Upholders of the Original Tradition might argue for the appropriateness of that denomination on the ground that, truth being uniform, 'alternative' traditions too must form a collectivity. The phrase thus comes with the caveat that the varying movements it encompasses will – apart from their common and increasing tendency toward an ever more secular view of man and the cosmos – be found to be often as much in conflict with one another as with the Original Tradition. It follows that to reject the Original Tradition, in whole or in part, is no guarantee of any consistent outlook – besides, and as we shall conclude, presenting an almost insoluble problem for public policy-makers.

For it would be a mistake to suppose that followers of either the Original Tradition or one of the alternatives – meaning those who aspire to view themselves as either enlightened, totalitarian or scientistic – follow their preferred tradition in its purest form. Most of us are still to an extent followers of the Original Tradition (as for example in claiming to respect human dignity); hence we have some vague belief that there are objective truths in ethics and aesthetics, yet dilute that tradition with overspill from incompatible alternatives while vehemently denying any backup from metaphysics. Or we may be armchair totalitarians still willing to claim some 'human rights' – provided it be without reference to God – perhaps indeed proposing 'rights' which the Original Tradition would reject as evils. (In much the same way we may be inclined to defend trends in music-making by appealing to difference of taste – while still wanting Bach to be a 'better' musician than Sir Michael Jagger.)

Not dissimilarly may those with Kantian inclinations in ethics be tempted to combine these with scientism – this being normally, as we have seen, the accompaniment of a Utilitarian mentality. Or they might view a 'categorical imperative' as awakening us to the duty of protecting badgers. (As we shall see in more detail, deniers of Natural Law may in effect appeal to it when needing to reach some 'obvious' conclusion.) In such ways does confusion increase exponentially while we all claim to know what we want for ourselves and for society.

Meanwhile, in a digital world of fake news and specious lies asserted as truths by – and directed at – those unqualified to distinguish them, rarely are we prompted to engage in the Socratic search for the 'examined life'; we rather incline to conclude all change – even change for change's sake and even if bringing with it more confusion – preferable to more circumspect social improvement. (Arrives a journal for alumnae, promoting Newnham College, Cambridge, and entitled 'Changing Lives'. One imagines Socrates commenting, 'Very interesting! Will that be changing them for the better – or for the worse?')

*

We have noted Auguste Comte theorising that the Age of Religion had been followed by the Age of Metaphysics and that in turn would be followed by the Age of Science. It might be helpful to apply Comte's distinguishing of these three types of society to three of the options confronting modern man: thus he can be religious or at least sympathetic to religion (in some sense still hanging on to the Original Tradition), or (rarely) metaphysical – or scientific. And as Plato and Aristotle identified three perverted parallels to three satisfactory forms of government – mob-rule, oligarchy and tyranny being alternatives to (moderate) democracy, aristocracy and monarchy – so a similar parallel can be proposed in the case of Comte's 'Ages', the perversions of religion, metaphysics and science being respectively: fideism and superstition, lofty-seeming profundities (perhaps in a translationese version of a German original) and scientism or 'pop-science' as purveyed to the ignorant by the less ignorant. Modern man has at least these six options to choose from or to blend together, however unconsciously, however incongruously. Further, in choosing he may assume or be led to believe that his 'feelings' rather than his mind should determine his preferences: in effect subscribing to eighteenth-century 'sentimentalism' with its concomitant risks of sentimentality and hypocrisy.

Within our six categories we can identify various problems and options, some of them common to many if not all societies, while others are specific to – or at least prominent in – the contemporary West. We shall glance at a selection of them, concentrating on the 'better' forms but also noting the perversions, before identifying a few of the more frequent if incongruous blends. Some features and antinomies of these are obvious, others more hidden.

Since the West was more or less Christian – and thus more or less of single religious mind – for more than 1,500 years, we shall limit our comments on important features of religious societies and a religious or ex-religious mentality to what is largely shared by the 'mainline' Churches, as well as by some recent 'branch-plants' – adding only brief reflection on the cultural changes resulting from the influx of large numbers of active believers in other gods and creeds. Yet diminished or perverted varieties of belief far from acceptable to earlier generations of Christian believers, but still claiming to be Christian, may now also be gaining ground and further churning up the conceptual mire. Even in the Catholic Church, matrix of the Original Tradition, swathes of the hierarchy have buckled under the pressures of Marxism and liberalism and are currently being led into basing the Church's continuing influence on presenting itself as the (even if pantheist) 'spiritual' arm of international moderation by the United Nations.

*

First let us consider that Trinitarian Unity of Persons referred to in English by the older pagan-Germanic name of 'God'. In the Original Tradition, although essentially beyond our ken, God has enabled us through revelation and natural reason to know certain truths: most notably that He created the world and ourselves *ex nihilo* (from nothing) and that Christ came at a specific point in historical time to 'redeem' us (meaning 'purchase' us again, buy us back) from our 'sins' (meaning moral faults, whether personal or of 'genetic' origin), so enabling us to enter His presence after death, and at the end of time to 'stand before Him' at His coming again in final Judgment at the General Resurrection. When Christians applied their human reason to that 'deposit', they mostly began to worship God as 'triune' (meaning three-in-one): that is as Father, Son and Holy Spirit. To the objection that few, if any, have offered an entirely plausible account of that theological conclusion, one can reply that we have no grounds to suppose that everything in our Universe – let alone beyond it – will be intelligible to the human mind: what is required in Christian doctrine is an overall conformity to 'right reason'.

Following on their triune account of God, Christians in the Original Tradition argued that the soul – source of life and the spiritual faculty by which religious, moral and aesthetic truths can be recognised as founded in God himself – is, though now flawed both in its intellectual capacities and its affectivity, formed, together with the body, 'in God's image and likeness': thence shares in the divine dignity and is possessed of whatever rights are compatible with the Providence of God, Whose nature is Love. Since, however, persons (that is souls and bodies) are 'fallen', they cannot claim to be always able freely to choose the good, the right or the true; believers who so claim are 'heretical' and known as Pelagians, after the British monk Pelagius who taught this (abidingly British-seeming) 'can-do' doctrine!

For not only have we been created by Another, but according to the Original Tradition we require the help of that other to live our lives well. Since we must humbly recognise this assistance as a necessity, we cannot coherently combine belief as to our moral weakness with notions of autonomy derived from Rousseau, Kant or any other: put simply, and contrary to the last-mentioned thinker, 'ought' does not imply 'can'. Nor can we choose to be other than we are – ruling out claims about humans as potentially transhuman or 'overmen' (*Übermenschen*). In conclusion, if a theory of virtue is developed from a combination of human dignity with 'humility' (which word, as also 'human', derives from the Latin for 'earth'), it cannot coherently reject 'human' incompleteness.

Though the historical and theological claims of Christianity as instantiated in the Original Tradition cannot be 'proved' in the way adolescents (of whatever age) may think required, they can be shown to be coherent, such that if they were incoherent there would be little reason (wishful thinking apart) to accept them. In that case, different solutions to the problems they address would have to be proposed – and these would have been judged acceptable or unacceptable in accordance with secular preconceptions that rule out the divine: otherwise would fail as circular and question-begging. On the other hand, the wider the range of problems the Original Tradition can be seen to solve or relieve, the more likely is confidence in it justifiable, puzzling detail notwithstanding.

To take a Biblical example: if Jesus is what Christians claim him to be, he had the power to predict the destruction of Jerusalem and its temple years before these events took place – as is recounted in the Gospel. If he was no more than a remarkable Jewish teacher, then claims that he could foresee the future look less plausible. As we have observed, Hume's argument against miracles: that miracles cannot happen therefore they do not happen, clearly begs the question. Yet while the Original Tradition must be shown to be coherent on its own terms, a 'static' coherence in and of itself is not enough, since to show that a theory is coherent is to allow that it is possible, not that it is true. Upholders of the Original Tradition will accept that it must always (eventually) be able to provide a solution compatible with its own principles for new problems that arise. They will also justly assert that it has already resolved or relieved so many problems more coherently than any of its competitors that their confidence in its continuing success is more rational than the sceptical alternative. Every new problem it can be seen to shine light on makes this view more plausible – and *ex hypothesi* we may assume that so it will be to the end of time.

*

The Original Tradition held that human beings, given a degree of autonomy compatible with their being created but fallible (able to fall), have misused their freedom, choosing their own apparent advantage rather than that good which the Creator God designed for them: hence need to recover the ability to live as images of God and trusting in the divine providence. With God removed, the sense of dependence persists and leads to disaster when we give ourselves (or are compelled to give ourselves) over to some 'Big Brother' or totalitarian structure imposing its demand for loyalty as if in parody of obedience to the life-giving precepts of a Creator God whose nature is Love. From which historically oft-repeated experience we can, if we will, learn that claims about the uniqueness of each person cannot be coherently combined with any form of totalitarian homogenising (*Gleichschaltung*), whether Marxist, Fascist, Nazi or claimed as 'left-liberal'. Persons are not mere members of a set and to be manipulated as such. In the Original Tradition that factual claim is explicated.

Writing in this part of our human story on Armistice Day 2020, we have been reminded that while for certain purposes (such as national defence against aggressors) aspects of such uniqueness may have to be 'put on hold' in the interest of a discipline necessary for survival – and indeed to a limited degree as required for any just arrangements in civic society – yet for the Original Tradition all such arrangements are a *pis aller*. Full human dignity may be shelved – perhaps one may use the honourable term 'sacrificed' – but not eliminated. Thus any attempt to make something like martial law a permanent feature of a society – more especially a society based in the Original Tradition – will be recognised as incoherent and arbitrary – as suggestions that the purpose of military training is to turn people into killing machines will always be suspect.

Similar incoherences must, for the Original Tradition, be eliminated from all moral and political structures, such that all practices, commendations and condemnations fall into a consistent pattern. There can, for example, be no conflict between love and justice; thus if love seems to override justice, clarification must be sought and here Judaeo-Christian religious leaders, not lawyers or judges, may be called upon for tricky decisions in individual cases. 'Dirty hands' – Sartre's '*Mains Sales*' – are an inevitable concomitant of what Augustine calls 'this darkness of social life', and responsible people will be faced with choices where every option – including the option of doing nothing – necessitates regret at a situation in which one irrevocably finds oneself. The word 'responsible' means 'answering to a call upon us'. Latterly, with the fading from public life of the sense of religious obligation to what is objective because truth is of God, the tendency among decision-makers, religious as well as secular, has been to duck this responsibility.

In a polity established only more or less in terms of the Original Tradition – as in other societies – the relation of pleasure and happiness will almost inevitably cause trouble. Secular identifications of happiness as pleasure, or even as the minimising of pain, cannot be accepted, but where happiness and pleasure conflict, pleasure must still yield – the paradox 'hopefully' being modified by the sense of doing the right thing. Apparently painful decisions can be accounted for as within the purview of divine providence; obviously in any secular world-picture such a resolution, if offered or implied, is incoherent. Yet though pleasure is not happiness, it will often accompany virtuous acts: this Aristotle notes in his *Nicomachean Ethics*.

In any society basing itself on the Original Tradition, a specific and coherent account of love, as the primary virtue, is prerequisite. Though love is accompanied by emotion, it is not to be identified with it: a common but thoughtless assumption that actually diminishes love. For while love will involve emotional – but permanent emotional – commitment, it must consist with a sense of duty and a rational behaviour in line with other virtues that are objective and not dependent on the feelings of fallible humans. As with rights, so with duties and obligations, a coherent and rational outlook is indispensable.

Those who, following the Original Tradition, accept that it must always be coherent, must ever avoid yielding to a compartmentalism which in other traditions may provide a solution to moral conflict. Financial integrity must be upheld even in the City of London, on the New York Stock Exchange – or in Vatican City. Socrates, shown by Plato in the *Symposium* as master of pleasure, appears in the *Phaedo* as master of pain: he thus never wears two hats – the philosophic ideal parodied (at least according to urban myth) by Wittgenstein's claim that he never minded what he ate so long as it was always the same!

Plato, standing, pagan and religious, near the beginning of the Original Tradition, also noted a frequent case where compartmentalism is notably hard to avoid. Part of his point, near the end of the *Republic*, about possible conflicts between art and morality, is that the better the artist – in his instance Homer – and the greater his 'aesthetic' appeal, the more dangerous he may be to morality. The beautiful, that is, may at times be the enemy of the good. Though that might be because the morality appealed to is too narrow, the danger of excess is more to the fore in literature and more especially in the performing arts, where having a fourteen-year-old enact the part of a prostitute may produce scenes of tragic beauty and *Lolita* be a book to elicit serious thought, but where the encouraging of – 'paedophilia' apart – the precocious sexualising of an adolescent should raise moral question. For while in Utilitarian terms this might be considered and accepted under a claim of 'the greater good of the greater number', in the Original Tradition that is not acceptable reason for doing harm, nor may those who suppose themselves to adhere to that tradition dodge such a problem by relapsing into an incoherent compartmentalism.

We have already noted two significant features of contemporary thought and culture which encourage such compartmentalism. First, a rootlessness tied both to the plethora of traditions available and to the displacement of local loyalties (for which one might be prepared to die) by a globalised internationalism whose claims on individuals will tend to seem less than urgent, more easily put 'on the back-burner' (or even dumped) in newly inconvenient circumstances. Aristotle offers a pithy comment: 'Better a real cousin than a Platonic son' – which is to say that personal ties will be stronger than more abstract alternatives.

The second factor increasing rootlessness, and in this case a certain *chronological* compartmentalism, is the theory of 'serial selves' deriving from Locke and Hume – though not necessarily with direct reference to these as it is by now part of the air we breathe. Its impact is assisted by an expectably extended life-span which presents us (and should present us) as very different from our youthful selves. But difference does not imply lack of continuity, nor should it encourage irresponsibility toward our own past. We may have changed our views; we are still responsible in varying degrees for past actions. If Klaus was a concentration camp guard and is now a United Nations official, he was still once a concentration camp guard – more especially if he has evaded detection and repentance. If Jill was twenty years ago married (at least if in accordance with traditional Christian teaching and procedures) to Jack, and Jack has turned out to be more from hell and less from paradise than she hoped, she was and still is married to Jack.

*

The Original Tradition assumed that death did not mark the end of human existence – despite the prospect after death hardly looking appealing for many believers who must rely on deathbed confession and absolution. Nevertheless, to live in a world where post-mortem existence is accepted as certain will produce a very different mentality from a world where the end is assumed (if not explicitly) to be extinction: not least in that the unambiguous assumption that there is ultimate purpose to human existence implies that some life choices are better and indeed happier than others. True, the Epicureans of antiquity claimed to find the prospect of extinction more appealing than an alternative pretty uniformly depicted as fear-generating for the vast majority; by contrast the Christian hope of immortality gives a purpose to life which the prospect of extinction, inducing feelings of the pointlessness, triviality or banality of human endeavour, cannot supply. The increase in suicide in contemporary Western (and Westernising) societies is surely an outcome of a sense of the transience and so worthlessness of oneself and everything besides.

It thus is no accident that we have found two 'modern' philosophers making great play of the 'hope' of becoming extinct: Heidegger, who held the ultimate (in every sense) 'authentic' act to be the recognition of the finality of lonely death, and Parfit who, from proffering an early example of a full-blooded atheist morality, came to recognise that to argue that we should diminish our high evaluation of our place in the scheme of things may lead to a conclusion that nothing matters. Indeed, even if what matters in a religious setting may be unwelcome and inhibiting to many, the 'scientific' picture as offered by Stephen Hawking, namely that we are mere 'scum on the surface of a medium-sized planet' and fated like other life forms to disappear, is likely to lead to disillusion, despair and thoughts of getting out of the misery of life as soon as possible – even though Hawking himself seems to have clung on particularly tenaciously. When attitudes to death in the Original Tradition are compared with those in alternatives now largely replacing it, we find basic beliefs at their most irreconcilable. We conclude that belief or non-belief in a providential God makes a radical difference – at least over time – to society's expectations for itself and its members, and thus one thing that certainly matters is whether God exists.

Max Weber dubbed the times of the Original Tradition the Age of Enchantment, this being succeeded by the ages of disenchantment. Recent times have witnessed an attempted, if futile, modification of that analysis, holding that for re-enchantment we should identify not with God but with the immanent natural world of which we are part: as a recent Vatican coin depicts, the Virgin Mary should conceive not the Divine Child but the earth. Those who walk this path will to endow nature – contrary to Weber's predictions – with a sort of substitute-sacredness: indeed 'sacred', as we have noted, is now regularly applied to all sorts of human experiences and institutions to which there is no reason to attach it except to add a spurious emotional flavour. Here again we can recognise confusion of two radically different value systems – much of it to be laid at the door of Kant's 'holy' Will.

We conclude this section on those fragments of the Original Tradition which have survived into an alien world – and which some few are still setting themselves to reassemble and replace where they rightfully belong – with brief attention to the downside of the 'religious' tradition. For certainly fideism may become the resort of the perverted intellect surfing on a wilful ignorance to insist (for example) that the world was created in a literal Biblical six days – evidence to the contrary (such as the recovery and dating of dinosaur bones) being discounted as the fantasy or plot of power-crazed scientists. Such assertions serve only to bring faith into contempt.

That said, it should be noted that, as with other words analogously misused – such as (currently) 'racism', 'homophobia', 'fascism', 'medieval' – the term 'fideism' may be deployed to stifle discussion of unpopular but important features of religious and other traditions, indeed of truth more generally. In defusing this aggressive sophistry, upholders of the Original Tradition need to deploy a Newmanesque theory of the development of religious doctrine that is intellectually coherent – and not the actual replacement of fundamental teachings in some 'paradigm shift' (as the authors heard it latterly – unintelligibly and indeed heretically – proposed by no less than a Cardinal of *Sancta Mater Ecclesia*).

By 'Newmanesque' we evoke an account of the history of doctrine which neither tries to obscure real changes – as about religious freedom (while making allowance for the cultural setting which led to the promulgation of errors needing later correction) – nor (and as does Newman himself) to canonise the fourth century and hence read back from that sophisticated theological epoch into pre-Constantinian times. But from such an intelligible account of the development of Christian thought – falling like the seed of the Gospel Parable in wayward places – devotees of the Alternative Tradition will prefer to turn away, rejecting out of hand that to follow such an approach is to 'be led into all Truth'.

As for superstition, that too flourishes. A survey not many years ago concluded that there are more practising astrologers in France than priests: evidence at least that some features of the universe which might issue in more rational religious belief have to find alternative explanations. It is perhaps unlikely that a high proportion of English nationals will turn out for midsummer jollies at that primitive circle of monoliths that has been dubbed 'Stoned-henge', in preference to packing the shopping malls, football stadia or gaming outlets; still, the seemingly ineradicable desire for some alternative to these more blatant forms of materialism will, and in despite of scientistic promises, ensure that superstition – New Age, Gnostic or other – continue to find scope in the souls 'swept and garnished' of the Gospels (*Matt.* 12: 44; *Luke* 12:45).

*

According to our Comtean-style analysis of social mentalities, a religious tradition – in its Western version our Original Tradition – will be replaced by a metaphysical alternative. That too often looks to be an abstraction without history and humanity; however we need to pay it some attention, since though the age of metaphysics detached from religion has passed, it has left a few eccentric remainders. Iris Murdoch attempted to revive an 'unreformed' (i.e. non-theistic) Platonism to account for Goodness and Beauty, though inevitably neglecting Plato's own later problem as to how to instantiate such Ideas in a Divine Mind. Murdoch has found a number of admirers of her courage in bucking alternative more philistine trends in philosophy, but few have accepted her attempt to revert – like a contemporary Giordano Bruno – to some sort of pre-personal Platonism where Minds are subordinated, and ontologically inferior, to the reified qualities by which they themselves are – as Plato himself put it – divinised.

More in evidence perhaps are admirers of Roger Scruton's attempt broadly to limit the 'transcendent' to the aesthetic (thus at least reducing clashes between the aesthetic and the moral) through tying it to a vaguely spiritual version of religious practice. As example of the attraction of this kind of incoherence we might take English national attachment to the annual Christmas Eve broadcast of 'Nine Lessons and Carols' from the great Chapel planned by a Christian king for his College in Cambridge – and providing for an aesthetic appreciation of the choir and ambience readily detached from the Christian message of the words sung and read: nor irrelevant the local joke about a man rebuked by a verger for singing along with the choir – to whose affirmation 'But this is God's house!' comes the retort, 'No, sir, this is not God's House; it is King's College Chapel'. Relevantly too one may note that the Chapel – which has now the status of a Cathedral of the Church of England – though begun by the still medieval Henry VI, was completed under the auspices of that Henry VIII whose role in the evolution of post-Christian modernity we have already noticed – and whose monogram, entwined with that of his ill-fating and ill-fated second Queen, proximate cause of that role, adorns the majestic interior.

Nor will perversions of a universe evoked typically in high-flown jargon intimating metaphysical depth or (as with Wagner) neo-pagan fantasy, win over more than a few drawn to such obscure (if alluringly 'satanic') mystification. A semi-educated public will dismiss such aesthetic productions as too intellectually challenging for entertainment – though might be tempted to embrace them in more popular form as science fiction. If Heidegger could hail (or Heil!) the mechanisation of the *Wehrmacht* as a metaphysical event (presumably in terms of the inevitable March of History), then the sub-metaphysical introduction of a certain boy-wizard is understandably popular not as mere food for the imaginations of children but as pointer to an ambivalent universe beyond our ken.

*

We leave behind Comte's age of metaphysics and pass quickly to more contemporary scientistic times, attending particularly to those areas in ethics and anthropology where solutions offered by the Original Tradition have been rejected. We need to look out for contradictory revisions and points at which elements of the older world picture may be slipped in incongruously to keep the faltering 'Western' show on the road.

The fundamental question arising with regard to the Alternative Tradition relates to truth as informative about what things really *are*. In the older world-programme – aspects of which survive into the new and uncongenial setting – truth came to be explained technically and in accordance with some sort of Aristotelian format as the correspondence of an idea to the form of that to which it refers; hence it was normally supposed that we could speak of the 'essence' of something: the 'what-it-is-to-be-something'. Let us return to knives: they are shaped for a set of purposes which indicate what they are for and so essentially *are*, namely instruments for cutting. We know what we want if we go to buy a knife. We would not expect the shopkeeper to ask whether we wanted a good one; we would assume – as he would assume – that we wanted a knife which could cut: the essence of a knife is its ability to cut; a knife that is satisfactory *qua* knife cuts well. Blunt knives won't cut well, so perhaps are only derivatively and rather misleadingly still called knives: so Aristotle holds that a dead hand is not a hand.

If we ask the same question about human beings, whose 'essence' (in Aristotelian terms) is dynamic, the answer of the Original Tradition involves reference to man's overall nature. Man may be viewed as intended to glorify God, to obtain likeness to God, to develop his capacities so far as he is able, and so forth; whatever answer was preferred, it was assumed that human life had some sort of purpose and the task of the philosopher was to identify that purpose so far as possible, even though complete success could not be expected.

In our own times, such notions of truth jostle with other claims. Some would have truth to be simple coherence. Certainly truths must be part of a coherent whole if they are to count as at all intelligible – and it is hard not to see our world as proffering at least a degree of intelligibility. One surely indisputable feature of man is that he is the speaking and syntax using animal – and syntax requires grammar, and grammar, as Nietzsche realised, intimates a Universe of coherent sense. (One might add that man is thereby the thinking and recording animal and hence the writer of books – as well as shopping lists or the palace inventories of more primitive societies.)

Here arises a further problem. Truth as simple coherence will give us the logical inference of a set of proposed realities; it does not and could not guarantee their existence. And if neither the identity of a thought with the form of its object nor its coherence will stand up as truth, then we seem left with the conclusion that truth must be 'relative'. Perhaps this can be said to be true of hypotheses in physics, where Einstein's 'truth' differed from Newton's as knowledge of the universe advanced; it yet seems difficult to universalise that conclusion: hard to see how what we in English call a knife could be any other kind of object than that to which in German/Italian, etc. is given the word Messer/coltello. The word 'knife' is thus what in more technical language Kripke denoted a 'rigid designator'.

Perhaps relativity fares better in aesthetics and ethics. We might argue that although killing, more especially killing those considered 'innocent', is frowned on and judged inappropriate or even 'wrong' in our own society, it could be regarded as a good and reasonable thing to do in Aztec Mexico. To find the Aztecs 'wrong' about this, we will have logically to introduce Original Tradition objectivism about right and wrong. Relativist accounts of such problems will be seen as clearly contradicting common sense.

Perhaps then we might fall back on the wider axiom that though killing the innocent is inappropriate – indeed wrong – in post-Christian Birmingham or Chicago, it is to be held appropriate – indeed right – where religion demands and custom sanctions. That would render any promotion of 'reform' in such cultures (let alone of opting out of them) inadmissible unless those in control of religious observance were to agree or at least be pressured into agreement – making reform depend upon changed obedience, not on a newly recognised 'right'. An Aztec devotee of human sacrifice going to Spain must accept to forego his religious practice and earlier conscientious supposition that without such ritual sacrifice the world would come to an end, and so turn relativist. This theoretical dilemma raises important questions about the legitimacy of elite or even majority rule – including in 'liberal-democratic' societies. This we reserve for further and final comment.

For first we must distinguish claims that all judgments about moral and aesthetic behaviour are subjective or otherwise relative, from claims that, although relativity is all we can 'know', there must *be* a deeper truth, even though inaccessible to us. Why *must* there be – unless we are to commit to the idea that what is inaccessible to the human mind may be accessible (like the Trinity for Christians) through revelation? Yet if without revelation we cannot recognise the right course (even if we have heard about it), we will be still dependent for any – albeit subjective and elusive – moral 'truth' on our choices and decisions. Introduce 'deeper' if inaccessible truths and you are on the road back to the Original Tradition.

Relativist discourse will imply that the only reason not to commit murder, if I feel like so doing, would be fear of punishment or other inconvenient consequence, or perhaps the view of the majority, or of the ruling elite, can be invoked to keep me in check. Thus if someone should ask, 'Why, if I can kill at whim, should not others do likewise?', I would have to reply that they could if they thought they could get away with it (adding an Hobbesian appeal to self-interested prudence). The only way to cut through – though hardly out of – the maze will seem to be that each of us must muddle along, forming whatever varying patterns of behaviour and belief seem helpful in securing the life that seems desirable to us. This indeed is pretty much what we are brought to. Even if our choice is for something 'idealistic', it will have been made in no principled fashion – difficult though we may by now find it to recognise random idealism as a contradiction in terms!

There are more than such immediately threatening restrictions on the limits of choice. What if we 'decide' to fly, or to live to 100, or to be a man and a woman at the same time? We might need to learn what it is at least intelligible to choose: Aristotle pointed out that it was pointless for Athenians to deliberate about what to do in Scythia. It looks as though theories about the relativity of truth condemn us either to the nihilistic belief that we cannot rationally determine what to do *or* that we must rely on local and variable conventions *or* must 'plump' as we feel like from time to time. Indeed we are sometimes invited to do just that, as when anti-natural-law jurists tell us that although statistical evidence shows that the use of drugs or pornography is harmful in the longer term, we should always be allowed to indulge in such since we cannot know that this will apply in the more measurable short run or in any particular instance.

In such cases, it may be that to evade relativist or perspectival accounts of truth offering us to base our actions either on the conventions and demands of others or on our immediate feelings and preferences, we shall fall back, knowingly or not, on truth as understood in the Original Tradition – even though we thought we had discarded that. The only other alternative, as we have observed, will be to give up on any coherent narrative of our lives: indeed should lead us – logically – to ask why we should even want or expect consistent behaviour in ourselves or others; rather let us accept to make decisions according to the perceived demands of pleasure and pain.

Those, it so happens, are the very criteria which Greek thinkers identified as primary deflectors from the good life: a conclusion that should worry any who aim to conduct their lives in avoidance of self-deception or illusions that may turn out to be guiding them by default. All which implies that if we try to appropriate any part of the Original Tradition about goodness or rightness without its related vision of truth, we commit ourselves to the non-ethic of wishful thinking: in the words of a great Teacher, to 'a house built upon sand': alternatively to some 'bias' – in the sense of that word as has been heard used to their teachers by the more aggressive and unmannerly among students: 'What's your bias?'

*

One of the best examples of what happens when objective truth is sidelined and delusion and 'virtual' morality becomes the only option, can be found in contemporary language and belief about 'human rights'. In the Original Tradition human dignity allows for the possession of human rights, though by secularists the two are assimilated only at the price of further incoherence. In fact, the difference between having a human right and possessing human dignity can readily be recognised: thus although one can claim that a woman (or man) has the right to be a prostitute, it is hardly regarded as a mark of human dignity to exercise this right – as is indicated by the ordinary language ('whore', '*putain*') used to denote those who do so. Thus rights (as also 'rights') may be instantiated under 'positive' (secular) laws, which will vary between places and times. Human dignity, properly understood, will be – if 'theoretical' – a norm unchanging with time and place.

So at least with the Original Tradition – and although human rights can be derived from its teaching as to human dignity, yet that Tradition's dignity-language will rule out rights claims incompatible with its account of the proper relationship between man and God. As in the example above, rights claims can be made which are incompatible with dignity at least as traditionally understood. Let us attend therefore to some of the rights claimed in the Alternative Tradition and the incoherences they entail; to relieve which difficulties, we will be supposed to be living still upon capital from the outmoded Original Tradition.

Modern human rights theories are the descendants of principles of Natural Right developed in the early modern period from earlier accounts of human dignity – at which point they depended still on the will of God: thus according to Grotius, God has given us rights as a means of protecting ourselves against the aggressions of others and as an aid and condition for dealing commercially with not only fellow-Christians but all members of the human race. That rights are for our protection implies that we must apply to human institutions, such as courts of justice, to assert them and to identify those committed to accepting them: it follows that, all rights being against someone or other, they must always be instantiated in legislation. Still, in the background and supporting these rights, for Grotius there lingers God, and God at least is not subject to legislative order.

If Grotius' natural rights were primarily commercial, those of John Locke were both religious and political; still, he was not above suggesting that they could be used to annexe the property of others, provided each man leaves 'enough and to spare'. Thus if in the vast expanses of North America we appropriate the lands of the native 'Indian' tribes and 'mix' them with our labour, there will be plenty more land – perhaps even 'as good' – for them to occupy elsewhere: or there would seem to be for the foreseeable future.

A convenient conclusion: nevertheless, Locke's account of rights against both Church and State still depends on God's authority. With the coming eclipse of God, why are we to accept Locke's conclusion, lacking Locke's God-premise? Possession will be (at least) 'nine tenths of the law' – and how should we defend, say, the right not to be subject to arbitrary arrest, torture, imprisonment, summary execution? Little effective attempt has been made to answer such questions, leaving confusion to reign. After 'natural rights' we have tried positing the Rights of Man (Rousseau, Kant and the Jacobins), then human rights as upheld by national and international organisations in our contemporary world. We have assumed, that is, that we had (the right to) whatever rights we could maintain.

And why? Presumably we saw 'rights' being denied, thought that obnoxious – anyway 'inappropriate', even 'wrong' – even though we had discarded the foundation for believing anything simply wrong. (R.M. Hare, once a prominent philosopher with a distinguished anti-Nazi war record, when asked whether Hitler had actually done anything wrong admitted – to incredulous jeers – that he could not say that.) We normally claim the 'right' to protect our 'rights' and fail to notice that we are defying one of the rules (derived from Hume) of much modern thought: namely that one cannot derive 'ought' from 'is': values from facts; rights from acts perceived as abuses.

Nor is finding ourselves better off with rights a justification for claiming them as possessed of objective status: what it provides is a motive to try to get them, by force if need be. The inadequacy of this approach becomes clearer when we consider which 'rights' we might want to use force to claim. Suppose we claim (with a Toronto student newspaper) that every student has the right to get drunk: we then have to recognise that someone must supply (even be compelled to supply) enough alcohol for every student who wishes to get drunk and can pay enough to do so. To enforce that will requires legislation or 'hard' power.

That kind of rights claim surely looks absurd. Even with God's absence granted (*etsi Deus non daretur*, as the schoolmen were already putting it), surely rights must be based on more than the power to enforce our demands; surely, that is, they are other than reified desires! Perhaps they rather are derived from needs; since Plato, as we have noticed, philosophers have distinguished between necessary and unnecessary desires, the former being for basic needs, as for food and shelter. That suggestion is more reasonable, not least because it is easily universalisable; thus it would seem absurd to suppose, even if every student has the right to get drunk, that every human being has the right to get drunk (students being some special subset of humanity).

'Every student has the right to a healthy diet' raises the stakes; then the student is not a special but a typical subset of humanity: thus every student, *because* every human being, needs a healthy diet. Does that entail that everyone has *the right* to a healthy diet? Certainly it suggests the claim that someone (perhaps the State) should guarantee everyone a healthy diet. Still the question arises: Why *ought* the State (or anyone) to be so obligated? To say that everyone has the right to a healthy diet is to assume that such a claim is not absurd, that it speaks both to genuine existential need and to human solidarity. But, analogously with the case of unnecessary desires, you cannot argue even from the fact that people need a healthy diet that they have a 'natural' right to it unless you invoke old-fashioned Natural Law.

In a value-free universe, nature (or if you prefer, Nature) does not recognise such rights; it rather is 'red in tooth and claw'. What can, of course, be argued is that in the case of a healthy diet there are better reasons to demand a *legal* right. Yet only in light of the Original Tradition can the move from 'is' to 'ought' be acceptable; otherwise, and as Kant should have recognised, rationality, though important, does not guarantee universal and objective moral truths: does not in itself construct a moral 'nature', only the codification – not the reification – of human, and so desirably rational, beliefs. If the distribution of rights is to be explained in terms of obedience to a just God's necessarily benevolent command and a logical corollary of His nature, it is unquestionably a legitimated inference; without that it is at best a reasonable and kindly – whatever that means – request.

Outside the Original Tradition, we have come to relieve the logical difficulties that arise – both for what might seem reasonable rights and for more absurd rights claimed as the mere reification of random desires, by resort to wishful thinking and wilful delusion; this we do by telling ourselves that states – or now (at least since Kant) international bodies – have the authority to pass laws granting us more than merely constructed rights. Yet if challenged, on what can their authority be shown to rest? Even where dominated by mass murderers, we grant them authority to legislate into shadowy existence an indefinitely expandible set of 'naturally' (but better, 'virtually') binding claims on us, thus lending them a quasi-transcendental authority.

Indeed, some rights have for centuries been labelled 'sacred', and those who have taken over the claiming of them have taken with it the word to use for their own purposes, as if the organisations which – replacing the God of Locke – can distribute rights must have some quasi-divine ('sacred') authority. Here rights in the Alternative Tradition can be seen to depend on an assumption (whether made in bad faith or out of an uncritical mentality) of the 'divinity' – anyway divine prerogative – of Man. But though, with Nietzsche, I might claim that were there gods I would have the right to be one, we must remember that Nietzsche 'knew' there are no gods. Let us be thus far, at least, consistent.

Still, perhaps we can fall back on a quasi-priestly caste who can declare truth in place of the now discredited theologians: those 'scientists' who (turning a blind eye to the fact that it is constantly changing and developing) assume that eventually 'science' will make us for all practical purposes omniscient – even though the more we learn about our universe, the more we realise remains to be known. The word 'science' (from the Latin *scire*, meaning to know) originally meant a (more or less systematic) 'knowledge' about some subject: hence what we *know* about it. In this essay we have distinguished by the term 'scientistics' all pretentious would-be 'scientists' (and their camp followers) from those, in accordance with contemporary usage, properly designated (and properly humble) scientists.

True, our categories may overlap: there may be scientists who choose – to gain notoriety or other reward – to prognosticate scientistically. In so doing, such a one will be performing not as a scientist but as a new variety of social engineer. Thus in the Alternative Tradition 'progressive' ideas need no longer depend on manipulating the structures of society (as in Communist states), nor even on propagandising the minds and 'souls' of individuals, but may be advanced by propagation of the faith that science, given enough time, will solve all problems and we (or our descendants) will all live in an earthly paradise: odd this, in light of some of the things scientific work has produced: the hydrogen bomb, cities choking with pollution, marine life choking on plastics, perhaps even a virus to kill us off or at least shut us down – and who knows what next! As superstition to religion, so scientism to science: providing the up-to-date confused manifestation of fideism.

*

Theories of rights are not the only area in which the Alternative Tradition is hard put to account for its *desiderata* for society without surreptitious recourse to aspects of that Original Tradition to which, logically, it has forfeited entitlement. We may cite a particularly striking example concerning justice – that being closely related to the problematic of 'rights'. After the World War II, a number of leading Nazis were condemned as war criminals at Nuremberg and the defendants' arguments that they were simply obeying orders legitimately given by the Nazi state were rejected – entirely properly if you hold by Original Tradition accounts of Justice and Human Dignity. Yet many, perhaps most, of the judges who condemned them would by then have denied natural law theory and natural justice as earlier understood. In effect, the Tribunal invented 'natural-law' crimes (as 'crimes against humanity') anew, awarding itself authority to formulate them.

Our point, of course, is not that the Nazis were the victims of justice-as-the-law-of-the-victor, or that they should have been acquitted, but that those who condemned them did so by appropriating principles about natural justice based in metaphysical claims to which a secularist jurisprudence did not logically entitle them. A Roman poet observed that though you may expel Nature with a pitchfork, she will return; even so at Nuremberg we see 'natural law,' as understood within the Original Tradition, return unacknowledged.

Similar reality-inventing procedures are invoked in aid of the Alternative Tradition in aesthetics, together with their more obvious abuses. Though we must admit that problems of 'taste' can be even more challenging than those of ethics, it is reasonable to ask whether we are entitled to complain when – as happened in Ottawa some years back – an art prize was awarded to an 'artist' (evidently of the 'fast-buck' variety) who, having received his financial reward, boasted that he had simply fired paint onto canvass at random with a spray gun. Though he saw in this no reason to return his winnings, we may reasonably ask whether the judges should have cancelled the prize and if so, on what grounds. Perhaps they could not honestly have done so because they knew no way of identifying what could count as art unless by those fusty old canons which would have led them to reject this exhibit however they supposed it to have been painted!

Plato long ago contrasted skill with knack and distinguished inspiration from meretricious appeal, but the Alternative Tradition lacks any authoritative way of evaluating artistic productions: it matters little what is produced, or whether the object produced is in any way 'inspiring' or even informative or intellectually challenging, but mainly that it appears something a bit different: in particular, it may help if it is blasphemous or otherwise designed to offend, the artist thus showing him or herself 'liberated' from 'bourgeois' taste, while his or her picture or statue disseminates its nihilistic message.

Such difficulties arise conspicuously with architecture. We can all know what a particular building is 'for', but unless we simply identify technical skill with artistic merit, on what principle do we decide whether it is beautiful or ugly – even 'easy on the eye'? Are we to conclude that in labelling a given building 'brutalist', we are merely describing and not evaluating it? And if not, by what standards are we making our evaluation? Under the Alternative Tradition the 'philistine' can have a field day: indeed it seems that the designation 'philistine' has lost its former reference.

One finds analogous problems arising in every area of both morals and aesthetics, suggesting it is high time to ask whether underlying such examples as the above is not a set of social shibboleths achieving dominance in 'liberal-democratic' societies and spawned out of that uncertain medley of wishful thinking we here refer to as the Alternative Tradition. Nor is our problem solved if, like Oriana Fallaci and many another art- and European-culture devotee, we want the 'Catholic' tradition without the Catholic faith. A 'cultural Catholic', though recognising traditional wisdom, is not a coherent follower of the Original Tradition.

That said, the outstanding virtue of Oriana Fallaci is to be recognised in her *daring to speak out*, firstly to and against dictators, finally and powerfully against Islamist violence. Some called her 'Islamophobic' (among other honorific epithets), not least in Western universities; in despising such craven attempts to censure her, she asserted the *raison d'être* of any university as contradicted by its reducing itself to a factory for the production of servants of the existing or prevailing regime of whatever stripe. Those in charge of our Western universities need to recognise that they are being tempted – and are often yielding to the temptation (which arose first in the revolutionary sixties and is now back in vogue) – to pander to groups inside and outside their ivory towers whose proceedings can be compared to those of the judicial murderers of Socrates in the early days of Western intellectual life: that is, in intending to kill off argued dissent.

Part of the charge against Socrates was that he 'worshipped gods other than those which the city worshipped' (a politically-motivated half-truth at best). We should ask who in contemporary universities represents the gods of our City which, as we have argued, worships not Wisdom but Choice (where tolerated within the limits of prevailing fashion), assisted by Deceit, Humbug and, reigning over all, Confusion. They will turn out to be the manipulators of the 'snowflakes' of the younger generation who, though so far unable to arrange the execution or otherwise 'elimination' of any new Socrates who might appear (and we shall soon be pointing to a case approaching that), would at least attempt to 'cancel' him or (as Fallaci) her, or silence him with threats of prosecution – perhaps for 'hate-speech': the term already implying condemnation. (Compare the notice seen in many of our stores: 'Shoplifters Will Be Prosecuted'!)

Those holding dear the flourishing of our universities should remember what Socrates told their Athenian forerunners: that he would not be silenced; he would continue to think and speak regardless of the threats brought against him. Just as those who condemned him to death (by a larger majority than had found him guilty) showed themselves unfit to sit in judgment as jurors, so our contemporary haters of free thought and inquiry show themselves unfit to be among those privileged to be part of anything claiming to be a seat of learning. If not vigorously repudiated, they will tend to reduce our Universities (at least their humanities and social science departments) to institutions satisfying Oscar Wilde's characterisation of University teaching as 'casting fake pearls before real swine'.

*

There would be small point in concluding our investigations with Stalinism, Nazism or other blatantly tyrannical regime; few in the West still suppose these to be legitimate forms of the Alternative Tradition. And yet – like liberal democracy – they arose out of the totalitarian 'democracy' of the French Revolution as supposed correctives to the Original Tradition and were similarly claimed to relieve an alienation and oppression coupled with servile dependence on God which older ways promoted.

We blithely assume our proudly 'liberal' democracy to be the legitimate successor, with the dominant successor mentality, of an original Christendom transformed first into a melange of Christian sects expanding in number in the West and beyond – and almost from the outset morphing, via deism, then agnosticism, into either anti-religion and atheism or a society inclined (if not committed) to the relegation of religion to private life. We by now feel our choice to lie between a tolerance of the theistic past at best less contemptuous than Hume's or an assault upon those bits of it remaining – especially the moral bits: in this latter case pursuing – if updated – the route embarked on by the French *philosophes*, the Jacobins and their successors.

The atheists and agnostics now dominating the secular state, having determined that religion and state must be kept apart (unless perhaps or perforce if the religion turn terrorist) should be required to justify the first principles of that state – and that while we still are permitted to enquire into their premises. For although they regularly deny any 'foundationalism', they do in fact have their own foundational principles. These assumed, they have sought to justify the liberal-democratic secular state (some as, in Churchill's famed words about democracy, 'the least worst option') as more 'enlightened', more respectful of man's autonomy, more 'free' – with freedom understood as a trade-off between public safety and the maximising of individual choices, without 'prejudice' as to whether or not those choices make for the individual or the common good. Thus they may signal virtue: for example by requiring a warning on cigarette packages that 'Smoking kills', but (and Bernard Mandeville would have approved) not too seriously discouraging it by punitive taxation, because it benefits the public purse – once, presumably, we discount the costs of the illnesses produced by smoking (or other thus far illegal habits). Humbug – or just convenient confusion?

*

The best exposition of the dominant ideology of the modern liberal-democratic state is to be found in John Rawls' widely acclaimed *Political Liberalism*. Rawls – in an earlier avatar a distinguished philosopher – has *qua* public intellectual concluded there is to be no privileged place in society for many of the principles on which the Original Tradition – hence Western civilisation as earlier envisaged – was based. Nor is it difficult to understand why he has come to this radical conclusion. One reason is that the increasingly rootless West, from its display of a 'humanism' still deriving from a divided Christianity, is now faced with assimilating a jumble of sometimes violently jostling traditions arriving with large numbers of immigrants to whom much of both the Original Tradition and its successor mentalities is alien or to be spurned.

This problem is strictly political in that the numbers of such immigrants into Europe now run into millions – in this being wholly different from the arrival of the conquering Normans in the England of 1066 or a few hundred Jews from Eastern Europe in the late nineteenth century. The Jews at least related to a culture that notionally still believed in the God of the Old Testament: indeed had previously been positively encouraged by a Cromwell with both millenarian and economic aims. The Normans were few and, sharing the Catholic culture of their conquered people, eventually were blended with and enriched it; hence in England (and far beyond) we still speak a tongue based in Anglo-Saxon. None of our latest arrivals have come as conquerors, yet they comprise large enough numbers to compel attention: whether they are accepting of democratic processes, or – as has begun to appear, especially in France – by the threat or actual deployment of aggressive force. And we write at the point that the debacle in Afghanistan means the absorption of considerable numbers of refugees from what has traditionally been a backwater of the *Dar al Islam*, the Islamic world.

Immigration alone, however, does not account for the confusion at the heart of that modern liberal democracy that finds itself challenged by such numbers increasing in its midst. A deeper problem arises from activist sub-groups far from limited to newcomers. To appease them, some of our self-proclaimed 'enlightened' advisers think it best to encourage the majority citizenry to accept the depiction of themselves as oppressors and of the various neo-Marxist subgroups as victims (self-styled) to whom should be displayed a sympathy wavering between the sentimental and the hypocritical.

To choose to view yourself as a victim is not to *be* a victim, and talk of repenting ancestral oppressions easily morphs into sentimental humbug. Nor should we suppose that our Western cultural identity crisis is to be compared with difficulties which will from time to time arise and can result in a readiness to sacrifice foundational features of Western society when we may be called upon to 'pull together' against threats from outside our borders – as in World War II Britain suspended the Habeas Corpus Act. In the contemporary world, the

State of Israel offers an object lesson in such pulling together – at least while the threat to its nationhood lasts.

Rawls' solution presents the liberal-democratic state as neutral between all factions, its task only to maintain order and not – as in the Original Tradition at its best – also to promote virtue in its citizenry. Indeed, and leaving aside the incomers, among the original inhabitants of contemporary liberal-democratic societies there remains – as this book we trust will have shown – little agreement on what, if anything, can be denoted virtue or virtuous. Therefore is Rawls' solution no better than an agreement or species of social contract to manage society on the basis of a lowest common denominator – perhaps consumerism (or if not, what else)? Even so, his concept of a neutral state is impossible to be realised in the actual world where both rulers and ruled will ever have agendas of their own and attempt to mould the 'neutral' state to suit these. Such a 'neutral' state would inevitably soon cease to be neutral and would rather reflect the mentality and aims not of the incomers, nor necessarily of the majority of the earlier population (though that might be brought about by media manipulation of 'news' and opinion) but of the dominant elites: those smart enough, aggressive enough, deceitful enough or simply lucky enough to control powers both 'hard' and 'soft' within society.

In practice the theoretically neutral state is controlled by a 'deep state' composed of lobby groups: that is to say of Hobbesian individuals writ larger plus social media gurus and other manipulators of mass opinion, in a contemporary world where few can distinguish between well-publicised falsehoods – often of anonymous origin – and more accurate approximations to truth. In similar vein are such insidious techniques used to boost simultaneously the lust to buy of the necessary mass consumer and the envy of the homogenised and malleable citizen, dazzling him or her with choices far removed from any realistic needs and cluttering him/her with a plethora of scarcely useful 'goods'. (The ineluctable passage through glittering shopping malls at our major airports – continuing even during the recent Covid lockdown – provides ready illustration of this.)

For as Goebbels, master of propaganda, knew well, it matters little whether what you say is false; you can make it appear 'true' by repeating it many times and getting (by bribery or complicity) well known individuals – in the 'democratic' world often pop stars, actresses, footballers or other 'celebs' – to repeat it. Parroting prevails and the public can hardly be blamed for not knowing what to think – until some disaster is about to strike them, when it may be too late: even Goebbels eventually could not persuade Berliners that the Red Army was not closing in on them. Stalin went one better in so brainwashing and paralysing his entourage that when he lay dead they were too terrified to find out why he had not rung for breakfast.

So will it be brought about that even in emergencies the ordinary bloke will find it hard to understand either all the facts or who is responsible: Is it the government's fault or the government's misfortune in that its good intentions have been subverted? If one scientist tells us that 500,000 will die of Covid (or Mad Cow Disease: this happened), while another, apparently equally qualified, puts the figure at 50,000, who are we to judge?

Does this mean that Rawls and those who think like him are unprincipled in just encouraging us to muddle along? Not necessarily, but they have undertaken an impossible task. For their proposals to be carried forward peacefully – rather than be imposed by force or manipulation – would require many citizens to give up or 'finesse' their consciences. Rawls and his like seem unable to recognise that for some people there are non-negotiable beliefs, and it must follow, from the radical differences we have pointed out between the two Traditions as set out in this book, that the Rawlsian solution would work only if those following the Original Tradition, even feebly, could be induced to abandon it. Happily even sneers or the label 'divisive' will not always frighten stand-outs into submission.

This the history of abortion laws brings out clearly. Governments have had successive opportunities to pass, by seeming compromises, laws which eventually have opened the doors to legal abortion practically 'on demand' and even up until birth – deluding those opponents who little thought 'mission creep' intended. The law passes, the same 'forward' push can be repeated, only this time the starting point has been moved; we are on a slippery slope.

Here to the philosophic mind will occur Hobbes' (based on a story in Plutarch) 'Ship of Athens', which ship is gradually repaired until, all the timbers having been replaced, one is left with the question whether this is the same ship. Rather similarly, if you compromise between an honourable or moral policy and one that is neither moral nor honourable, the dishonourable side's activists, having won the first round, are well placed to win the ensuing bouts and emerge victorious – the technique known as 'salami tactics' – and we are left with an entirely different scenario. Meanwhile and cumulatively, many millions of unborn but indubitably human lives are sacrificed to aims essentially selfish and ultimately suicidal (if, that is, the maintenance of a 'Western' style democratic polity is thought desirable).

*

Toleration of the radical differences and confusions that this study addresses will be unsuccessful in solving the problems of liberal democracy, hence presaging the move we have already noted into more totalitarian habits – though still, and for a time, promoted as 'liberal'. For advocates of the Original Tradition to win out against such forces, they would have to recover a majority of their fellow citizens to a much closer approximation to something they might recognise as their own position than seems at all likely in a (Weberian) 'disenchanted' age.

Followers of some (or even any) Alternative Tradition have a better chance of success, in having less and less non-negotiable axioms: thus while the Original Tradition would be destroyed if (the Judaeo-Christian) God were denied or reduced to irrelevancy in public life, many followers of the Alternative Tradition (though not the more rabidly anti-Christian) will not object if He be the private hobby of a declining number of eccentrics. Many indeed have already adopted that position *vis à vis*, for example, those who say they are Catholics but reject swathes of Catholic teaching, especially on life-issues. In other words, those will be tolerated who can claim to have a foot in both camps. (The philosopher Charles Taylor might be one example, the politician Nancy Pelosi another.)

For the rest, the future looks bleak. For scratch that sort of lobby-driven liberalism and creeping totalitarian thought-control emerges. Even so does a Rawlsian neutrality produce apparent liberalism but an actual covert totalitarianism, with those who subscribe to more traditional morality required to act against their consciences or face prison – or worse.

No doubt for some – and Rawls himself is in this perhaps only another sort of 'useful idiot' – that is precisely the intent of a Rawlsian neutrality in ethics and politics: in defect, that is, of an actual *trahison des clercs*. One actual *'clerc'*, Cardinal George of Chicago has observed: 'I shall die in my bed; my successor may die in prison; his successor may be executed'.

Since then, a fellow Cardinal of the Catholic Church, George Pell, has been imprisoned a whole year on a trumped-up charge of paedophilia. Had not one (Jewish) judge dissented on appeal, finding the conviction 'unsafe', Pell's persecutors might have hoped he would not emerge e'er 'justice delayed' should be – and finally – 'justice denied': their victim banged up without further right of appeal and perhaps fulfilling his fellow Cardinal's prediction by dying in prison: not by direct murder but by a not improbable heart attack. Some have insolently claimed that the Cardinal 'deserved' this treatment as revenge against misdoings of other co-religionists. If that can be tolerated, then truly we are on the cusp of a turn to mob rule and its dictatorial consequences.

For the time being we merely have Confusion regnant in the West.

Selected Further Reading

Cambridge Companions offer good contemporary introductions to many of the thinkers named in this book, especially the Companions to:

Plato, Aristotle, Epicurus, The Stoics, Plotinus, Augustine (first edition), Aquinas, Duns Scotus, Ockham, Machiavelli, Descartes, Hobbes, Locke, Hume, Rousseau, Kant, Mill, Husserl, Heidegger.

The following studies – limited almost entirely to writing in English – might also be helpful. Only books are listed, with the exception of a single essential journal-article.

CHAPTER 1: CONFUSION INTRODUCED

Anscombe, G.E.M., 1958. 'Modern Moral Philosophy', *Philosophy* 53, pp. 1–19.

Chappell, T.J.D., 2015. *Knowing What to Do: Imagination, Virtue and Platonism in Ethics*. Oxford, Oxford University Press.

MacIntyre, A., 1981. *After Virtue: A Study in Moral Theory*. South Bend, IN, University of Notre Dame Press.

MacIntyre, A., 1988. *Whose Justice? Which Rationality?* London, Duckworth.

Rist, J.M., 2004. *Real Ethics: Rethinking the Foundations of Morality*. Cambridge, Cambridge University Press.

Ryrie, A., 2017. *Protestants: The Radicals Who Made the Modern World*. London, William Collins.

CHAPTER 2: ATHENS, ROME, JERUSALEM

Bobzien, S., 1988. *Determinism and Freedom in Stoic Philosophy*. Oxford, Oxford University Press.

Brown, P., 1988. *The Body and Society. Men, Women and Sexual Renunciation in Early Christianity*. New York, Columbia University Press.

Frede, M., 1997. *A Free Will: Origins of the Notion in Ancient Thought*. Berkeley, University of California Press.

Gerson, L.P. (ed.), 2010. *The Cambridge History of Philosophy in Late Antiquity (2 volumes)*. Cambridge, Cambridge University Press.

Inwood, B., 1985. *Ethics and Human Action in Early Stoicism*. New York, Oxford University Press.

Lear, J., 1988. *Aristotle: The Desire to Understand*. Cambridge, Cambridge University Press.

Long, A.A., 2002. *Epictetus: A Stoic and Socratic Guide to Life*. Oxford, Oxford University Press.

Rist, J.M., 1967. *Plotinus: The Road to Reality*. Cambridge, Cambridge University Press.

Rist, J.M., 2012. *Plato's Moral Realism: The Discovery of the Presuppositions of Ethics*. Washington, DC, Catholic University of America Press.

CHAPTER 3: FROM CONSTANTINE TO HENRY VIII

Allen, M., 1984. *The Platonism of Marsilio Ficino*. Berkeley, University of California Press.

Brown, P., 2000. *Augustine of Hippo (new edition with epilogue)*. London, Faber & Faber.

Byers, S., 2012. *Perception, Sensibility and Moral Motivation in Augustine's Stoic-Platonic Synthesis*. Cambridge, Cambridge University Press.

Cory, T.S., 2012. *Aquinas on Human Self Knowledge*. Cambridge, Cambridge University Press.

Cross, R., 1999. *John Duns Scotus*. New York, Oxford University Press.

De Libera, A., 2007. *L'Archéologie du sujet*. Paris, Vrin.

Finnis, J., 1980. *Natural Law and Natural Rights*. New York, Oxford University Press.

Hoffmann, T., 2021. *Free Will and the Rebel Angels in Medieval Philosophy*. Cambridge, Cambridge University Press.

Kent, B., 1995. *Virtues of the Will: The Transformation of Ethics in the Late Thirteenth Century*. Washington, DC, Catholic University of America Press.

Rex, R., 2017. *The Making of Martin Luther*. Princeton, NJ, Princeton University Press.

Rist, J.M., 1994. *Augustine: Ancient Thought Baptized*. Cambridge, Cambridge University Press.

Rist, J.M., 2008. *What Is Truth? From the Academy to the Vatican*. Cambridge, Cambridge University Press.

Rist, J.M., 2014. *Augustine Deformed: Love, Sin and Freedom in the Western Moral Tradition*. Cambridge, Cambridge University Press.

Sweeney, E., 2012. *Anselm of Canterbury*. Washington, DC, Catholic University of America Press.

Tierney, B., 1997. *The Idea of Natural Rights: Studies in Natural Rights, Natural Law and Church Law 1150–1625*. Atlanta, GA, Scholars Press.

Wippel, J., 2000. *The Metaphysical Thought of Thomas Aquinas*. Washington, DC, Catholic University of America Press.

CHAPTER 4: MAN ENLIGHTENED: MONTAIGNE TO KANT

Darwall, S., 1995. *The British Moralists and the Internal 'Ought': 1640–1740*. Cambridge, Cambridge University Press.

Gauthier, D., 1969. *The Logic of Leviathan*. Oxford, Oxford University Press.

Gregory, B., 2012. *The Unintended Reformation*. Cambridge, MA, Harvard University Press.

Haakonssen, K., 1996. *Natural Law and Moral Philosophy from Grotius to the Scottish Enlightenment*. Cambridge, Cambridge University Press.

Helm, P., 2004. *John Calvin's Ideas*. Oxford, Oxford University Press.

Hill, C., 1958. *Puritanism and Revolution*. Harmondsworth, Penguin.

Hundert, E.G., 1994. *The Enlightenment's Fable*. Cambridge, Cambridge University Press.

Kaufmann, W., 1974. *Nietzsche: Philosopher, Psychologist, Anti-Christ*. Princeton, NJ, Princeton University Press.

Korsgaard, C.M., 1996. *Creating the Kingdom of Ends*. Cambridge, Cambridge University Press.

Macpherson, C.B., 1962. *The Political Theory of Possessive Individualism: Hobbes to Locke*. New York, Oxford University Press.

Martin, R. and J. Barresi, 2001. *Naturalization of the Self: Self and Personal Identity in the Eighteenth Century*. London, Routledge.

Menn, S., 1998. *Descartes and Augustine*. Cambridge, Cambridge University Press.

Schneewind, J.R., 1998. *The Invention of Autonomy*. Cambridge, Cambridge University Press.

Yolton, J., 1970. *Locke and the Compass of Human Understanding*. Cambridge, Cambridge University Press.

CHAPTER 5: TOTALITARIAN MAN: THEORY AND PRACTICE

De Lubac, H., 1958. *The Drama of Atheist Humanism* (trans. E.M. Riley). San Francisco, Ignatius Press.

Fest, J., 1970. *The Face of the Third Reich*. Harmondsworth, Penguin.

Hartle, A., 1983. *The Modern Self in Rousseau's Confessions*. South Bend, IN, Notre Dame University Press.

Harvey, V.A., 1995. *Feuerbach on the Intelligibility of Religion.* Cambridge, Cambridge University Press.

Rauschning, H., 1939. *The Revolution of Nihilism.* London, Heinemann.

Sixsmith, M., 2012. *Russia: A 1000-year Chronicle of the Wild East.* London, BBC Books.

Starobinski, J., 1988. *Jean-Jacques Rousseau. Transparency and Obstruction.* (trans. A. Goldhammer) Chicago, Chicago University Press.

Talmon, J.L., 1986. *The Origins of Totalitarian Democracy.* London, Secker and Warburg.

Wheeler-Bennett, J.W., 1956. *Nemesis of Power: The German Army in Politics 1918–1945.* New York, Macmillan.

CHAPTER 6: SCIENTISTIC HUMANISM

Blackburn S., 1984. *Spreading the Word.* Oxford, Oxford University Press.

Nagel, T., 2012. *Mind and Cosmos: Why the Materialist Neo-Darwinian Conception of Nature Is Almost Certainly False.* New York, Oxford University Press.

Smilansky, S., 2000. *Free Will and Illusion.* Oxford, Oxford University Press.

Smith, S.D., 2010. *The Disenchantment of Secular Discourse.* Cambridge, MA, Harvard University Press.

Williams, B.A.O. and J.J. Smart (ed.), 1973. *Utilitarianism: For and Against.* Cambridge, Cambridge University Press.

Wright, T.R.,1986. *The Religion of Humanity: The Impact of Comtean Positivism on Victorian Britain.* New York, Cambridge University Press.

CHAPTER 7: WORLD WAR, BUREAUCRACY, CONSUMERISM

Frankfurt, H., 1988. *The Importance of What We Care About.* Cambridge, Cambridge University Press.

Murray, D., 2017. *The Strange Death of Europe.* London, Bloomsbury Academic.

Scruton, R., 2017. *On Human Nature.* Princeton, Princeton University Press.

Strawson, P.A., 1959. *Individuals: An Essay in Descriptive Metaphysics.* London, Methuen.

CHAPTER 8: SEXUAL LIBERATION AND THE SUBVERSION OF THE PERSON

Faye, E., 2009. *The Introduction of Nazism into Philosophy.* New Haven, CT, Yale University Press.

Malo, A., 2020. *Beyond Gender Ideology* (English trans. A. Pavey). Washington, DC, Catholic University of America Press.
Parfit, D., 1986. *Reasons and Persons*. New York, Oxford University Press.
Parfit, D., 2011, 2017. *On What Matters*. Oxford, Oxford University Press.

CHAPTER 9: PERSONALISM, VALUE ETHICS AND THE ORIGINAL TRADITION

Borden, S., 2010. *Thine Own Self: Individuality in Edith Stein's Later Writings*. Washington, DC, Catholic University of America Press.
Crosby, J., 1996. *The Selfhood of the Human Person*. Washington, DC, Catholic University of America Press.
MacIntyre, A., 2006. *Edith Stein: A Philosophical Prologue 1913–1922*. Lanham, Rowman and Littlefield.
Peroli, E., 2006. *Essere persona: Le origini di un idea tra grecità e cristianesimo*. Brescia, Morcelliana.
Rist, J.M., 2020. *What Is a Person?: Realities, Constructs, Illusions*. Cambridge, Cambridge University Press.
Sokolowski, R., 2008. *Phenomenology of the Human Person*. New York, Cambridge University Press.
Spaemann, R., 2012. *Persons. The Difference between 'Someone' and 'Something"* (trans. O. O'Donovan). New York, Oxford University Press.

CHAPTER 10: CULTURE, WHAT CULTURE? 2021

Arendt, H., 1952. *The Burden of Our Time*. London, Secker and Warburg.
Glendon, M.A., 1991. *Rights Talk: The Impoverishment of Political Discourse*. New York, Free Press.
Nagel, T., 1998. *The View from Nowhere*. New York, Oxford University Press.
O'Hear, A., (ed.) 2017. *Modern Moral Philosophy*. Cambridge, Cambridge University Press.
Oderberg, D. and T.J.D. Chappell, 2004. *Human Value: New Essays in Ethics and Natural Law*. London, Palgrave MacMillan.
Rawls, J., 1993. *Political Liberalism*. New York, Columbia University Press.

Index